Politics in West Bengal:

A Critical Study

Dr. Keshab Chandra Mandal, Ph. D.

Contents

Preface and Acknowledgments

The present volume is the result of my selfless and remorseless research. There might be a little reflection of my erudition and sobriety to the political leaders as well as the existing system, but no doubt this book will not leave any stone unturned to satisfy the needs of the further researchers of India and abroad on contemporary politics of Kolkata and West Bengal that remained the colonial capital of India till the first decade of the twentieth century. My interest and experience in research on national and sub-national politics will provide a fascinating portrait of political culture, socio-political condition, electioneering system, and legacy of violence in modern India and particularly in the state of West Bengal. For understanding the dilemmas, contradictions, and tensions of a modern democratic state, this volume will act as the dominant paradigm. The debate over the rationalization of growing corruption in modernization and ethical political system in modern times has become the focus of this book. Lucid, informed and accessible this book will be essential reading for students of Sociology, Political Science, and Public Administration. The urge I felt for writing and the backdrop of making this book is delineated hereunder.

After the 2006 Legislative Assembly elections, the West Bengal government led by CPI(M) took the vigorous initiative to remove its bad name and negative epithet of 'anti-industrial and 'anti-bourgeoise' stigma from public mind. And when the Marxist Communist party leaving behind its longstanding pro-proletariate and pro-farmer image started wooing industrialists and embarked on modernization and industrialization, the farmers and laborers waged movements and agitations against the anti-CPI(M) comrades. This anti CPI(M) sentiment was skillfully fanned by the opposition Trinamool Congress with active support from the so called 'civil society of Kolkata. The government machinery was completely paralyzed by the Trinamool Congress party-led movements, Maoist uprisings, and farmers' movements throughout the State and particularly in Singur and Nandigram.

On this backdrop, I conducted a research study between 2007- '09 and published the work with a pleasant title _West Bengal Government: the Issues and Constraints of_

Development in 2010. The Assembly elections in West Bengal was held in the following year, which was contested primarily between the then 'firebrand opposition leader' Mamata Banerjee and incumbent chief minister Buddhadeb Bhattacharya, whereas the Indian National Congress (INC) party as an alliance of Banerjee's TMC fought against the Communist parties, who had been ruling the State uninterruptedly since 1977. Toward the end of their 34 year-long rule, the Communist Party of India (Marxist) changed their class character and turned from ruler to 'tyrant' and from service provider to 'oppressor'. As a consequence, the average electors were disillusioned and dissatisfied with their performance and cast their votes with two specific purposes: (i) to throw the Communist party-led Left Front (LF) government from power, and (ii) to get respite from the CPI(M)'s the tyrannical rule. Resultant of that, Mamata Banerjee won a stupendous victory in the legislative assembly elections. The three-decade-old red citadel of power fell like a house of cards to the indomitable struggle of India's most visible, lively, and robust leader Smt. Mamata Banerjee. The major issues of the 2011 elections were misrule, corruption, deterioration of law and order situation, and unemployment problems of the youths in Bengal. Besides, the huge debt incurred by the LF government, acrimonious relation of the State government with the governor on one hand and with the Union Government on the other, frequent *bandhs*, closures of factories, the Maoist attacks on common people in Jungle Mahal area, the insecurity of life and property of general people, and finally the threat of eviction of poor farmers from the lands of Singur and Nandigram for setting up the chemical hub and industries ignited the fire of discontent among a large section of the people in Bengal, which the LF government failed to handle with connoisseurship, intelligence, patience, and wit. Gradually the fire of dissatisfaction spread like a wildfire that burnt the edifice of the Communist empire.

Taking the advantage of the common farmers' simplicity and their fear of losing cultivable lands, the dire poverty in Paschimanchal i.e. western parts of Bengal, and subsequently the Maoist movements, Mamata Banerjee initiated a vehement movement taking the confidence of the farmers against the LF government and particularly its land policy. Her movement in the second half of the first decade in the new Millennium almost paralyzed normal life and disrupted the freedom of people. The road blockades in

Singur and Nandigram, destruction of government property at Writers' Buildings, and her continuous fasting for 26 days at Dharmatalla ultimately gave her a dividend. She succeeded in her attempts to bring about destructive politics of anti-industry movements at Singur, where the Tata Company had already set up the world's smallest and cheapest four-wheeler Nano small car project, and anti-Petrochemical Hub movements in Nayachar and Nandigram. These two movements and other above-said factors were instrumental to her landslide victory with 190 seats alone (42 seats more than that of the minimum required to form the government in Bengal), whereas her principal ally the Indian National Congress (INC) won 39 seats, another election partner SUCI got 1 seat, and INC (Independent) won 1 seat; thus the total number of seats of the alliance became 228, while in 2006 this number was only 30. On the other hand, the Left parties were reduced to a mere 66 in 2011 from the boosting numbers of 233 in the preceding election. While the NDA bagged a total of 24 seats in 2006, it was diminished to only 3 after five years in 2011.

After a decade in the 2021 elections people completely rejected the CPI(M). The Indian National Congress was also completely abdicated, and the TMC alone attained 213 seats out of 294, while the BJP after a tough fight had to remain satisfied with only 77 seats. This latest election ushered a complete 'withering away' of both the former ruling parties of Bengal - CPI(M) and Indian National Congress - from the domain of Power i.e. *Nabanna* (originally the Writers' Buildings, which is now under renovation). From the above discussion, it can be presumed that the oppression and misrule of the LF government reached to such an extent that people were very displeased with the Communists; and secondly, the befooling and instigating of the poor and innocent farmers along with the active support of disgruntled civil society the Trinamool Congress party came to power. Further, the results of the 2021 elections substantiate that tyranny and misrule cannot sustain for long. There must be an end either today or tomorrow to the tyrants and oppressors; howsoever powerful, indomitable, and gigantic they may be.

In making this book, several people have been particularly helpful and influential in developing my intellectuality. Pinaki Sukul, my friend since my University days, has been a source of inspiration in forcing me to come out of my national and provincial paradigm to consider the changes taking place at local levels across the State. Bimal Shankar Nanda, a teacher of Political Science, also a political analyst, and a candidate in the just-concluded legislative assembly elections in West Bengal, has been both a friendly teacher and mine of information to me. Informal discussions with Mr. Ashok Santra, my good and respected friend, a District Committee Member of CPI(M) in Paschim Medinipur, and my reporter friends across the state have helped me to understand the ground reality of the political scenario in Bengal. Debasish, my school friend now living in Delhi, and Subhasish, my brother also from Delhi helped me immensely with their knowledge. Our debates on various issues relating to contemporary Bengal politics and particularly the extent of violence during and post-election period in the state, and their subsequent reactions among the general public in Delhi and other Indian states helped me to realize the image of Bengal in the eyes of others. Goutam Ray, a retired engineer of Indian Railways, also helped me with sharing public sentiments and ongoing incidents before the elections in the district of North 24 Parganas.

My friends Prabhangshu Halder and Debabrata Roy, both Deputy Magistrates working in two different districts of the State, were depot of information on political and electoral titbits and technicalities. Regular interactions with them enriched the contents of the book. When I was a student of Kalyani University three decades ago, my teachers Professor Amartya Mukhopadhyaya, Professor Dipankar Sinha, Professor Partha Pratim Bose, Professor Aneek Chatterjee, and Professor Uddolok Ray were important because they shaped my understanding of the politics of Bengal as well as India, and strengthened the theoretical base of my knowledge. Finally, my Ph. D. Supervisor Dr. Anil Kumar Jana, former Professor in the Department of Political Science with Rural Administration, Vidyasagar University, has provided an enormous stimulus to reinforce the essential character of rural local government bodies, participation of people and particularly women in three-tier local governments; the role of different stakeholders such as women's organizations, political parties, and family members in establishing women's empowerment. My colleagues – both former and present – have given me a stimulating atmosphere where I devoted myself to research and study along with teaching. My colleagues and friends of the Bengal Institute of Political Studies (BIPS) and the West Bengal Political Science Association (WBPSA) are the best sources of knowledge. I express my special gratitude to the Presidents of BIPS and WBPSA for their academic assistance and encouragement. I am also grateful to all the members and office-bearers of both institutions. Finally, I admit that this book would never have been published without the love and all-out support of Reba, my wonderful wife; Arka, my lovely son, and Roshni, my sweet daughter.

Kolkata

Keshab Chandra Mandal

Dated, the 2nd September, 2021

Chapter - I

Introduction

"Democracy is not so much a form of government as a set of principles."

-   Woodrow Wilson

Let us begin with a Weberian question: "What is the characteristic uniqueness of the times in which we live?"[1] To answer the very question, any modern rational citizen would answer - it is the rationalization of tradition, and rationalization of corruption, religious fundamentalism, political vendetta, intolerance, sexuality, infirm bureaucracy, tilted media, money power, muscle power, violation of democratic and human rights, and dominance of tainted criminals in Parliaments and Legislative Assemblies. Modern India is a democratic country. Is democracy a blessing or bane or India? Robert Dahl has rightly pointed out that, "It would be a grievous error to ask too much of any government, including a democratic government. Democracy cannot guarantee that its citizens will be happy, prosperous, healthy, wise, peaceful, or just. To attain these ends is beyond the capacity of any government, including a democratic government."[2]

Despite having so many limitations, modern democracy has many benefits that make democracy more desirable than any feasible alternative to it. These include: "1. Democracy helps to prevent government by cruel and vicious autocrats. 2. Democracy guarantees its citizens some fundamental rights that nondemocratic systems do not, and cannot, grant. 3. Democracy ensures its citizens a broader range of personal freedom than any feasible alternative to it. 4. Democracy helps people to protect their fundamental interests. 5. Only a democratic government can provide a maximum opportunity for persons to exercise the freedom of self-determination – that is, to live under laws of their choosing. 6. Only a democratic government can provide a maximum opportunity for exercising moral responsibility. 7. Democracy fosters human development more fully than any feasible alternative. 8. Only a democratic government can foster a relatively high degree of political equality. 9. Modern representative democracies do not fight wars with one another. 10. Countries with democratic governments tend to be more prosperous than countries with nondemocratic governments." With all these advantages, democracy is, for most of us, a far better gamble than any attainable alternative to it.[3] Now, let us examine how far these advantages are being realized in the context of West Bengal especially in the pre and post-election periods.

The legislative assembly election of 2021 was very crucial in the political history of West Bengal. Unlike the proceeding two assembly elections, this one was unique in character and context. The 2011elections were held on the backdrop of several movements and agitations like the 'save farmland movement of Singur and Nandigram', 'Nandigram killings of 14 TMC supporters', 'anti-TATA-industry movement at Singur,' 'anti-petrochemical hub movement at Nandigram' and 'people's committee against police atrocities movement in Jungle Mahal' etc. Besides, the Trinamool Congress Party was in alliance with the then UPA-II government and quite naturally it received the fullest support from the National Congress party and its stalwarts like Sonia Gandhi, Dr. Manmohan Singh, P. Chidambaram, and Rahul Gandhi. Then Mamata Banerjee herself was also the Union Railway Minister, and she had all support from Bengal's electors for her 'firebrand' and 'fighter' image. She received national political and administrative supports on one hand and garnered the general dissatisfaction and anger of the people against the CPI(M) led Left Front government on the other. So, all these factors favored her to win the minds and hearts of the Bengalee people, and materialize her dream of becoming the chief minister of West Bengal.

Further, the 2016 elections were fought in the absence of a virtual opposition-free battlefield, where the Trinamool Congress party had succeeded to win 207 seats alone. It was the continuation of TMC's promise to fulfill the unfinished tasks. The CM advised her opposition leaders to "Keep silence" for ten years after assuming power at Writers' Buildings. The ten years were over now. She has done a lot of works. She has said that

...t of the works. Since independence, West Bengal has ... an National Congress Party and it has tasted the flavor of ... parties, and the latest was the (mis)rule of the TMC

During ... years of Mamata Banerjee's rule, West Bengal has witnessed paranormal v... ce in Panchayat elections; while the elections to the urban local bodies were pending for a few years; more than 40% percent of schools have no formal managing committees; teachers' recruitment in permanent posts through School Service Commission has been halted since 2016; politics of dole; and the most momentous trajectory through which the state running was unbridled corruption; increase in the number of rich TMC leaders in the fastest speed; an abnormal increase of tolabali, extortion, syndicate raj and the such. But it could not be said that there was not physical, social, economic, and cultural development. The numbers of Universities, colleges, and institutions are now a matter of pride for Bengal's academicians; the roads, parks, electrification, beautification, decoration of roads and buildings, and many such areas make an average person plausible for Bengal's growth and development. Bengal's agriculture, information technology industries, urbanization, and extension of metros in suburbs have transformed the living standard of the rich people a lot. On the other hand, the poor are also happy with so many doles, and the middle class too with so many benefits from cradle to crematorium, and from education to marriage are gleeful with the government of Mamata Banerjee.

Major issues in the 2021 elections

The 2021 elections were fought on some fundamental and significant issues such as 'corruption vs. development', 'cut money vs. good governance', 'hired poll strategist vs. indigenous leaders,' 'national political power vs. regional political power', 'politics of inclusion vs. exclusion', 'constitutionalism vs. utopianism', 'dole politics vs. development politics' etc. The latest addition to the list was 'Jay Sri Ram' vs. *'Khela Hobe'*. The general electors of this State were puzzled with propaganda and counter-propaganda of various contesting political parties. Also, the uneducated and lowly-educated voters fail to understand the allegations of one party and count[er] their opponents. However, the power equation has been completely changed in 2[019...] has made stunning inroads in Bengal and emerged as the major opposition party in th[e] state after the 17th Lok Sabha elections in 2019 winning 18 seats out of 42, while the ruling TMC won 22 seats and the Congress party was satisfied with only 2. On the other hand, the CPI(M) could not send even a single representative to the Lok Sabha. This zero representation of CPI(M) from West Bengal in the highest decision-making body has cropped up for the first time since its foundation in 1964. The latest election was a triangle fight with the CPI(M) - Congress and Indian Secular Front (ISF) alliance, the ruling TMC, and the emerging BJP.

West Bengal witnessed an unforeseen and unholy alliance of CPI (M) and Congress, who are and were always at loggerheads for decades in different states including Bengal. The more blasphemous attempt of these erstwhile two political giants – CPI (M) in Bengal, and INC in India – had been explicit when they held hands on stage in a very large gathering at Brigade Parade ground and concluded a grand alliance with Indian Secular Front (ISF) chief Abbas Siddiqui, a pirzada (descendent of a pir) belonging to the popular pilgrimage site of Furfura Sharif in Hooghly district, who has earned a reputation of being a conservative and even a fundamental.[4] General voters, and especially the erstwhile supporters and members of the CPI(M) and Congress could not bear this insult, and their natural anger was reflected in the results of the elections giving them a big zero only.

Why West Bengal was a major focus of the BJP?

West Bengal is an integral part of the Indian Territory that occupies a special strategic position. It has glory and a reputation in the international arena. Since long back the saints and sages along with multiple scholars had illumined the prestige and dignity of Bengal. Many great souls that transformed the lives of millions, and still have been influencing the life of thousand of scores throughout the world took birth in this wonderful state. Rabindra Nath Tagore, Rammohan Roy, Bankim Chandra Chattopadhyay, Sarat Chandra Chattopadhyay, Ramkrishna Paramhansa Deb, Swami

Vivekananda, Ishwar Chandra Vidyasagar, Mother Teresa, Amartya Sen, Abhijit Vinayak Banerjee, and several others have brightened the name of this state with their universal thought, humanitarian work, and innovative action. Bengal was always at the forefront of the Indian freedom struggle. This is, also, the cultural hub of India, and gateway to North-East states. Netaji Subhas Chandra Bose, Deshbandhu Chittaranjan Das, Syama Prasad Mukherjee, Sir Ashutosh Mukherjee, Binay-Badal-Dinesh, Kshudiram Bose, Prafulla Chaki, Matangini Hazra, and thousands of other leaders have mobilized Indian politics since long past. That is why the great political leader and philosopher of India Gopal Krishna Gokhale once remarked, "What Bengal thinks today India thinks tomorrow". The National Library is the only situation in Kolkata, The Victoria Memorial Hall, the Alipore zoo, Birla Planetarium, the Indian Museum is only a fragment of the best places of the world visitors. The culture and heritage of Bengal are so rich that the world is envious of it. Recently, both the Prime Minister and the Union Home Minister "focused on West Bengal's rich heritage and some of its lost glory in a back-to-back address to people in the poll-bound state."[5]

In addition to the above, it must be highlighted that the soil of Bengal is renowned as a 'home of protest', 'mother of revolution', and 'abode of innovation' since the pre-independence period. West Bengal was illustrious since long past for its silk trade, cottage industry, jute and handloom industries, and bell metal industries, but it gradually lost its position in the wake of independence due to political reasons. While the old image of a prosperous Bengal was diminishing in the hands of a few political leaders, a new antagonistic and hostile image of Bengal kicked off in the mid-seventies after the formation of the Left Front Government in 1977. The uninterrupted 34-year-rule of the Left Front government suffered its worst debacle in the hands of the Trinamool Congress party in 2011. The TMC government was further reelected in the 2016 and 2021 assembly elections with a colossal margin.

Importance of the study
The present study was conducted with some specific aims in mind. It has a tradition to write the socio-economic, cultural, educational, and political system of a particular

region, and for a specific period. It carries valuable information regarding various dimensions of socio-cultural and politico-economic aspects to the future generation of students, researchers, and general readers who can obtain data and information of the past. Our next-in-line researchers would be able to make a comparison between their existing circumstances and that of the earlier to conclude. Besides, they could point out examples and learn lessons from the past. Thus this kind of writing makes a bridge between the present and the past.

The characteristics of a region help the researcher to develop a holistic understanding of the relationship between environment and people, their economic and social context. It gives an idea about the lives and livelihood, economic condition, social condition, political participation and political culture, educational pattern, health situation, as well as the problems they face together with their prescriptions about the development of the region, which is inhabited by them. The mere discussion of problems will burden the minds, almost all the politically conscious persons are aware of the problems to some extent. What is more necessary is the supply of prescriptions for those problems. The suggestions and recommendations together with the problems of the state regarding Sustainable Development and economic growth are very important at this juncture. These are perhaps the reasons for the study of this subject in many educational institutions in India. Some of the Universities of India and abroad even have been preserving the local or provincial historical and cultural works of scholars with the above specific aims in view.

The State now occupies a unique position in the country. After Rabindranath Tagore (1913), three more people with Calcutta Chromosome such as Mother Teresa (1979), Amartya Sen (1998), and Abhijit Vinayak Banerjee (2019) won Noble Prize. Out of the total of 10 Nobel Prize winners, four were from Bengal. Kolkata's Victoria Memorial, National Library, Monument, Museum, Writers' Buildings, etc. are unmatched with any other state in India. Bengal's industry, culture, theatre, films, music, literature are still a matter of envy to many other states. The courage of people, level of consciousness of its common masses, love for football, cricket, communal harmony, unity and integrity among different religions, and fellow-feeling have made it distinct from other regions.

Despite having so many advantages in Bengal and its many things to be proud of, Bengal is notorious for its political skirmishes, antagonistic politics, non-cooperative attitude, intolerance to opposition views, and violent politics of almost all political parties. The recent trends of horse-trading, criminalization of politics, unbridled corruption, cut money, political leaders and police nexus, etc. have been added in Bengal politics. The overall degradation of the quality of leaders, their administrative skills, and the low level of knowledge of some ministers exposed in the recent past have raised eye-brows to many political pundits and social scientists inter alia thousands of general electors. Lack of allegiance to the public interest, lack of sacrifice for the country and its people, lack of devotion, self-interest, and selfish money-making mental makeup of a large number of leaders have become explicit in Bengal politics. A very simple question was raised by general voters as to why these things were happening in Bengal? How long will these continue to eat up the Bengalees? Is there no respite from these dark and dirty politicians?

To find out the answers needs an in-depth study of the ideology of the party in power and its proper application in running the administration. If there is no ideology of a political party and its top leadership, the turret of party edifice is sure to smash like a sand-made palace either today or tomorrow. On the other hand, if a political party is based on a strong philosophy and ideology and having a strong discipline among its members and workers, and some office-bearers practice those ideals in their daily life and activities, the party is sure to last long. At the same time, it should be remembered that when a particular party remains in power for a long time, one type of 'don't care attitude' or 'bossism' is found explicitly among its leaders, ministers, and workers – the heat of which was experienced and felt by the general public and its malodor is spread in the political air of the State.

Once, West Bengal was the capital of India. It was the pinnacle of the culture, heritage, and political thoughts of the country. Bengal's industry was once famous in the world arena. But the glory of the then State had started to wane after the division of Bengal in 1905 and after independence due to various reasons. Further, it waned in the hands of Left parties' anti-industry slogans and disruptive politics. Buddhadev Bhattacharjee tried to repair the image in Bengal from 2006 but in vain. The Trinamool Congress's movement against the anti-Nano Car project in Singur further hit the image of Bengal. Besides, the shift of behavior from smiling face and politeness to rudeness with red eyes of a large section of comrades at different levels during their rule, and the same attitude in the TMC rule in the last 10 years was discerned, perceived, and experienced by thousands of sufferers in different fields. The TMC government and its leaders started their innings very nicely, but the end of their second innings was full of so bitterness that millions of people in large were annoyed with the performance of its local leaders all over the state. When the BJP emerged as a decisive power in the 2019 Lok Sabha elections, one by one the wickets of the Trinamool Congress party began to fall. Many heavy-weight leaders left the Trinamool Congress party and joined in the nationalist party to serve the people and the nation in a better and more democratic manner.

The game of power is very dirty. It seeks more and more. Absolute majority brings the vice of corruption and it proved true in the case of West Bengal. History teaches us that when the level of corruption is increased, public sentiments and feelings get hurt. When the attitude and behavior of the ruling party members become arrogant and hostile, the edifice of power is sure to break down. It is interesting that the ruling party as well as many of its followers become so blind that they could not see and feel the heat of public grievances, and even if understood they sometimes pretended that nothing wrong had happened. A few of them even began to blame the media and opposition parties as they were misleading the innocent masses. Thus, they not only underestimated the strength of common people, but they also started to dig their graves.

In West Bengal, the law and order situation has deteriorated, and life and property of people in a few areas were also at stake. They were continuously facing stiff troubles and losing their lives and property in political violence. What allegations were made against the Left Front Government, similar allegations were also being leveled against the TMC Government in 2021. Serious violation of fundamental rights enshrined in the Constitution was a common phenomenon in Bengal. How far the rights and properties of people were violated; what was the extension of violence in pre and post-election periods; what was people's perception about the performance of the state, and why the CPI(M), BJP, and INC were defeated in elections became important to understand. The study examined all these issues extensively. On the above circumstances, the present research study is very significant to the students and general readers.

Area of study

Selection of the area of study stands as a significant factor. The area should always be related to the topic, which may produce an accurate result. For the present study, the entire State of West Bengal was selected. West Bengal is situated in the eastern direction of India. The three bordering areas of the state are surrounded by land while the southern part is merged with the Bay of Bengal. The northern neighboring state and countries are Sikkim and Bhutan. On the eastern side, there are Bangladesh and Assam. Bihar, Jharkhand, and Orissa have fallen in the western part of this state. Nepal is situated in the northwest of West Bengal. The State is extended from Darjeeling on the northern border to the coast of the Bay of Bengal in the south. The length of the state is about 645 kilometers. Again, the 330 kilometers wide area has been extended from the western border of Purulia district to the eastern part of North 24 Parganas. This state has a very old tradition and it is full of diversity. Commerce and industry, cultivation, and service sectors are the main pillars of this state. Being the Gateway of Eastern Zone it carries extra importance.

West Bengal, which now consists of 23 districts, is one of the states of the Indian Federation, which further comprises 28 States and 8 Union Territories. India is a federal country with a strong centralization tendency. In case of emergency, it turns into a unitary country. Indian Parliament is the most powerful legislative body that can make any law except making a man a woman and a woman a man. With a two-thirds majority by a single political party or an alliance in both houses, the Indian Parliament turns into the most powerful law-making body. However, power is distributed among the states through the union, state, and concurrent lists whereas the Union Government enjoys most of the important powers such as defense, currency, railways, international relations, and others.

West Bengal is a very important State in India as well as in the sub-continent. After independence, the then Indian States were re-organized for facilitating smooth administration. The Governor-ruled Indian provinces were categorized in sections 'A' 'B', 'C' and 'D'. The first category included Assam, Bihar, Bombay, Madhya Pradesh, Madras, Orissa, Punjab, Uttar Pradesh, and West Bengal. The larger states were categorized into section 'B'. These included Hyderabad, Jammu & Kashmir, Madhya Bharat, Mysore, and Patiala (East Punjab). The 'C' category states were Ajmer, Bhopal, Bilaspur, and Kurg, while the Andaman and Nicobar Islands were included in the 'D' category. Thus the Indian Union of States was comprised of 18 States and one Union Territory initially. After the adoption and enactment of the Constitution on 26th January 1950, the States were further restructured. Kooch Behar was included in West Bengal in 1951. Again in 1956, Purulia of Manbhum districts and the eastern part of Purnia district of Bihar were annexed with West Bengal. The state of West Bengal then was formed with 16 districts.

In 1986, the district of 24 Parganas was divided into North 24 Parganas and South 24 Parganas. Barasat and Alipore respectively became the headquarters of these two districts. Similarly in the following year, the district of Dinajpur was segregated into North Dinajpur and South Dinajpur, and Raigunj and Balurghat were made their headquarters respectively. Again in 2002 for administrative reasons the erstwhile largest district of India Midnapore was divided into Purba Medinipur with headquarters at Tamluk, and Paschim Medinipur with Midnapore as its district headquarters. West Bengal was a state of a total of 19 districts till the TMC government came to power in 2011. The new chief minister further divided some districts only to form 23 districts which include the newly formed Alipurduar district (formed on 25 June 2014), Jhargram district (formed on 4 April 2017), Kalimpong (formed on 14 February 2017), and the splitting of the former Bardhaman district into Purba Bardhaman and Paschim Bardhaman districts (formed on 7 April 2017). These 23 districts are grouped into five divisions.

It is to be declared here that, the performances and promises of the Indian National Congress will not be discussed in the entire study because it has a very negligible presence and relevance in Bengal politics. But the Left Front's performance and lapses, as they were in ruling position for 34 years, will be examined thoroughly along with the promises and lapses of the ruling TMC government. To understand the big talks of big bosses of politics, and how far they have transformed the life and status of people so far, this study was undertaken. In addition to this, the following are the main objectives of the present study.

Objectives of the study

In every study, there are certain aims and objectives. The present one is not an exception. The main objectives of the study are:

1. to understand the social, economic, political, educational, health, and industrial status of West Bengal;

2. to investigate the achievements of the Trinamool Congress government;

3. to explore the nature and extent of violence in elections;

4. to understand the causes of defeats of the Congress, CPI(M), and BJP;

5. to comprehend people's perception regarding the performance of the TMC Government; and

6. to recommend some policy prescriptions to the 'people in power'

Methodology

The present study is partly historical and mainly empirical. The study is based on both the secondary as well as primary sources of data. The secondary sources comprise books, journals, newspapers, evaluative studies, and periodicals. The primary sources include Government records, Acts, Manuals, Reports, and Statues. To supplement the theoretical knowledge, an empirical study has also been undertaken. Primary data have been collected through online interviews of some Government officials, members of different political parties, academicians, and general voters with the help of an interview schedule. The survey was conducted online through a Google questionnaire circulated in social media like Facebook and LinkedIn. The process of data collection continued from September 2020 to November 2020 during the lockdown period in India. The interview schedule was framed in English so that the respondents feel free to respond conveniently.

The questionnaire containing 4 broad sections was prepared exclusively for the purpose of this study. The first section was related to the socio-economic background of the respondents. The second part sought information on political matters. The third section examined the level of consciousness of general voters regarding the recent performance and policies of the Government; the nature and functioning of the leaders of the State; chances of coming back in the power of the Government etc. The fourth section provided suggestions of the general respondents regarding their hopes and aspirations and demands to the government. This part focused on public demand for better governance, transparency, sustainable development, and inclusive growth of the people in the State. The questions were finalized after ensuring their relevance through a pilot study. All the respondents were interviewed with the same questionnaire. All questions were open-ended and that they are quantified as per the standard categorizations available. The signature of each respondent could not be taken as the research was done through an online survey. Now, let us examine the socio-economic background of the respondents as was availed through the survey.

Socio-Economic background of the respondents

A total of 372 people participated in the online survey. The age group of the respondents was categorized into five sections. It is found that a total of 356 (95.65) people were exposed their age, while a small number of respondents 4.4% preferred to remain silent on this question. It is evident from the following table (Table 1.1) that 27 percent of respondents belonged to the age group of 18-30 years, and 24.7 percent respondents belonged to the age group of 31-45 years, while the majority respondents (32.6%) come under the age group of 46-60 years. Only 8 respondents comprising 2.2 percent were in the age group of 70 years and above.

Table: 1.1 Age of respondents

Age	Number of Respondents	%
18-30	96	27
31-45	88	24.7
46-60	116	32.6
61-70	48	13.5
70 & above	8	2.2
Non Respondents	16	4.4
Total	372	100

Source: survey data

Further, it was intended by the researcher to know the sex of the respondents. The survey data show that 68 respondents comprising 18.2 percent only are women, while the majority of respondents (76.34%) are male. Interestingly 4 transgender people comprising 1.07 percent were included in the survey, while 4.30 percent of respondents said that they were not interested to expose their gender identity.

Table: 1.2 Sex of respondent

Sex	Number of respondents	%
Female	68	18.2
Male	284	76.34
Prefer not to say	16	4.30
Transgender	4	1.07
Total	372	100

Source: survey data

The religion of the respondents was also identified through the survey. It comes to light that the majority of respondents comprising 332 persons (89.24%) belong to the Hindu, while only 4.30 percent of respondents are Muslim. Only four persons were Christian, but not a single person was Buddhist, while the religion of 20 respondents (5.37%) was not known, and hence, they have been included in the 'Others' category.

Table: 1.3 Religion of respondent

Religion	Number of respondents	%

Hindu	332	89.24
Muslim	16	4.30
Christian	4	1.07
Buddhist	0	0.00
Others	20	5.37
Total	372	100

Source: survey data

Most of the respondents were told about their marital status. The data show that the majority of respondents i.e. 232 respondents are married, while 29.03 percent of respondents are unmarried, and 1.34 percent of respondents are divorced. There was not a single widow in the survey, and 27 respondents (7.25%) did not like to expose their marital status.

Table: 1.4 Marital status

Status	Number of respondents	%
Married	232	62.36
Unmarried	108	29.03
Divorced	5	1.34
Widow	0	0.00
Do not like to say	27	7.25
Total	372	100

Source: survey data

The personal income of individuals is a very vital indicator of the economic empowerment of the voters. The survey data show that a lot of people do have not any income at all. This number of respondents is 56 which consists of 15.05 percent of the total respondents. On the other hand, 6.45 percent of people have only income between Rs.500.00 and Rs.2000.00. Only 1.07 percent of respondents have income between Rs.2001.00 and Rs.5000.00. The next higher income group is represented by 5.37 percent of respondents who earn Rs.5001.00 to Rs.10,000.00 per month. The next higher income group (from Rs.10,001 to Rs.25,000) is 7.52 per cent population, while 16.12 per cent population comprising 60 respondents earns between Rs.25,000.00 to Rs.50,000.00. The higher income group who earns between Rs.50,001 to Rs.1,00000.00 in a month is 17.20 percent population. Again, it is found that 6.45 percent population earns between Rs.1 lakh to Rs.1.5 lakh per month. And, another 64 people comprising 17.20 percent of total respondents earn between Rs.1.50 lakh and above. Interestingly 28 respondents (7.52%) did not respond and write their personal monthly income in the survey form.

Table 1:5 Personal monthly income

Income	Number of Respondents	%
Nil	56	15.05
Rs. 500-Rs.2000	24	6.45
Rs. 2001-Rs.5000	4	1.07
Rs. 5001-Rs.10000	20	5.37
Rs. 10001-Rs.25000	28	7.52
Rs. 25001 -Rs.50000	60	16.12
Rs. 50001-Rs.100000	64	17.20
Rs.100000- Rs.150000	24	6.45
Rs.150000 & above	64	17.20
Non respondents	28	7.52
Total	372	100

Source: survey data

A personal bank account is very important nowadays. Hence, it was intended to know if the respondents were having a personal bank account or not. It came to light that, majority respondents comprising 331 respondents (88.97%) have a bank account, while only a small number of respondents (9) were not having a bank account to date, only 1.1 percent respondents said "May be", and 7.52 percent respondents did not want to expose their bank account status.

Table: 1.6 Personal bank account

Bank Account	Number of respondents	%
Yes	331	88.97
No	9	2.41
Maybe	4	1.1
Non respondents	28	7.52
Total	372	100

Source: survey data

During the COVID-19 pandemic period, the Government of India has repeatedly asked for downloading various Apps including Arogya Setu to avoid public gatherings. Besides, the other intention of the author was to examine how far the digital India campaign of the Union Government has been successful in our country. So, it was intended by the researcher to see if people were using various apps for information, and transactions with banks or other financial, or educational institutions. It came to the fore that, 59.13 percent of respondents were using digital apps, while 32.25 percent were not using at all, and 8.60 percent did not like to say anything.

Table: 1.7 Use of digital app

Digital App	Number of respondents	%
Yes	220	59.13
No	120	32.25
Maybe	0	0.00
Non respondents	32	8.60
Total	372	100

Source: survey data

When asked "Do you have two-wheelers", the majority of respondents comprising 204 in number (54.83%) said that they have two-wheelers with them, while 144 respondents comprising 38.70 percent people do not have two-wheelers. On the other hand, 24 respondents (6.32%) did not say anything in this regard.

Table: 1.8 Ownership of two-wheeler

Ownership of two-wheeler	Number of respondents	%
Yes	204	54.83
No	144	38.70
Maybe	0	0.00
Non respondents	24	6.32
Total	372	100

Source: survey data

When asked "Do you have a four-wheeler", the majority of respondents comprising 279 in number (75.00%) said that they have not four-wheelers with them; while 62 respondents comprising 16.66 percent answered that they have four-wheelers. Only 31 respondents (6.33%) did not respond to the question.

Table: 1.9 Ownership of four-wheeler

Bank Account	Number of respondents	%
Yes	62	16.66
No	279	75.00
Maybe	0	0.00
Non respondents	31	8.33
Total	372	100

Source: survey data

After discussing the socio-economic background of the respondents, we will turn to the physical background of the state of West Bengal. A brief picture of the topography can be enumerated hereunder.

Physical Background

Location and situation

West Bengal is the fourteenth largest state of India with a total area of 88,752 sq. km. having a national share of 2.70 per cent as per Census report of 2011.[6] The geographical area of the state is extended from 21 ° 38' to 27°10' in the north latitude and from 85 ° 50' to 89 ° 50' east longitude. As per 2011 census total population of the state is 9,13,47,736 comprising 4,69,27,389 males and 4,44,20,347 females who live in 23 districts (in 2021). Out of this total number of Scheduled Caste (SC) population is 1,80,73,260 comprising 99,69,962 males and 81,03,298 females. Sex ratio (females per 1000 males) in the state stood at 947 against 940 at the national level. Literacy rate in the state has also gone up by 77.08 per cent. West Bengal is the fourth populous state after Uttar Pradesh, Maharashtra and Bihar.[7] In 2011 there were 2,14,63,270 Scheduled Caste population, which was 23.51 per cent of the total population of the State. Also it has 52,96,953 Scheduled Tribe (ST) population comprising 26,49,974 males and 26,46,979 females, which is about 5.8 per cent of total state population.[8] Density of population per sq. km. is 1100 per sq km. It is one of the earliest and beautiful states in India. It was established with the attainment of independence and falls in 'A' category.

Distance of Kolkata from some important places (in KMs)

1. Delhi   1469 kms by road &1304 kms by flight

2. Mumbai   1972 kms by road & 1655 kms by flight

3. Hyderabad   1530 kms by road & 1122 kms by flight

4. Bangaluru   1915 kms by road & 1561 kms by flight

5. Cochi   2388 kms by road & 1906 kms by flight

6. Chennai   1706 kms by road & 1308 kms by flight

Source: Yatra.com

Air ports in West Bengal

1. Netaji Subhash Chandra Airport (CCU) (International)

2. Bagdogra Airport (IXB) (International)

3. Kazi Nazrul Islam Airport (RDP) (Private Airstrip)

4. Balurghat Airport (RGH) (Domestic)

5. Behala Airport (Domestic).

6. Cooch Behar Airport (COH) (Domestic)

7. Malda Airport (Domestic)

8. Panagarh Airport

Name of the air base

Kalaikunda

Sea ports in West Bengal

1. Kolkata port

2. Haldia port

3. Farakka port

4. Sagar port, and

5. Tajpur port

Topography

Diversification of land in West Bengal

The State of West Bengal has been divided into five geographical lands. They are (1) the northern mountains and hills, (2) the plateau region of the west, (3) the silted plain land, (4) the Ganga delta, and (5) the sandy coastal plains of the south.

(1) The Northern Mountains and Hills: It is mainly the Himalayan hilly region. It consists of the whole entire Darjeeling district and the northern part of the Jalpaiguri region excluding the Siliguri Sub-Division. The height of this land is about 2000 meters to 3000 meters from sea level. Coming out from the Jemu glacier of Sikkim the river Tista has bifurcated the Darjeeling Hilly region into – (a) western part and (b) eastern part. Sandakafu, Falut, Sabargram, etc. are the important peaks of the Singalila Mountains. Other important peaks are Reniganga (1885 m.) and small Sinchula (1,726 m.). Singalila is the highest peak of West Bengal. A few important hills and mountains of this region are Takda hill, Ghum hill, Sinchula Mountain. These are very beautiful and attractive tourist spots of the state. People from different parts of the world come to view Tiger Hill from Darjeeling. The temperature is cool throughout the year. Mainly these areas are very good and comfortable in summer.

(2) The Plateau Region of West: This area comprises the whole of Purulia, Bankura, Midnapore, Birbhum, and the western part of Burdwan district. It is adjacent to the Chotonagpur plateau of Jharkhand. The average height of the western side is 300 meters while the mean height of the eastern sector is 50 to 100 meters. A few important hills are also visible in these areas. Ayodhya and Chandi hills of Purulia, Beharinath (439 m.), and Susunia (447 m.) of Bankura are important hills. Besides, Mama Bhagne hill of Birbhum is also famous. Gorgaburu is the highest peak of the western plateau region.

(3) The Silted Plain Land: Excluding the northern hilly and western plateau regions, most of the areas of West Bengal fall in this region. This region is formed with silted soil of the Ganga and a lot of its tributaries. The silted soil is also of two types e.g. (1) plain land of North Bengal and (2) plain land of South Bengal. The North Bengal region is formed of North and South Dinajpur, Coochbehar, and Maldah districts. It is a little higher than the southern plain land. On the other hand, the southern plain land consists of the total Murshidabad, Burdwan, Hooghly, Howrah, Bankura, and Midnapore districts.

(4) The Ganga Delta: The Ganga delta region consists of plain land of the districts of Kolkata, Nadia, North and South 24 Parganas. The region has been created with the silts of Ganga and its other tributaries. A lot of canals and rivers are found in this region. The

most southern part of this area is very much popular by the name of Sundarban. The great Royal Bengal tiger is seen in this forest. This area is fertile.

(5) The Sandy Coastal Plains of South: The sandy coastal plain land is situated at the coastal areas of Kanthi of Purba Medinipur district. High sandy hills and hillocks are visible in the areas. Digha and Shankarpur are two important tourist spots of the State. The seashore is very attractive to tourists. People go for a change in this area.

Rivers of West Bengal

Ganga, the great river is flowing through the state. West Bengal is abounded in rivers. Most of the rivers have emanated from the northern Himalayan region. The main tributaries of the Ganga are the Bhagirathi and the Hooghly. The rivers of West Bengal can be divided into four sections. They are (1) northern rivers of West Bengal, (2) Ganga and its tributaries, (3) the rivers of rarh and plateau region of west, and (4) the rivers of southern Sundarban.

(1) The Northern Rivers: The main river of the northern region is the Tista. It has been originated from the Jemu glacier of Sikkim. Besides, the other rivers of this region are Torsa, Jaldhaka, Sankosh, Raidak, Mechi, Rangit, Balason and Tangon. These rivers are fed with melting ice. Therefore, the rivers are ever flowing and full of current.

(2) The Ganga and its Tributaries: The main river of this state is Ganga. It has emanated from the Gomukh ice cave of the Himalayan Gangotri glacier. Flowing through Uttar Pradesh and Bihar it has entered West Bengal. Near Dhulian of Murshidabad district, a part of the Ganga has entered into Bangladesh by name of Padma while the other part has been renamed as Bhagirathi and has merged with the Bay of Bengal flowing through West Bengal. The southern part of Bhagirathi is known as Hooghly. A few tributaries of the Ganga-Padma are Ichhamati, Churni, Mathabhanga, and Jalangi.

(3) The Rivers of Rarh and Plateau Region of West: Most of the rivers of this region are fed with rainwater. The main rivers of this sector are the Mayurakshi, Damodar, Rupnarayan, Ajoy, Dwarakeshwar, Silai, Kangshaboti, and Subornorekha. Most parts of

...pur and Paschim Medinipur are affected by floods every year due ...se rivers.

(4) The Rivers of Southern Sundarban: This region is comprised of many big and small rivers and estuaries. A few important rivers of this region are the Matla, Gosaba, Piyali, Thakurani, Hariabhanga, Ichhamati, Kalindi, Saptamukhi, and Roymangal. These rivers are fed with the saline tidewater of the Bay of Bengal.

The climate of West Bengal

Though the climate of West Bengal is monsoonal in character, variation in climate is observed from the rainfall and temperature data of different zones. This variation is due entirely to the topographical variations of the place. The topography of the northern and western portions is different from that of the southern and eastern sectors.

Hot summer, high relative humidity, and well-distributed rainfall during the monsoon season are the main characteristics of the climate of the state. The cold weather begins from about the middle of November and lasts up to the end of February. The summer season lasts from March to September. October and the first half of November constitute the post-monsoon season.

The rainfall is controlled chiefly by the cyclonic storms, which form in the northwest angle of the Bay of Bengal. The inland depressions influence the weather. During the hot season, thunderstorms occur commonly, mostly in the afternoons. Associated with the heavy rains, occasional hail and severe squalls occur. The thunderstorms called Norwesters are locally known as 'kal baisakhis'. The squalls associated with them usually come from the northwest. A sharp drop in temperature is experienced during the storm.

In the cold weather months of November and December, the rainfall is only a fraction of an inch. The northward movement of cyclonic storms from the south of the Bay of Bengal causes this type of rainfall. From about the end of December, the northern wind forms. Cold season storms are caused by shallow depressions, which originate in the northwest of the bay and move eastward. During their passage, they cause general cloudy weather and rainfall.

Temperature

The temperature during the summer months is higher in the surrounding districts. The temperature begins to rise rapidly from about the middle or end of February. April-July is the hottest month with the mean daily maximum temperature of 38° - 40° c. But the temperature of the Darjeeling hill region remains 14-17 degrees during this season. However, there is a welcome relief from the scorching heat in the plain land, though temporary, when thunderstorms occur, on some days in this season.

With the arrival of the southwestern monsoon in early June, the daily temperature drops appreciably, but the night temperature remains high. With the withdrawal of the monsoon by about the first week of October the temperature begins to fall more rapidly. And from about the middle of November, through December and January, the coldest months continue with the mean daily minimum 8°-13° c temperature.

Briefly, it can be said that the climate of the state is dry, humid, and healthy. December is the coldest month while May is the hottest month. Recently the temperature of the World including the state has tremendously increased. In a recent study, U.S scientists have proved that the world witnessing a hot fever which is the highest in the last four hundred years. It was reported in Business Standard[9] that, in 2019 Asansol recorded West Bengal's highest temperature of the day at 41.2 degrees Celsius, while Midnapore, Bankura, and Sriniketan recorded above 40 degrees Celsius temperature. On the other hand, Kolkata recorded its highest day temperature of 2019 at 39.6 degrees Celsius. The State witnessed occasional rainfall in the evenings and at nights. The winter is not felt so heavily. The temperature comes down to 13.1-degree centigrade to 26.9 degrees centigrade and rarely does it fall to 8 degrees. The spring lasts for a few weeks only here. Most of the rainfall takes place due to southwest monsoon wind. Nearly 71 percent of rainfall (125 CM) of the year is held due to this wind. The humidity in the air is 60-90 degrees. The average rainfall in the state is 175 CM.

Soils

Edaphic condition exerts considerable influence on the land use pattern of any state. Crops and soil patterns are closely interrelated. For example, rice does not favor sandy soils because of its high porosity. Soils of a place are locally classified by the peasants through the long-continued experience of cultivation, on the basis of situation, elevation, composition, and productivity. Classification according to the elevation is following:

Jala land - The land below the water level is known as 'Jala'. This is usually covered by the fields.

Danga land - It is located at a higher level than the 'Jala'.

Texture - the soil is composed of particles of different sizes together with some amount of organic matter. The main bulk is composed of particles of different sizes and the size of the particle determines the texture of the soil.

In a typical alluvial tract, the soils consist mostly of sandy, silty or clayey loams or riverine origin. The following soil types are recognized in this state. These are (1) alluvial soil, (2) laterite soil (3) loamy soil and 4) hilly region soil.

(1) Alluvial Soil: The soil mixed with sand, silt, and clay is called alluvial soil. Being a river-centric state, most part of the soil of West Bengal is of this nature. On the basis of the creation, the alluvial soil is divided into three classes e.g. (a) old alluvial soil, (b) new alluvial soil, and (c) salinity alluvial soil. The old alluvial soil is found in South Dinajpur, the eastern part of Maldah, the western part of Murshidabad, Birbhum, Bankura, the eastern part of Burdwan, and the western part of Hooghly. The color of this soil is a little reddish. Paddy, sugarcane, wheat, jute, mulberry, and mango are produced in this soil.

Originally the soil of the tract was highly productive, which gradually diminished in fertility due to continuous use of land for ages. The organic matters such as humus content are less in the soil. According to agriculturists, most of the alluvium contains lime (CAO), Potash (K2O), and Phosphorous (P2O5).

The new alluvial soil is seen in the districts of Cooch Behar, North Dinajpur, Nadia, North and South 24 Parganas, Howrah, and the eastern part of Hooghly. Normally this is found in grey color. This type of soil is very fertile and rice, paddy, jute, etc. are produced in this kind of soil. On the other hand, the saline alluvial soil normally exists near the sea areas. The coastal Sundarbans and Kanthi are the places where it is found. Salt and clay remain much in this soil. It is very conducive for the cultivation of coconut, palm, betel nut, etc. but nowadays watermelons, sunflowers and cotton are also being produced.

(2) Laterite Soil: The soil of Purulia, Birbhum, Bankura, some parts of Paschim Medinipur, and Burdwan is known as laterite soil. It is full of gravel and its color is red. As there is much iron in the water of this region, the soil has become red. It is not healthy for cultivation. However, the laterite soils may be cultivable with the use of irrigation and fertilizer.

(3) Loamy Soil: This is found in most of the Ganga delta region of West Bengal. This soil is exclusively devoted to aus, which in some areas is now replaced by market gardening and Rabi crops. It has got moisture retentive capacity and hence favors the growth of aman paddy.

(4) Soil of Hilly Tract: It is completely different from the above types of soils. The podsol soil is made with hard stones and fallen rot leaves. It is almost barren and gets depreciated. The color of this soil is red and brown. However, tea, cinchona, and tobacco can be produced on this type of land.

Mineral resources of the state

West Bengal occupies an important position in the mineral production of the country. During 1989 and 1990 the state produced 3.8 percent minerals and holds the seventh position in the country. The metallic and non-metallic deposits of the state are coal, china clay, fire clay, apatite, dolomite, limestone, silica sand, base metals, wolframite, which are very much important in terms of economy. A brief account of the mineral resources is given hereunder.

Apatite

The apatite-magnetite mineralization is visible in the southern part of the district of Purulia. Most of the valuable apatite occurrences are situated in Beldih and Medinipur in the western part and Chirugora, Purtaha Kutni, and Dandodih-Gamardih in the eastern part. The ore bodies at Beldih have a reserve of 4.56 million tonnes of ore containing an average grade of 13.17 percent P_2O_5 has been estimated up to a depth of 150m. This includes a high grade of 1.56 million tons of ore with an average grade of 21.62 percent P_2O_5. It has direct application in fertilizer industries. Thin lensoid apatite in Medinipur has a reserve of 0.19 million tons of ore with an average grade of 7.00 percent P_2O_5 has been estimated for a vertical depth of 50m. Similarly, in the western sector, a reserve of 1,862 million tonnes of ore with an average grade of 10.58 percent P_2O_5 has been estimated up to a vertical depth of 50m, and in the eastern sector, 0.521 million tons of ore with an average of 7.33 percent P_2O_5 has been estimated up to a vertical depth of 100m. In Kutni, a total of 4.26 million tons of ore with an average of 8.87 percent P_2O_5 has been estimated from this area up to a vertical depth of 100m. In Dandodih-Gamardih deposit of west has a total of 4.48 million tons of ore with an average grade of 8.04 percent P_2O_5 has been estimated up to a vertical depth of 50m. In the northern part of the Purulia district apatite-magnetite quartz rock is reported to occur at Pankridih where apatite mineralization is extended over a strike length of 300m.

Asbestos and barytes

It is estimated that there is a reserve of 111 tons of asbestos ore within a depth of 10m over 500m strike length in Chirugora and Birmadal areas of the Medinipur district. Barytes veins are found in Malthal in the east to Ukma in the west of Purulia district, which is white and off-white in color ad lensoid in nature. They contain 59.80 percent to 63.50 percent BaO, 31.20 percent SO_3, 2.72 percent to 3.20 percent SiO_2, and 0.20 percent Fe_2O_3. It is estimated that approximately there is a reserve of 165 tonnes of barites in Belna, Kanisitanr (Raghudih), and Malthal areas and 268 tons in Ukma, Husi, and Gunja areas up to a vertical depth of 10m.

Base metals

Purulia, Darjeeling, and Jalpaiguri districts are places where base metals are mainly found. Most of the important base metal deposits for lead and zinc are found in the Sukha Khola blocks, Khar Khola, Mal Khola, Daling Chu areas of Himalayan terrain near Gorubathan, Darjeeling district. In the Gorubathan deposit, an estimated reserve of ore is likely to be the order of 3.7086 million tons with 3.77 percent Pb and 3.87 percent Zn. Above 1.66 million tons of magnetite is available as a major by-product from the ore. Minor deposit of Copper ore is reported from Pedong and Peshok areas of Darjeeling district. Copper mineralization has also been located in the Tamakhun area of the Purulia district.

China clay

In parts of Birbhum, Bankura, Medinipur and Purulia have a large deposit of clay while the district of Bardhaman has a few small but potential clay deposits. Clay deposits of Muhammad Bazar (Birbhum) area are scattered over 450 sq. km. areas and are clustered in two separate belts. The district has a total reserve of 141.47 million tons of clay deposits inclusive of all grades. In the district of Bankura, a total of all clay deposits have been estimated to be 141.470 million tons inclusive of all grades. The clay pockets of the district of Purulia are covered under the soil, varying in thickness from 1.8m to 6.0m. It is estimated that there is a total reserve of 23.882 million tons of clay in the district. In the district of Midnapore the persistence of the clay bed is traceable up to 13m. depth and here a total of 0.135 million tons of clay of all grades has been estimated. But in the district of Bardhaman, a total of 85.54 million tons of clay deposits of all grades have been estimated.

Coal

Though the two large coalfields of the state are situated in Ranigunj and Birbhum to date, Ranigunj coalfield is the only coal-producing area of the state. There are a few other minor coal fields in the state e.g. Darjeeling, Barjora, Hematpur, and Tangsuli. Ranigunj coalfield covers a vast aerial stretch of over 1900 sq. km. and a major portion of which is located in Bardhaman district. "….the total known reserves of different qualities and categories of coal in Ranigunj coal field down to a depth of 1200 m. from the surface, as assessed on 1.1.98 amount to 22149.39 million tones".[10] The Coalfield of Birbhum was discovered by the Geological Survey of India during 1983-84. It is anticipated to have an aerial spread of over 200 sq. km., and the coal from this coalfield is non-cooking, having high moisture, medium volatile, and of inferior grade. However, the total reserve of coal from the so far explored part of this region has been assessed to 3613.83 million tons down to the depth of 1200m. Darjeeling coalfield is stretched 77 kilometers between Pankhabari to the west and Jaldhaka to the east. A total of 15 million tons of coal down to a depth of 300m have been estimated in this area. Barjora coal field of Bankura district occupies about 40 sq. km. areas with a total reserve of 114.27 million tons down to a depth of 300m.

Dolomite

In the Jainti area of Jalpaiguri district, extensive deposits of dolomite have occurred. Two distinct bands of dolomite are found in this area. The most important deposits of this district are located at Mahakal, Machia Khola-Baje Khola, Chunia Jhora, and Hathipotha-Phoaskhawa Nala blocks. The thickness of the individual dolomite bands varies between 0.6m to 38.0m. The dolomite which is banded massive, crystalline, and also cherry in appearance, very fine-grained to medium-grained, dark to bluish-grey in color, has a total reserve of 293 million tons up to a depth of 50m within an area of nearly 5 sq. km.

Fire clay

Fire clay deposits are mainly associated with the coal seams over a wide area in Ranigunj and Birbhum coalfields. Also, some of the China clay quarries of the Muhammad Bazar and Chandidaspur in the district of Birbhum yield fire clay. The thickness of fire clay seams varies from 0.61m. to 4.9m. In West Bengal, there is a total reserve of 64 million tons of all grades of fire clays and out of which the Ranigunj coalfield has an approximate reserve of 4.139m tons up to a depth of 6.1m.

Limestone

In the district of Purulia limestone is found in Jhalda and Tansa areas. Also, it is visible around Kudagara, Tutu Pahar, Subarnarekha river, Dankagarha Nala, Balamu, and Maramu areas of Purulia district and Harirampur and Salaipahar areas of Bankura district. Jhalda deposits are situated roughly about 13 km NE and 16 km NW of Jalda which has a total reserve of 13.76 million tonnes of crystalline limestone of different grades. The total reserve of limestone of Digardih-Chhota Baked area has been estimated at 4.76 million tons up to 30m depths. In the Tansi area, a crystalline limestone band is exposed for a strike length of 25m. and an average thickness of 4.5m. It is estimated that 0.54 million tons of limestone are reserved up to a depth of 30m. In the Kudagars area, a total reserve of 0.174 million tons of limestone have been estimated up to a depth of 30m and in the Maramu-Balamu area, a total reserve of 0.226 million tons of limestone up to 30m depths has been estimated. Jabar area has an estimated reserve of 7.2 million tons of limestone up to 30m depths while the Hanspathar has a total of 4.19 million tons of crystalline limestone. The limestone deposits of Harirampur-Salai Pahari of Bankura district have a total reserve of 2.154 million with an average grade of 12.57 percent insoluble, 35.46 percent CaO and 13.16 percent Mg O is available from this area up to a depth of 30m.

Silica sand, moulding sand, and glass sand

From the beds of many rivers in the northern and western parts of West Bengal, huge reserves of sands are available. Though most of the sands are impure and of inferior quality, the sands of Damodar and Ajoy rivers are in great demand for stowing in the coal mines of Ranigunj Coalfields. It is estimated that there are 589.3 million tons of sand in Damodar River from its junction with Barakar River to Pinjrapols and 294.64 million tons of sand in Ajoy River. In the Andal-Dubchuria-Gopalmath area of Bardhaman district, the reserve of molding sands is estimated to be 1.5 million tonnes down to a depth of 3 to 4 meters over an area of 1.0 sq. km. A probable reserve of 4.89 million tons of molding sand is available in the Bardhaman district and 0.5 million tons of molding sands are estimated in Bankura district down to a depth of 3 meters. But there is a lack of good quality glass sands. Most of the glass sands are impure, mixed with iron oxides, and suitable for colored glasses. However, fairly large occurrences of quartzite of the Proterozoic are available in the district of Bardhaman and Purulia, which may be suitable for its utilization in glass factories. It has a reserve of 0.53 million tons of quartz down to a depth of 10m.

Wolframite

The areas of Chhendapathar and Porapahar in the district of Bankura are full of wolframite. There are three mineralized zones situated at Dhajuri North, Dhajuri South, and Ghattusel. The total reserve of 0.4 million tons of wolframite ore with a variable grade containing 0.002 percent to 0.5 percent WO3 is estimated in these areas. In the Porapahar area there is a reserve of 0.15876 million tons of ore with an average of 0.01 percent WO3.

Organization of the Study

The book contains a total of nine chapters including an ***Introduction***, wherein the major issues of the 2021 assembly elections; the importance of the study; the area of study, objectives of the study, and methodology have been presented. The socio-economic background of the respondents has been arranged in some tables. After the tables, I have discussed the physical background of the area of study that includes location and situation, ports of Bengal, etc. These were followed by the topography, diversification of land, rivers, climate, temperature, soils minerals, etc.

The Second Chapter - ***Socio-Economic and Political Status of West Bengal*** - enumerates the existing social, economic, and political status of the State. A comparative method was adopted to highlight the veritable status of the State under study. Year-wise and state-wise data were analyzed for understanding Bengal's real position in terms of other states, and analysis of inter-district data of the State will help the readers to understand the actual position of its various districts too. Again some tables were used to highlight the education status, state-wise population and growth, industry and economic growth and how poverty and inequality are related, and the current poverty scenario in West Bengal.

Thereafter, the political participation of people has been highlighted. In this part, I have prepared a table to show the participation of women in politics. In this table, the rate of women's participation in comparison with their male counterparts in Lok Sabha, Rajya Sabha, Legislative Assembly have been delineated. Thereafter, I have written the current status of participation of people in local governments. This chapter ends with a conclusion.

The Third Chapter – *Achievements of Mamata Banerjee* - deals with the achievements of Mamata Banerjee as a chief minister of the state for the last decade. It will help readers to make an assessment as to why she was re-elected despite the prime minister-home minister-led entire union ministry and many key political heads of various states stormed campaign on the eve of elections. Her achievements in the economic field, tourism industry, and industrial sector have been enumerated. The agriculture and allied sectors, health and family welfare, inclusive health for all have been illustrated one by one in figures and diagrams. At the end in a long list of three dozens of important welfare schemes, either new or borrowed from the Centre, have been presented with a brief description. That will increase the level of awareness and enthusiasm of readers about the welfare schemes and services introduced by the government, which touched upon the life of almost every person from cradle to crematorium. The chapter concludes after highlighting additional inputs on the government's newly formulated policies made through the latest budgets.

The 2021 elections and their different phases have been highlighted in the Fourth Chapter – *The Legislative Assembly Elections - 2021*. Also, it gives a brief description of the Constitutional provisions relating to the elections of the State Assemblies in India. Further, the dynamic role of the Election Commission of India has been discussed. In addition to these, some measures and provisions of the ECI that have been taken by them have been presented. These include the restriction on media coverage; measures of ECI to curb the money power in elections, confiscation of illegal items during election days, violation of Model Code of Conduct, etc. The following part discussed what the model code of conduct is and how it was violated by various political parties on the eve of elections. This chapter ended with a wonderful conclusion.

In the Fifth Chapter – ***Violence in Pre and Post-Poll Bengal***, I have traced out the roots of violence in Bengal, and fostering of violence in Bengal since the days of sixties of the previous century. The citation of Naxalite movements and the mention of TMC's Terror on CPI(M) from 2011-2021, violent politics in Bengal during the TMC regime, violence on BJP workers by TMC in the pre-poll period etc. were nicely pointed out. The other things discussed in this chapter are as follows: clashes and killings in 2nd phase of elections – attacks on BJP's candidates - violence in the 3rd phase of elections - attacks held on candidates - fourth phase of elections and violence at Cooch Behar. How tension increased in Cooch Behar after bombs were recovered, extents of violence in the fifth phase of elections, exorbitant violence in 6th phase of elections, violence in the 7th phase of elections, firing during the sixth phase of elections and violence in the 8th phase of elections have been enumerated. Not only that, but post-poll violence in West Bengal has also been discussed to show the unethical, unconstitutional, and unfair practices adopted by the leaders and supporters of Trinamool Congress leaders.

The Sixth Chapter – ***Perception Regarding the TMC Government*** - deals with the perception of people regarding the performance of the TMC government. I have asked questions to the respondents and on the basis of their responses, I have prepared 24 Tables. In this chapter, the respondents have expressed their opinions in different issues and welfare schemes of the government that are not encouraging at all.

Next, I examined the probable reasons for BJP's defeat in the Bengal elections. In the Seventh Chapter - ***Arguments for BJP's debacle in Assembly Elections***, the reasons were highlighted under the sub-heading - Reasons for Deplorable Defeat of the BJP in Bengal.

The Eighth Chapter – ***Understanding the Rise and Fall of CPI(M) and Congress in Bengal*** – examines the significant rise of the Indian National Congress after the independence, and how the CPI(M)-led Left Front (LF) rose through the violent and disruptive political actions in the '60s of the previous century, and how the miserable defeat of the both in the 2021 elections have happened. I have enumerated the reasons for withering away of the Left Front and the Congress from the West Bengal Legislative Assembly in 2021. The ***Concluding Chapter*** provides some general as well as specific recommendations. The book wraps up with a magnificent conclusion.

Chapter - II

Socio-Economic and Political Status of West Bengal

"Wealth flows from energy and ideas."

- William Feather

Introduction

After discussing the importance of the study, its aims and objectives, and the methodology followed by the physical background of the state, it is necessary to enumerate the existing social, economic, and political status of West Bengal. In this chapter, we will adopt a comparative method to highlight the veritable status of the State under study. Year-wise and state-wise data will be analyzed for understanding Bengal's authentic position in terms of other states, and analysis of inter-district data of the State will help us to understand the actual position of its various districts too. Every government intends to provide as many benefits and facilities as possible to its voters, because it is the voters who always hold the determinant role in the Parliamentary system of elections.

Therefore, West Bengal Government has also been endeavoring to provide various amenities to its people as per capacity, goodwill, and resources since independence. History demonstrates that the works of development were frequently interrupted in Bengal due to the over activism of a few political parties with idiosyncratic ideologies. The people of this state witnessed cumbersome political turmoil after the 14-years' fruitful administration of Dr. Bidhan Chandra Roy between 1948 and 1962, and another 5 years up to 1967 under the chief minister of Prafulla Chandra Sen. Before the beginning of Jyoti Basu's ruling in 1977 that continued up to 2000, only the 7th Assembly was dominated by the Congress Party under the chief minister of Siddhartha Shankar Ray (1972-77) that worked for full five years term. But the decade from 1962 to 1972 was the decade of political turmoil and circus in Bengal including 2-time President's Rule in

1971 and 1972. Buddhadeb Bhattacharya stepped into the shoe after relinquishment of the chair by Jyoti Basu in 2000 and continued in office until the Communist parties were badly defeated by the Trinamool Congress-Indian National Congress Party alliance in the fifteenth assembly elections held in 2011. Mamata Banerjee, the only woman chief minister in Bengal, is the incumbent for the last 10-plus years now. However, the following part seeks to deal with the socio-economic and political situation of this state under her administration, and it begins with the educational scenario in the state.

Education scenario in West Bengal

We are living in the 21st century. This century is the centuplicate of the youths; also it is the age of science and technology. "The world today has more knowledge than ever before, but not everyone can benefit from it. Globally countries have made major strides in increasing access to education at all levels and increasing enrolment rates in schools, and basic literacy skills have improved tremendously."[1] Education is the backbone of a state. It determines the character and future growth of a state. Further, it can be said that "Education is a dynamic process that starts from birth."[2] (It is education that starts even prior to birth i.e. from the mother's womb. "A child surrounded by parents and other siblings experiences her surroundings and responds accordingly."[3] Pramanik and Singh[4] consider that "Education is the mirror to the society and is the seed as well as the flower of the socio-economic development. It transforms human beings from ignorance to enlightenment, from shades of social backwardness to light of social amelioration and a nation from underdevelopment to faster social and economic development."

In India primary school starts from Class I and continues up to V, while Upper Primary runs between Class VI to VIII. To understand the school education system in Bengal fully, one should know the perplexing segregation of the school education system that comprises all the primary schools, upper primary schools, primary with upper primary, secondary and higher secondary, upper primary with secondary and higher secondary only, primary with upper primary and secondary, and upper primary with secondary school. West Bengal is now divided into 23 districts which include the newly formed Alipurduar district (formed on 25 June 2014), Kalimpong district (formed on 14 February 2017), Jhargram district (formed on 4 April 2017), and the splitting of the former Bardhaman district into Purba Bardhaman and Paschim Bardhaman (formed on 7 April 2017). The districts are further grouped into five divisions. Now let us examine the elementary education scenario first. It is to be noted that the available data of the National

Institute of Educational Planning and The administration is of 2016-2017; hence, quite naturally the mention of some of the present districts might be absent from the report.

The following table (Table 2.1) highlights elementary education in West Bengal. It comes to light that in West Bengal, the total numbers of schools are 96,418 including 82,993 governments, 10,404 private and 3,021 madrasas and unrecognized schools. However, district-wise population, a total number of schools including government, private, Madarsas and unrecognized as well as private schools in rural areas has been segregated in the following table. It is revealed that maximum numbers of schools are available in Paschim Medinipur (9,702) followed by South 24 Parganas district (7,464), North 24 Parganas (7,452), Bardhaman (6,942), and Murshidabad (6,820). Madarsas and unrecognized schools are mostly found in North 24 Parganas followed by Cooch Behar, Murshidabad, and Bhibhum. Interestingly, private schools are mostly set up in rural Maldah. South 24 Parganas hold the second position in establishing private schools, and it is followed by Purba Medinipur, Murshidabad and Paschim Medinipur. This proves that even the rural guardians are showing their interest in private and expensive education for their kids. It is pointed out by several guardians that, in government schools the quality of teaching and discipline education are

Table: 2.1 Elementary education report card 2016-17

District	Total Population	Total Schools	Government Schools	Private Schools	Madarsas & Unrecognised Schools	Government Schools - Rural	Private Schools - Rural
1. Alipurduar	1,501,983 (2011)	1,969	1,624	332	13	1567	313
2. Bankura	3,596,674 (2011)	5,213	4,936	261	16	4,751	218
3. Barddhaman	7,723,663 (2011)	6,820	6,204	403	213	5,280	224
4. Birbhum	3,502,404 (2011)	4,253	3,838	149	266	3,642	112
5. Dakshin Dinajpur	19,76,276 (2020)	2,285	2,075	184	26	1979	168
6. Darjeeling	1,846,823 (2011)	1,812	1,545	262	5	1407	218
7. Howrah	1,077,075 (2011)	3,678	3,039	570	69	2,378	388
8. Hooghly	5,519,145 (2011)	4,592	4,173	339	80	3,514	248
9. Jalpaiguri	3,872,846 (2011)	2,683	2,246	395	42	5,051	329
10. Cooch Behar	2,819,086 (2011)	3,580	3,198	18	364	3,059	15
11. Kolkata	4,496,694 (2011)	2,789	2,094	645	50	00	00
12. Maldah	3,988,845 (2011)	4,561	3,176	1,273	112	3,041	1,216
13. Murshidabad	7,103,807 (2011)	6,949	5,963	659	327	5,533	593
14. Nadia	5,167,601 (2011)	4,539	3,996	502	41	3,468	396
15. North 24 Parganas	10,009,781 (2011)	7,452	5,878	972	602	4,096	355
16. Paschim	5,913,457 (2011)	9,702	8,846	636	220	8,378	531

Medinipur							
17. Purba Medinipur	5,095,875 (2011)	6,640	5,874	736	30	5,612	665
18. Purulia	2,930,115 (2011)	4,964	4,332	433	199	4,195	380
19. Siliguri	470,275 (2011)	1,161	812	293	56	696	194
20. South 24 Parganas	8,161,961 (2011)	7,464	6,182	1,021	261	5,781	907
21. Uttar Dinajpur	3,007,134 (2011)	3,312	2,962	321	29	2,824	294
Total	**89,781,520**	**96,418**	**82,993**	**10,404**	**3,021**	**76,252**	**15,528**

Source: Elementary Education in India: Where do we stand? District Report Card 2016-17 Volume – II, National Institute of Educational Planning and Administration, New Delhi.

poorly imparted. At the same time, it needs to be highlighted that there is no dearth of government-aided or sponsored schools in rural Bengal. A total of 8,378 numbers of government schools were set up in rural Bengal. South 24 Parganas has the second-highest number of government schools followed by Purba Medinipur, Murshibadad, Bankura, and Purulila.

Table: 2.2 District-wise student enrollments in different schools

District	Total Enrolment (2016-17)	Enrolment in Government Schools	Enrolment in Private Schools	Enrolment in Madarsas and Unrecognised Schools
1. Alipurduar	197,378	1,63,512	31,886	1980
2. Bankura	494,439	461,863	27,462	5,114
3. Barddhaman	889,854	805,284	57,366	27,204
4. Birbhum	507,428	461,845	13,715	31,868
5. Dakshin Dinajpur	2,32,282	207,335	18,716	6,231
6. Darjeeling	81,052	72,896	8,156	00
7. Howrah	524,630	449,084	58,035	17,511

8. Hooghly	566,356	501,666	47,409	17,281
9. Jalpaiguri	328,838	284,734	40,043	4,061
10. Cooch Behar	425,612	385,149	3,603	36,860
11. Kolkata	366,489	250,227	53,840	2,089
12. Maldah	786,686	579,920	132,108	74,658
13. Murshidabad	1,226,441	1,036,547	83,546	106,348
14. Nadia	621,268	562,297	48,671	10,300
15. North 24 Parganas	940,683	904,503	12,001	24,179
16. Paschim Medinipur	828,947	761,512	51,964	15,471
17. Purba Medinipur	675,777	599,705	70,335	5,737
18. Purulia	441,162	421,535	14,601	5,011
19. Siliguri	163,887	120,823	36,446	6,618
20. South 24 Parganas	1,149,613	989,378	113,291	46,944
21. Uttar Dinajpur	545,533	482,660	45,854	17,019
Total	**1,19,94,355**	**1,05,02,525**	**9,69,048**	**4,40,724**

Source: Elementary Education in India: Where do we stand? District Report Card 2016-17 Volume – II, National Institute of Educational Planning and Administration, New Delhi.

Table: 2.3 District-wise numbers of teachers in West Bengal

District	Total Teachers (2015-16)	Teachers in Government Schools	Teachers Private Schools	Teachers in Madarsas & Unrecognised Schools	Female Teachers (2016-17)	Schools with SMC (2016-17)
1. Alipurduar	10,923	8,022	2,473	132	49.7	33.2
2. Bankura	24,827	22,093	2,351	180	31.4	59.8
3. Barddhaman	41,693	34,192	4,216	1,789	42.6	57.7
4. Birbhum	21,668	18,067	1,415	1,976	34.1	13.8
5. Dakshin Dinajpur	11,254	9,529	1,007	325	35.3	69.1
6. Darjeeling	8,710	6,733	2,097	49	48.3	96.2
7. Howrah	26,396	20,020	5,453	842	51.09	48.6
8. Hooghly	29,243	26,296	2,626	793	41.3	54.4
9. Jalpaiguri	15,570	12,012	3,058	182	49.5	36.1
10. Cooch Behar	19,076	15,284	204	2,740	36.8	95.5

11. Kolkata	27,038	16,047	10,402	456	68.0	69.1
12. Maldah	28,249	17,612	10,741	1,806	37.9	58.6
13. Murshidabad	44,239	33,983	6,567	3,975	36.9	100.00
14. Nadia	31,127	25,603	4,969	485	44.1	24.9
15. North 24 Parganas	48,782	39,776	5,233	3,381	47.3	33.9
16. Paschim Medinipur	47,003	39,711	5,268	1,583	39.7	40.9
17. Purba Medinipur	38,519	31,387	6,526	355	41.3	49.1
18. Purulia	19,350	17,498	2,570	1,213	27.4	57.6
19. Siliguri	9,167	5,240	2,938	196	55.9	34.6
20. South 24 Parganas	44,629	33,318	9,143	2,306	48.6	73.3
21. Uttar Dinajpur	18,183	15,391	2,665	453	41.5	57.2
Total	**5,65,646**	**4,47,814**	**91,922**	**25,217**	**43.27**	**55.40**

Source: Elementary Education in India: Where do we stand? District Report Card 2016-17 Volume – II, National Institute of Educational Planning and Administration, New Delhi.

It is found that in West Bengal total numbers of teachers are 5,65,646 including 4,47,814 in government schools and 91,922 in private schools and 25,217 in Madarsas and unrecognized schools. In West Bengal, there are substantial numbers of female teachers (43.27%). But the most disheartening fact is that in more than half (55.40%) of the schools in West Bengal there are not valid school managing committees. There are some districts where the percentages of valid School Managing Committees (SMCs) are very negligible. The topmost district in the list with SMCs (in a negative sense) is Birbhum, where only 13% of schools are having Managing Committees in 2016-17. Birbhum is followed by Nadia (24.9%), North 24 Parganas (33.9%), Siliguri (34.6%), and Paschim Medinipur (40.9%). Without the president of a valid managing committee, a lot of problems have emerged in a school such as – the school cannot distribute school uniforms to the students, no library books can be purchased from library grant, no 18-years service benefit can be given to the teachers, and many administrative, as well as financial works, remain pending in school. The School Education department, the local MLAs, and the office of the District Inspector of Schools are quite well aware of the fact, but no affirmative action has been taken by any of them. The government only extended the term of the managing committee (MC) at the expiry of the term of the existing MC. Interestingly, where the president has resigned, in most of the cases no new president has been appointed thereafter. The District Inspector of Schools has the authority to appoint DDO or Administrator. How the order of the DI of Schools is violated can be understood from the following fact. One SI of Schools in Maheshtala (West) Circle in 2018 defying the order of the then District Inspector of Schools of South 24 Parganas threw one School in the midst of chaos and disharmony. Thus by the whim of the higher authorities, many Schools in Bengal are in the middle of uncertainty, and complex administrative crux.

When examined it was observed that maximum numbers of teachers are working in North 24 Parganas district (48,782). The second-highest number of teachers are found in Paschim Medinipur district i.e. 47,003, and these teachers include 39,711 in government schools, 5,268 in private schools, and 1,583 in Madarsas and unrecognized schools. The third position is held by Bardhaman district where the total numbers of teachers are 41,693 comprising 34,192 in government schools, 4,216 in private schools and 1,789 in Madarsas and unrecognized schools. On the other hand, the lowest numbers of school teachers are found in Darjeeling i.e. 8,710. This includes 6,733 teachers in government schools, 2,097 teachers in private schools, and only 49 in Madarass and unrecognized schools.

Another interesting aspect of the education system in West Bengal is the large number of female teachers. Most of the female teachers are engaged in Kolkata (68.0%), followed by Siliguri (55.9%), Howrah (51.09%). The opposite trend is found in rural districts such as Purulia (37.4%), Bankura (31.4%), Birbhum (34.1%), Dakshin Dinajpur (35.3%) etc.

Table: 2.4 Teachers by educational qualification (Other than contractual teachers)

District	Ph.D./M. Phil Degree Holders			Post-graduate Teachers		
	Pry. Teachers only	U. Prim. + Sec.+H.S.	Contractual	Pry. Teachers	U. Prim.+ Sec.+H.S.	Contractual
1. Alipurduar	3	7	1	388	837	194
2. Bankura	20	68	2	1,110	3,309	301
3. Barddhaman	133	272	45	1,918	5,618	651
4. Birbhum	27	67	7	1,002	2,662	267
5. Dakshin Dinajpur	4	18	5	502	1,316	191
6. Darjeeling	8	18	12	90	533	371
7. Howrah	56	131	8	1,205	4,051	635
8. Hooghly	57	100	8	1,474	4,003	459
9. Jalpaiguri	24	40	14	463	1,669	276
10. Cooch	55	70	23	784	2,630	168

Behar						
11. Kolkata	25	196	5	1,168	3,833	384
12. Maldah	28	48	8	1,164	3,099	486
13. Murshidabad	25	73	17	1,730	5,201	1,188
14. Nadia	32	117	11	1,517	4,518	1,174
15. North 24 Parganas	47	265	24	1,789	8,838	551
16. Paschim Medinipur	53	118	10	2,327	6,103	599
17. Purba Medinipur	75	118	22	2,025	5,415	855
18. Purulia	30	50	9	764	2,567	288
19. Siliguri	8	49	2	235	1,065	100
20. South 24 Parganas	105	116	37	1,391	5,945	518
21. Uttar Dinajpur	19	111	68	750	2196	412
Total	**834**	**4104**	**328**	**23796**	**75408**	**10068**

Source: Elementary Education in India: Where do we stand? District Report Card 2016-17 Volume – II, National Institute of Educational Planning and Administration, New Delhi.

Now, let us see the educational qualification of the teachers. West Bengal is a cultural state and its educational heritage is age-old. It comes to light from the District Report Card 2016-2017, Volume-II, published by the National Institute of Educational Planning and Administration (NIEPA), New Delhi that, in total 834 Primary school teachers only are having Ph. D. or M.Phil Degrees; 4104 teachers in Upper Primary, Secondary, and Higher Secondary schools are qualified with the highest University Degrees; and 328 contractual teachers are similarly qualified. On the other hand, 23,796 teachers are teaching with post-graduate degrees in the Primary schools; 75,408 teachers in Upper-Primary, Secondary and Higher Secondary schools are engaged with post-graduate qualification and the numbers of contractual teachers in different schools across the state are 10,068.

When we see the district-wise number of Ph. D./M.Phil qualified teachers it comes to light that, the 'rice bowl of Bengal' i.e. Bardhaman district is having the highest numbers of Ph.D/M.Phil degree holder teachers in different levels – in Primary level 133 teachers; in Upper Primary, Secondary, and Higher Secondary level 272 teachers and even there are 45 contractual teachers in the district with the highest degrees of India. South 24 Parganas district is also having a good number of teachers with Ph.D. and M. Phil degrees. In Primary Schools, only a total of 105 teachers are very highly qualified, while in Upper Primary, Secondary, and Higher Secondary levels we find 116 teachers with M.Phil/Ph. D. degrees and 37 contractual teachers are also having the same degrees. The smallest numbers of highly qualified teachers are engaged in Alipurduar – only 3 teachers are three with Ph. D./M. Phil degrees, 7 teachers with similar degrees are working in Upper Primary, Secondary and Higher Secondary level while only one is a contractual teacher.

Postgraduate degree holder teachers in Primary schools are mostly engaged in Paschim Medinipur district, where the rate of education is always encouraging. From the available data in Table 2.3 we find out that, 2,327 teachers with Master's Degrees are teaching in Primary Schools and this number is 6,103 in Upper Primary, Secondary and Higher Secondary Schools. Even 599 contractual teachers are teaching with Master's Degrees in different schools in the district of Paschim Medinipur. The second position in this regard is held by its sister state – Purba Medinipur where total Primary teachers and Upper-Primary, Secondary, and Higher Secondary teachers with Post-Graduation Degrees are 2,025, and 5,415 respectively.

Table: 2. 5 Number of College per Lakh Population (1823 YEARS), Average Enrolment per College

States/UTs	No. of College	College per lakh population	Average Enrolment per College
1. Andaman & Nicobar Islands	6	12	492
2.. Andhra Pradesh	4780	48	493
3. Arunachal Pradesh	19	11	1943
4. Assam	485	13	1009
5. Bihar	629	5	1794
6. Chandigarh	27	18	805
7. Chhatisgarh	574	20	646
8. Delhi	184	8	1081
9. Gujarat	1815	27	624
10. Haryana	1054	33	766
11. Karnataka	3098	44	414
12. Kerala	962	29	557
13. Madhya Pradesh	2009	23	611

14. Maharashtra	4512	35	756
15. Odisha	1089	23	600
16. Punjab	956	29	724
17. Rajasthan	2435	29	725
18. Tamil Nadu	1985	27	574
19. Tripura	36	8	1086
20. Uttar Pradesh	4049	17	1351
21. West Bengal	857	8	1655

Source: All India Survey on Higher Education 2010-2011, 2013, Ministry of Human Resource Development, Department of Higher Education, Government of India, p. T-4 (54)

Table: 2.6 State-wise Enrolment in Universities Teaching Departments and its Constituent Units/Off-campus Centres

Sl. No.	State	No. of Universities (2010-11)	No. of Universities (2020)	Ph. D.			M. Phil.			Total Post Graduate
				Male	Female	Total	Male	Female	Total	
1	Andhra Pradesh	46	28	5279	2743	8022	1366	715	2081	178866
2	Assam	9	24	1053	701	1754	39	47	86	20596
3	Bihar	20	21	1150	407	1557	0 0	0 0	0 0	45682
4	Delhi	26	32	3906	3102	7008	2430	1994	4424	308519
5	Gujarat	36	59	1431	770	2201	485	343	828	38496
6	Karnataka	43	59	4991	2496	7487	436	403	839	126722
7	Kerala	16	20	1071	1177	2248	184	408	592	27666
8	Madhya Pradesh	28	54	598	312	910	382	318	700	23075
9	Maharashtra	44	53	3158	1310	4468	960	584	1544	135001
10	Odisha	18	26	349	154	503	330	413	743	14062
11	Punjab	17	30	892	1020	1912	140	292	432	82494
12	Rajasthan	43	71	1816	1148	2964	85	110	195	30114
13	Tamil Nadu	59	53 **	4708	2834	7542	1440	1749	3189	317255

14	Tripura	3	3	81	30	111	00	00	00	11531
15	Uttar Pradesh	56	75	3556	1622	5178	645	576	1221	71525
16	West Bengal	26	42	1969	828	2797	651	749	1400	112032

Source: All India Survey on Higher Education 2010-2011, 2013, Ministry of Human Resource Development, Department of Higher Education, Government of India, p. T-13 (61)

At present the numbers of recognized universities in West Bengal are 42 including 29 state universities, 2 deemed universities, 1 national law university, and 11 private universities. All the 11 private universities, and state-run universities such as Kazi Nazrul University (2012), Mahatma Gandhi University (2020), Bankura University (2014), Cooch Behar Panchanan Barma University (2012), Diamond Harbour Women's University (2013), Raiganj University (2015), the Sanskrit College and University (2015), West Bengal University of Teachers' Education, Education Planning and Administration (2015) and Kanyashree University (2020) were established during the last decade. In Andhra Pradesh, there were 46 universities, but after the bifurcation of the state Telangana was created, and in the newly formed state at present, there are 21 universities. In Assam, there is a total of 21 universities including 2 central universities, 1 deemed university, 15 state universities, and 6 private universities. In Delhi, this number is 32. Out of them, there are five central universities, seven state universities, and 13 deemed universities. The status of one institute, the National School of Drama, is unclear. Delhi also has an international university established by the eight-member nations of SAARC. Gujarat has total 59 universities at present that include 18 state universities, 4 agriculture universities, 3 central universities, 2 private aided, and 32 private universities. Tripura is the third smallest state in India. The state has one Central University (Tripura University) and one private university which is a branch of the Institute of Chartered Financial Analysts of India.

In terms of Ph. D. registration, it can be found that Andhra Pradesh Universities hold the topmost position, where total enrolment in Universities' teaching department is 8,022 including 5279 males and 2743 females. The second position is occupied by another South Indian state Tamil Nadu where the figure is also quite encouraging – total 7,542 teachers comprising 4708 male and 2,834 female. Delhi is not far behind its' southern counterparts. It is found that Delhi has a total of 7,008 enrolment in Universities Teaching Department comprising 3906 male and 3102 female. But out of the above 16 states, West Bengal (total 2797) comes behind its other counterparts such as Karnataka (total 7542), Uttar Pradesh (total 5178), Maharashtra (total 4468), and Rajasthan (total 2964).

Table: 2.7 Education Budget in some States

State (Year)	Total amount (in crore)	% of the total budget
Delhi (2020-21)	15,815	24.33
Gujarat (2020)	31,955	N/A
Maharashtra (2019-20)	71,302	19
Karnataka (2020-21)	29,768	11
Tamil Nadu (2020)	34,100	19 (% rise)
Kerala (2020)	20,862	14.46
Bihar (2020)	35,191	16.62
West Bengal (2020)	37,059	14.49

Source: Compilation from various sites

The education budget of a few states shown in Table 2.6 indicates that, West Bengal's budget in the year 2020 was the highest i.s. Rs.37,059 crore which is 14.49 of the total state budget. The highest allocation in the education budget was done by the Maharashtra government (Rs.71,302.00 crore) followed by Bihar (total Rs.35,191 crore), Gujarat (Rs.31,955 crore) and Karnataka (Rs. 29,768 crore). Delhi's allocation in the education sector was Rs.15,815 crore, which was 24.33 percent of the total budget amount of that state, while Kerala spent Rs.20,862 crore which was 14.46 percent of its total budget in 2020. Education is the only weapon by which we can defeat so many social, and political evils. The first Education Minister of Independent India, Maulana Abul Kalam Azad said in the parliament in 1948 that, "I need hardly say that whatever be our program for industrial, scientific, agricultural, commercial or material progress and development, none of them can be achieved without an improvement of the human material which is the basis of our national wealth. That human material is largely conditioned by the training and education which it receives. It seems to me that whatever we think of defense or food or industry and commerce, we must take every step to see that education is given the priority among our national requirement."[5] Amartya Sen also envisaged that the solution of all problems, be they related to the economy, development, or population, lies in education.

Population and education

It is necessary to understand that population and education are correlated. It is education that empowers a general and poor child from rural areas or urban huts along with the urban-born rich students. Through the enhancement of education, one can be transformed from a burden of society to the wealth of the society and the country as a whole. When the population is more, the infrastructural expenditure and budgetary allocation are also high. Thus the growth of population affects the inequitable allotment of developmental money to the institutions. A controlled population is always desirable and necessary for the better and quicker development of a state. But a controlled or limited population always holds good for the economic growth of a nation.

The relationships between population growth and growth of economic output have been studied extensively[6] by Headey and Hodge. Many analysts believe that economic growth in high-income countries is likely to be relatively slow in coming years in part because population growth in these countries is predicted to slow considerably[7] On the other hand, it is argued by another section of scholars[8] that population growth has been and will continue to be problematic as more people inevitably use more of the finite resources available on earth, thereby reducing long-term potential growth.). Population growth affects many phenomena such as the age structure of a country's population, international migration, economic inequality, and the size of a country's workforce. These factors both affect and are affected by overall economic growth.

Table: 2.8 State-wise population and growth share

R n k	State/U T	Population		Growth (2019-2011)		Share (%)
		2019	2011	Absolute	%	2019
1	Uttar Pradesh	237,882,725	199,812,341	38,070,384	19.05	17.35
2	Bihar	124,799,926	104,099,452	20,700,474	19.89	9.10
3	Maharashtra	123,144,223	112,374,333	10,769,890	9.58	8.98

4	West Bengal	99,609,303	91,276,115	8,333,188	9.13	7.26
5	Madhya Pradesh	85,358,965	72,626,809	12,732,156	17.53	6.22
6	Rajasthan	81,032,689	68,548,437	12,484,252	18.21	5.91
7	Tamil Nadu	77,841,267	72,147,030	5,694,237	7.89	5.68
8	Karnataka	67,562,686	61,095,297	6,467,389	10.59	4.93
9	Gujarat	63,872,399	60,439,692	3,432,707	5.68	4.66
10	Andhra Pradesh	53,903,393	49,576,777	4,326,616	8.73	3.93
11	Odisha	46,356,334	41,974,218	4,382,116	10.44	3.38
12	Telangana	39,362,732	35,004,000	4,358,732	12.45	2.87
13	Jharkhand	38,593,948	32,988,134	5,605,814	16.99	2.81
14	Kerala	35,699,443	33,406,061	2,293,382	6.87	2.60
15	Assam	35,607,039	31,205,576	4,401,463	14.10	2.60
16	Punjab	30,141,373	27,743,338	2,398,035	8.64	2.20
17	Chhattisgarh	29,436,231	25,545,198	3,891,033	15.23	2.15
18	Haryana	28,204,692	25,351,462	2,853,230	11.25	2.06
NCT	Delhi	18,710,922	16,787,941	1,922,981	11.45	1.36
UT1	Jammu & Kashmir	13,606,320	12,258,433	1,347,887	11.00	0.99
19	Uttarakhand	11,250,858	10,086,292	1,164,566	11.55	0.82
20	Himachal Pradesh	7,451,955	6,864,602	587,353	8.56	0.54
21	Tripura	4,169,794	3,673,917	495,877	13.50	0.30
22	Meghalaya	3,366,710	2,966,889	399,821	13.48	0.25
23	Manipur	3,091,545	2,855,794	235,751	8.26	0.23
24	Nagaland	2,249,695	1,978,502	271,193	13.71	0.16
25	Goa	1,586,250	1,458,545	127,705	8.76	0.12
26	Arunachal Pradesh	1,570,458	1,383,727	186,731	13.49	0.11
UT2	Puducherry	1,413,542	1,247,953	165,589	13.27	0.10
27	Mizoram	1,239,244	1,097,206	142,038	12.95	0.09
UT3	Chandigarh	1,158,473	1,055,450	103,023	9.76	0.08
28	Sikkim	690,251	610,577	79,674	13.05	0.05
UT4	Dadra & Nagar Haveli and Daman & Diu	615,724	586,956	28,768	4.90	0.04

UT5	A.& N.Islands	417,036	380,581	36,455	9.58	0.03
UT6	Ladakh	289,023	290,492	-1,469	-0.51	0.02
UT7	Lakshadweep	73,183	64,473	8,710	13.51	0.01

State-wise population in 2019, the growth rate in comparison with the 2011 census result, and percentage of population share in India has been shown in the above table (Table 2.8). The data show that Uttar Pradesh is the most populous (total population 23,78,82,725 persons in 2019) state with a growth rate of 19.05 percent between 2011 and 2019; its share of the population in India is 17.35 percent. Bihar is the second most populated state with a population of 12,47,99,926 constituting 9.10 percent of the total population in India, while the third and the fourth positions are occupied by Maharashtra and West Bengal, where total number of population in 2019 were 12,31,44,223 and 9,96,09,303 persons respectively. These two states are having a population share of 8.98% and 7.26%. Out of 28 Indian states, Sikkim is the smallest populated state with a population size of only 6,15,724 persons, while Lakshadweep, with only 73,183 persons occupy the lowest position in terms of population size of the Union Territories.

Industry and economic growth

Once upon a time West Bengal was known for its industrial achievements. But since the 1960s of the preceding century, the destructive politics initiated by the Communist parties gradually diminished Bengal's industries and factories. One by one the big manufacturing industries either locked down or shifted to other states. The Times of India reported that "It was one of British India's most industrial regions, but during the 1960s West Bengal fell behind economically. Its per capita income declined."[9] However, we have discussed in detail the type and nature of movements and agitations of militant communists in Chapter VIII. Further, the status of the Industrial achievements of this State in the last decade has been delineated in the following chapter (Chapter III). Now, we may have a glimpse of the existing industrial status of West Bengal.

It is learned from the India Brand Equity Foundation (IBEF)[10] that, West Bengal is India's sixth-largest state in terms of economic size, and its Gross State Domestic Product (GSDP) is expected to reach Rs. 14.44 trillion (US$ 206.64 billion) in 2020-21. The average annual GSDP growth rate is about 12.62% between 2015-16 and 2020-21. West Bengal with a GSDP of USD 155.32 billion is the 4th largest contributor to India's services GDP and 6th largest contributor to India's manufacturing GDP.[11]

West Bengal is the largest producer of rice in India. Rice production for the state totaled 14.99 million tonnes in 2017-18. West Bengal is also a major producer of fish. During 2018-19, the state produced a total of 1.85 million tonnes of fish. As of November 2020, West Bengal had a total installed power generation capacity of 11,061.85 MW, of which 6,497.95 MW was under state utilities, 2,883.28 MW (private sector) and 1,680.62 MW (central utilities). Of the total installed power capacity, 9,097.62 MW was contributed by thermal power, 1,396.00 MW (hydropower) and 568.23 MW (renewable power).

The state is the second-largest tea-growing state in India. Total tea production in West Bengal stood at 415.48 million kgs in 2019-20, accounting for 29.27% share of India's total production.

According to the Department for Promotion of Industry and Internal Trade (DPIIT), Foreign Direct Investment (FDI) inflow in West Bengal, along with Sikkim and Andaman and the Nicobar Islands, totaled US$ 6351 million during April 2000 and September 2020. Some of the major initiatives are taken by the Government to promote West Bengal as an investment destination are:

The state received an investment of Rs. 4.45 lakh crore (US$ 63.13 billion) in the large industry from five Global Summit organized in the state so far.

- The State Government introduced West Bengal Information Technology and Electronics Policy 2018 to make West Bengal one of the leading states in India in IT & ITeS, ICT, and ESDM sectors.
- In the State Budget 2020-21, Rs. 1,158.40 crore (US$ 164.34 million) has been allocated to the Industries, Commerce, and Enterprises Department.
- The government introduced Tea Tourism and Allied Business Policy, 2019, to utilize unused tea gardens and boost tourism in the state.
- West Bengal plans to raise its share in the country's IT export to 25% by 2030. Total export from the IT sector of the state crossed an estimated Rs. 22,897 crore (US$ 3.28 billion) in 2018-19.

- As per State Budget 2020-21, the Government of West Bengal has allocated Rs. 260 crore (US$ 36.88 million) for the development of the IT and Electronics department in West Bengal.
- In December 2020, the state government approved construction of a deep seaport in Tajpur, which will be built for Rs. 15,000 crore (US$ 2,028 million).[12]

Poverty and inequality

But, poverty is a major issue in India and this state too. Aristotle said, "Poverty is the mother of revolution and crime."[13] The Economic Survey 2019-20 argued that ethical wealth creation – by combining the invisible hand of markets with the hand of trust – provides the way forward for India to develop economically. An often-repeated concern expressed with this economic model pertains to inequality. In the advanced economies, it was argued by economists that, "…higher inequality leads to adverse socio-economic outcomes but income per capita, a measure that reflects the impact of economic growth, has little impact. Some commentary, especially in advanced economies post the Global Financial Crisis, argues that inequality is no accident but an essential feature of capitalism."[14]

It comes to light from a report of The Hindustan Times that, annual per capita income growth in real terms between1993-94 and 1999-2000, West Bengal's growth rate was 5.5 percent while the all India average was 4.6 percent. During the next decade, West Bengal's growth rate fell to 4.9% while the all-India average went up to 5.5. Between 2011-12 and 2019-20, West Bengal's growth rate fell further to 4.2%, and although the all-India average growth rate fell to 5.2%, the gap has marginally increased. Further, it was pointed out that, as 72% of people in the state live in rural areas, this improvement in rural expenditure levels is reflected in the percentage of people below the poverty line. In 1999-2000, 27% of the people were below the poverty line in West Bengal while the national average was 26.7%. During the next decade, poverty fell by 7 percentage points to 20% in the state, while the national average fell to 22%. However, in the last decade poverty fell to 14% in the state (similar to the drop in the previous decade) while nationally poverty went up marginally to 23%.[15] If we compare West Bengal with some other states, it will be clear our status. SDGs India Index[16] reported that the percentage living below the poverty line (BPL) in Kerala is 7.05 percent; in Punjab, it is 8.26 percent; in Tamil Nadu this rate is 11.28 percent; in Gujarat, this rate is 16.63 percent and in Uttar Pradesh BPL rate is 29.43 percent.

State GDP

From the report of the Ministry of Statistics and Programme[17] we come to know that, Maharashtra has the highest GSDP among 33 Indian States and Union Territories. As of Financial Year 2018-19, Maharashtra contributes 13.88 percent of India's GDP at current prices, followed by Tamil Nadu (8.59%) and the most populous state Uttar Pradesh (8.35%). Other states in the top 5 are Gujarat (7.92%) and Karnataka (7.87%). West Bengal holds the sixth position with Rs. 12,53,832 crores (5.77%) followed by Rajasthan Rs.10,20,989 crores with a share of 4.99 percent. The top 5 states share 46.6 percent of India's total economy. Five states of South India together accounts for close to 30 percent. Eight states of North-East India shares 2.8 percent of the total India's GDP. Andaman and Nicobar Islands have the lowest GSDP in the list of 33 States/UTs. Next, in line comes to Mizoram, Arunachal Pradesh, Nagaland, and Manipur.

Foreign direct investment

Foreign direct Investment (FDI) scenario in some states has been highlighted through the following table (Table 2.8). The quarterly fact sheet on FDI from April, 2000 to September 2000 shows that Gujarat has been successful to attract the highest share of FDI which is Rs.1,38,530.00 crores constituting 35 percent of the total FDI in India from October 2019 to September 2020. Maharashtra, the economic hub of India attracted the second-highest amount of FDI during the same period, which was 20 percent of the total FDI in India. South Indian state Karnataka was the third-highest attractive state of the investors, who invested Rs.58,204.00 crore comprising 15 percent of the total Indian FDI. But unfortunately, West Bengal remained in the last position of the list of 10 states are given in the above table (Table 2.9) with merely Rs.3,348.00 crores, which is only 1 percent of the total FDI in India. Thus, we find that Bengal's position in terms of FDI is disheartening. Maybe this is due to several reasons including extortion of some political leaders of the ruling Trinamool Congress party, ideological and political rivalry of the center and the state, violent and disruptive political activities of the Left parties including the Communist Party of India (Marxist).

Table: 2.9 States/UTs attracting highest FDI equity inflows

Amount in Rupees Crores (in US$ Million)

S. No.	State	2019-20 (October – March)	2020-21 (April – September)	Cumulative Inflows (October, 19	%age to total Inflows (in

				- September, 20)	terms of US$)
1	Gujarat	18,964 (2,591)	1,19,566 (16,005)	1,38,530 (18,596)	35%
2	Maharashtra	52,073 (7,263)	27,143 (3,619)	79,216 (10,882)	20%
3	Karnataka	30,746 (4,289)	27,458 (3,660)	58,204 (7,949)	15%
4	Delhi	28,487 (3,973)	19,863 (2,663)	48,350 (6,635)	12%
5	Jharkhand	13,208 (1,852)	5,990 (792)	19,198 (2,644)	5%
6	Tamil Nadu	7,230 (1,006)	7,062 (938)	14,292 (1,944)	4%
7	Haryana	5,198 (726)	5,111 (682)	10,310 (1,408)	3%
8	Telangana	4,865 (680)	5,045 (668)	9,910 (1,348)	3%
9	Uttar Pradesh	1,738 (243)	1,680 (225)	3,418 (468)	1%
10	West Bengal	1,363 (190)	1,985 (261)	3,348 (451)	1%

Note: (i) Cumulative State-wise/UT-wise FDI equity inflows (from October 2019 to September 2020) are at – Annex-'C'. (ii) %age worked out in US$ terms & FDI inflows received through FIPB/SIA+ RBI's Automatic Route + acquisition of existing shares only. (iii) Figures are provisional.

Source: Quarterly fact sheet on Foreign Direct Investment (FDI) from April 2000 to September, 2020, p. 3.

Political participation of people

Democracy becomes vibrant with the participation of people. I wrote in 2010 in one of my research studies that, "People's participation in a decentralized political system is most vital for its survival."[18] Political Participation ensures people's empowerment. In this regard Renana Jhapvala[19] envisaged that, "Empowerment is the process by which the disempowered or powerless people can change their circumstances and begin to have control over their lives." Further, Valsamma Anthony[20] holds that "Empowerment is a multidimensional process, which should enable the individuals or a group of individuals to realize their full identity and powers in all spheres of life…Empowerment of women may also mean equal status to women, opportunity, and freedom to develop her." On the other hand, Archana Singh considers "Empowerment is a process of change by which citizens or groups acquire power and ability to take control over their lives."[21]

Political participation of people is considered as the highest ingredient of participatory democracy. The following part deals with people's participation in some high levels of democratic decision-making bodies. It comes to light that in the newly constituted West

Bengal Assembly, there are 43 women MLAs out of 292 seats. A total of 2,132 candidates were in the fray. The election in 2 constituencies had to be postponed to 16 May because there was the death of one candidate each in major parties.

Table: 2.10 Participation in politics

Area	Total Members	Male	Female (%)
W.B. Legislative Assembly	294	251	43 (14.62%)
MPs of Lok Sabha from West Bengal	543	32	10 (23.80%)
MPs of Rajya Sabha from West Bengal	238	12	3 (20%)
Ministers in West Bengal	44	35	9 (20.45%)

Source: Compilation from different sources

West Bengal sends 42 Members to Lok Sabha. The Indian National Congress Party won and sent only 2 MPs from West Bengal, while Bharatiya Janata Party sent 18 MPs to the Lok Sabha in the 2019 general elections. On the other hand, the Trinamool Congress party became the largest party to send its 22 MPs to the Lok Sabha. The gender bias is clearly visible in the list of MPs from Bengal. It is found that 8 women MPs have belonged to the AITC such as Aparupa Poddar, Kakoli Ghosh Dastidar, Mahua Moitra, Mala Roy, Mimi Chakraborty, Nusrat Jaha Ruhi, Protima Mondal, Sajda Ahmed, and Satabdi Roy, while only 2 MPs - Debashree Chaudhuri, and Locket Chatterjee represented the BJP from Bengal.

The Rajya Sabha i.e. the "Council of States" is the upper house of the Parliament of India. West Bengal elects 16 Members and they are indirectly elected by the state legislators of West Bengal. The numbers of seats, allocated to the party, are determined by the number of seats a party possesses during the nomination and the party nominates a member to be voted on. Elections within the state legislatures are held using single transferable and with proportional representation. Presently the Rajya Sabha has 15 MPs from West Bengal, and out of them, 3 are women – Arpita Ghosh (AITMC), Shanta Chetri (AITMC) and Dola Sen (AITMC). And out of 15 MPs from West Bengal, only 1

Member was elected from the Communist Party of India (Marxist) and the two other Members belong to Indian National Congress Party.

On 10.05.2021 the ministers of West Bengal took an oath and from the list it is observed that a total of 44 ministers have been inducted in the newly formed ministry of Mamata Banerjee-led government. Out of total 25 cabinet ministers, only Mamata Banerjee is the single cabinet minister. Her portfolios are – Home & Hill Affairs, Personnel & Administration, Health and Family Welfare, Land and Land Reforms, and Refugee and Rehabilitation, Information and Cultural Affairs, and North Bengal Development. Chandrima Bhattacharya, Ratna De Nag, Sandhyarani Tudu, Bulu Chik Barik were made Ministers- State (Independent Charge), while Seuli Saha, Yeasmin Sabina, Birbaha Hansda, Yotsna mandi were given the charge of Ministers-of-State.

Participation in local governments

Local governments are the governments situated at the local level. There are two types of local governments – Urban local bodies (Municipalities, Corporations) and Rural Local Governments (Gram Panchayats, Panchayat Samities, and Zilla Parishads). "The institutions of local governments being key components of representative democracy provide the scope and platform for citizens to be involved in the planning and implementation process of local affairs and monitoring public service delivery."[22] Various scholars have defined the term political participation in different ways. But there is a common thread that connects all of them. It is closely related to power and it very much exists in democratic societies. Miller[23] holds that "It is the activity which aims at bringing government to bear in a particular direction, to secure particular results". Lassswel[24] assumes that "Political the process is the shaping, sharing, and exercise of power".

Table: 2.11 State-wise representations of women in panchayats

State/ UTs	Total PRI Representatives	Total EWRs
Andaman & Nicobar Islands	858	306
Andhra Pradesh	156050	78,025

Arunachal Pradesh	9383	3,658
Assam	26754	14,609
Bihar	136573	71,046
Chhattisgarh	170465	93,392
Dadra & Nagar Haveli	147	47
Daman & Diu	192	92
Goa	1555	571
Gujarat	144080	71,988
Haryana	70035	29,499
Himachal Pradesh	28723	14,398
Jammu & Kashmir	39850	13,224
Jharkhand	59638	30,757
Karnataka	101954	51,030
Kerala	18372	9,630
Ladakh	NA	NA
Lakshadweep	110	41
Madhya Pradesh	392981	196490
Maharashtra	240635	128677
Manipur	1736	880
Odisha	107487	56,627
Puducherry	NA	NA
Punjab	100312	41,922
Rajasthan	126271	64,802
Sikkim	1153	580
Tamil Nadu	106450	56,407
Telangana	103468	52,096
Tripura	6646	3,006
Uttarakhand	62796	35,177
West Bengal	59229	30,458 (51.42%)
Total	**31,87,320**	**14,53,973**

Local governments are of two types in India i.e. rural local government and urban local bodies. Rural local bodies are called panchayats, which have three tiers – 1. Gram Panchayats - the lowest level local government, 2. Panchayat Samities - the middle-tier local bodies and 3. Zila Parishads - the highest tier of the rural local bodies. On the other hand, urban local bodies are the Municipalities and Corporations. However, the Panchayat, being "Local government", is a State subject and part of State list of Seventh Schedule of Constitution of India. Clause (3) of Article 243D of the Constitution ensures participation of women in Panchayati Raj Institutions by mandating not less than one-third reservation for women out of a total number of seats to be filled by direct election and number of offices of chairpersons of Panchayats. So far, the 20 States namely Andhra Pradesh, Assam, Bihar, Chhattisgarh, Gujarat, Himachal Pradesh, Jharkhand, Karnataka, Kerala, Madhya Pradesh, Maharashtra, Odisha, Punjab, Rajasthan, Sikkim, Tamil Nadu, Telangana, Tripura, Uttarakhand,
and West Bengal have made
provisions of 50% reservation for women in Panchayati Raj Institutions in their respectiv e State Panchayati Raj Acts.

Further, in terms of clause (4) of Article 243D of the Constitution, the offices of the Chairpersons in the Panchayats at the village or any other level shall be reserved for the Scheduled Castes, the Scheduled Tribes, and women in such manner as the Legislature of a State may, by law, provide, provided that the number of offices of Chairpersons reserved for the Scheduled Castes and the Scheduled Tribes in the Panchayats at each level in any State shall bear, as nearly as may be, the same proportion to the total number of such offices in the Panchayats at each level as the population of the Scheduled Castes in the State or of the Scheduled Tribes in the State bears to the total population of the State provided further that not less than one-third of the total number of offices of Chairpersons in the Panchayats at each level shall be reserved for women.[25]

The participation scenario of women in the three-tier rural local bodies in different states of India has been highlighted in the above table (Table 2.9). It is found from the above table that the total number of representatives in three-tier Panchayats are more than three million i.e. 31,87,320, while several elected women representatives (EWRs) are

14,53,973 (45.61%). Andhra Pradheh has total 1,56,050 numbers of elected representatives in PRIs, but women hold 78,025 seats in the three-tier PRIs which is just 50 percent of its total representatives. In Kerala, we find 18,372 elected representatives, and women represent 9,630 seats, which is 52.16 percent of the total seats of PRIS in the state. On the other hand, in West Bengal, though the government has reserved 50 percent of seats for women, it has more women representatives than the minimum reserved seats in its rural local bodies. The available data show that, out of 59,229 total elected representatives, women occupy 30,458 seats in three-tier PRIs. This figure indicates that 51.42 percent of women are now elected in West Bengal at different tiers of Panchayati Raj Institutions, which further proves women's political empowerment in the state.

Conclusions

From the above discussion it can be said that the state of West Bengal is one of the most progressive and major economically, socially, and politically advanced states in India. The education scenario is both bright and dark. Students' enrolment is satisfactory and the teacher-student ratio is also up to the mark. New universities, schools, and classrooms have brought the students to the campuses of educational institutions. But, the politicization of education, corruption in recruitment, and non-existence of valid managing committees in more than forty percent of schools need government attention. Bengal's GSDP is in a reasonable position and it is ahead of more than twenty-six States and Union Territories. West Bengal's budgetary allocation in the education sector is also pretty satisfactory, but in terms of foreign direct investment, the share is pathetically low. Women's participation is also better than in many other states in India. Women's share in State Ministry is more than 20% of the total seats. Total MPs in Lok Sabha and Rajya Sabha from West Bengal are also more than twenty percent of the total seats. More than fifty percent (51.42%) of women are found in the three-tier local government bodies.

Chapter – III

Achievements of Mamata Banerjee

"Inner gentle way you can shake the world."

- *Mahatma Gandhi*

-

Introduction

Under the Left rule for 34 years West Bengal turned to a non-performing or lowly performing state, where the development engine was almost halted or at best staggering. The level of corruption, lack of decent job opportunities, de-industrialization, politics of '*chakka jam*', violent trade-unionism, and deterioration of law and order has disgruntled the majority electors of this state. The deficiencies and loopholes of the LF government facilitated the Trinamool Congress supremo to put an end to the '*Dadagiri*' of the so called mighty, muscular, and gigantic communist rulers in Bengal. After defeating badly the pithy Communist rulers in 2011 assembly elections, the Trinamool Congress government led by Mamata Banerjee swam into action for the holistic development of the state. The state was almost paralyzed in the last few years of the Buddhadeb Bhattacharjee regime. The LF government became notorious for its slogans like '*cholche na, cholbe na,*' '*bhenge dao guriye dao*', '*manchi na, manbo na,*' etc. In consequence of the ultra leftists' anti-industry and anti-bourgeoise agitations, long processions, violent strikes, and policies of *chakka jam, hartal*, and *gherao*, the industrialists one by one either started to wind up their establishments or left this state in search of better working atmosphere and peaceful running of their trade, business and manufacturing activities. Professor Dipankar Sinha[1] has excellently highlighted the hyperactive politics of the communist regime in one of his articles published in The Economic and Political Weekly where he asserted, "…the Bengal brand of politics was as much associated with high action orientation, including the most radical and violent kind as with utter non-action orientation. While the hyperactive phase reached its peak with the Naxalite movement and the hyper-reactive counteractions of the Congress government in the late 1960s and 1970s, the non action phase, which followed it, had a longer run. The latter phase was significantly marked by "popular" slogans – *cholche na cholbe na* (nothing moves, nothing would move) and *bhenge dao, gunriye dao* (break, demolish) – which would seek to bring anything and everything under the sun to a screeching halt."

Thus West Bengal's development took a U-turn, and it reduced its glamour from an industry-based economy to an agro-based economy. A decade ago, prior to the transfer of power of the Writers' Buildings, this author argued that, "Agriculture still occupies the largest source of livelihood of the people in India. People - both male and female - participate in the agricultural activity. But there is risk and uncertainty relating to profitability from agriculture. Besides, the kind of labour, amount of money and time of persons invested in agriculture, return does not come from it up to that extent."[2] This being a fact is believed by all reasonable persons from Professor Amartya Sen to Muhammad Yunus. Samit Kar also mentioned this reality in his words such as "Agriculture is becoming less remunerative along with the passage of time and as a result, poor farmers are compelled to become dependent on non-agricultural livelihood."[3] But Bengal was reduced to a deindustrialized state under the LF government. People, as a whole, were fallen in this crux. Majority of the rural people, despite unwillingness and lower rate of earning, had little option than to engage themselves in agriculture for livelihood.

On the above backdrop, after the transfer of baton from Jyoti Basu to Buddhadeb Bhattacharjee, the latter realized that without industry it would not be possible to make real human progress and growth of economy. Bhattacharjee rightly believed in the concept that, if agriculture is the base of economy, industry is future. Out of this realization he approached to the industrialists in the dawn of the new Millennium. But the Trade Unions of his own party and some Big Bosses at Alimuddin were reluctant to approve his initiative. However, his approach to the Indonesia based Salem group, and

Tata group chairman was a right step for industrialization even prior to 2006 elections. But the political situation in Jangal Mahal and Darjeeling was deteriorating day by day. The Maoists began to disrupt the normal life and property of people in certain pockets of Bengal, particularly in Jungle Mahal areas. Finally, the incidents of forceful attempt to land acquisition in both Singur and Nandigram for fulfilling his dream of industrialization put the last nail in the coffin of the Bhattacharjee-led government. Keshab Chandra Mandal[4] (this author) in his *West Bengal Government: The Issues and Constraints of Development* pointed out that, "During the industrialization process of the state there were chaos and disturbance. The government tried to acquire land from the villagers with old land acquisition laws. But they little bothered to arrange for rehabilitation of the homeless villagers. There were no alternative arrangements for their livelihood." This added fuel to the fire of the aggrieved farmers.

Mamata Banerjee, the then firebrand leader and Indian Railways Minister under UPA-II Government mobilized the people. In reality, people were desperate to get rid of the anarchic situation in Bengal. They were seeking a respite from the clutches of the Communist rulers. Mamata Banerjee realized the public sentiment and wasted not time to seize the opportunity. She promised for better governance and better future for the people of Bengal. The people wooed her, embraced her, accepted her, and finally blessed her with their votes in 2011 Legislative Assembly elections. In this chapter, we will discuss a few major achievements of Mamata Banerjee from 2011 to 2020. Though the size and dimension of development and growth is much bigger, it is not possible to pinpoint all the information and data in this small chapter. However, an attempt has been made to highlight some important achievements, schemes and programs taken by the Mamata Banerjee-led Government.

Economic Achievements

It is evident from the following figure (Figure:1) that in 2010-11, when the Left Front Government left office, total Gross State Domestic Product was Rs. 4,60,959 crores, and that has been increased to Rs. 9,89,965 crores in six years. This shows the remarkable increment of economic activities of the state. Further, in terms of the Gross State Domestic Product (GSDP) the total size of West Bengal's economy in FY 2021 and FY

2022 is estimated to be Rs. 13.5 lakh crore and Rs. 15.1 lakh crore. Bengal's most recent budge, presented in February, 2021 forcast a sharp uptick in nominal (inflation-unadjusted) growth of 8.5%.[5]

Figure: 3.1 GSDP (In crores)

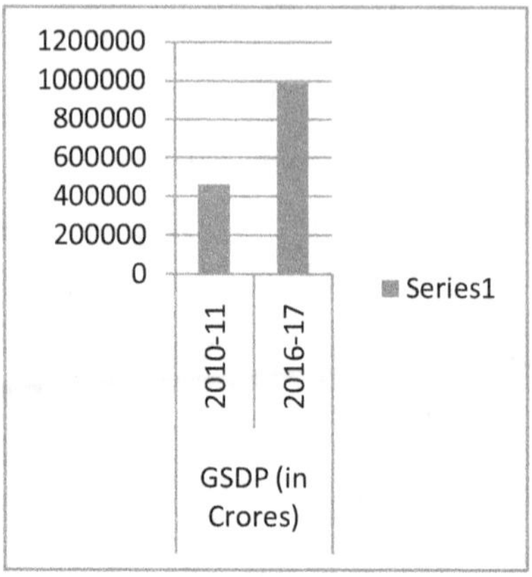

Source: Paschim Banga, Year 50, Vol. 1-3, May-July, 2017, p. III.

Further, it is observed that, while the growth of Gross Domestic Product of India was 7.6%, the Gross State Domestic Product has been increased to 12% in 2017. It indicates that the growth rate of Bengal is higher than that of India. According to data from the ministry of statistics and program implementation, the state's average growth of gross state domestic product or GSDP, the most common measure of income at the state level, between 2012-13 and 2017-18 — which coincide, partly, with Banerjee's first and second term — was around 5.5%, lower than the national average of 7.1%. The state's budget documents show 2018-19 was a turnaround year. West Bengal grew 10.7% in 2018-19 in real terms compared to the 6.8% growth rate of the country as a whole.[6]

Figure: 3.2 Comparison of GDP between Centre and State

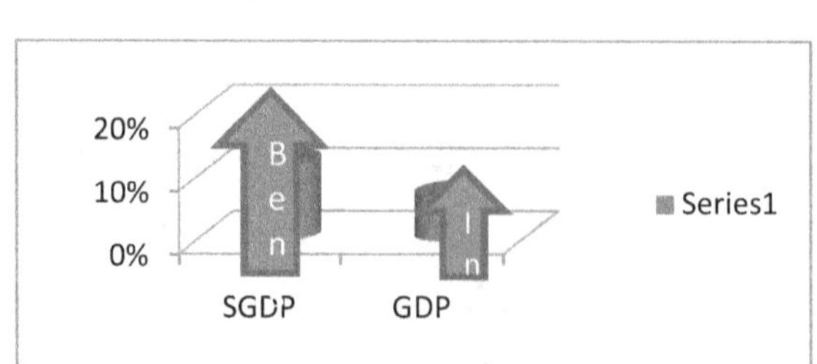

Source: Paschim Banga, Year 50, Vol. 1-3, May-July, 2017, p. II.

In the years between 2010-11 to 2016-17, the collection of online tax has been doubled in West Bengal. In 2010-11 the total online collection was only 21,000 crores; this rate had been doubled to 42,000 crores in 2016-17. It is learned from a report of The Economic Times[7] that, recently the GST collection in West Bengal is improving with growing economic activities in the state and the revenue from the indirect tax at Rs. 1,212,44 crore in July (2020) was higher than that of the previous months. The Goods and Services Tax collection was getting stabilized in the state. Because companies have started making deferred payments which the authorities had allowed till September 2020 given the coronavirus crisis.

Figure: 3.3 Collection of online tax

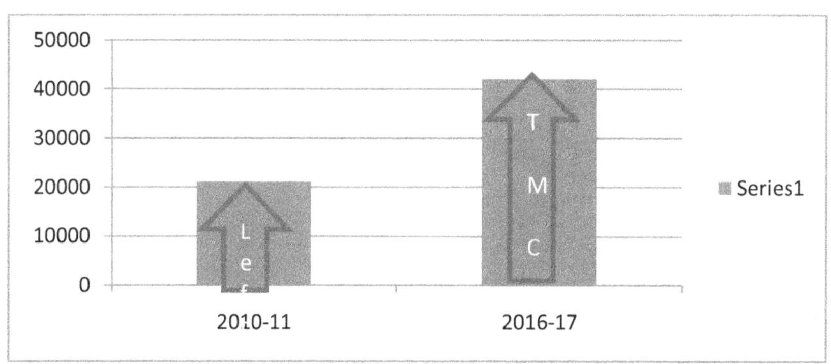

Source: Paschim Banga, Year 50, Vol. 1-3, May-July, 2017, p. II.

Tourism Industry

The tourism sector is a major engine of economic growth that contributes significantly in terms of GDP, foreign exchange earnings, and employment. India is one of the most attractive tourist places in the world. It is interesting to note that, "The top five states attracting foreign tourists are Tamil Nadu, Maharashtra, Uttar Pradesh, Delhi, and West Bengal, accounting for 69.4 percent of -the total foreign tourist visits in the country in 2019."[8] Under the Trinamool Congress government, the tourism industry has made remarkable progress in Bengal. Not only the tourists from different parts of India are visiting Bengal, but a substantial number of visitors are coming to have a glimpse of the 'Beauty Queen' of India. West Bengal's location is strategic from the point of view of tourism. It is situated in eastern India and shares its borders with Jharkhand, Bihar,

Odisha, Sikkim, and Assam. The state also shares international borders with Bangladesh, Bhutan, and Nepal. The Bay of Bengal is in the south of West Bengal.

West Bengal has the most magnificent hill station in the world, Darjeeling, which is dubbed as the "Queen of the Hills'. Its' beauty is world-famous, its tea plantation and ancient buildings and architecture attract visitors from across the world. Other Hill Stations are Kurseong, Kalimpong, Lava Lolenaon, Mirik, Sandakphu etc. The Beauty of Howrah bridge at night, the ferry ghat at Howrah in the lap of Mother Ganga, the Victoria Memorial, National Library, American Library, British Library, the Birla Planetarium, the Museum, the zoo, the IT hub at Rajarhat, the roads and parks of Kolkata and major cities in the state are now fantastic. The largest mangrove forest in the world is located in the Sundarbans. The Dooars foothills, Bengal Heritage sites, Coastal Bengal, and the Sundarbans are the major tourist circuits in Bengal. The Sundarbans has been declared as a World Heritage site by UNESCO. Bengal's Digha, Shankarpur, Bakkhali, Gangasagar, Tajpur, and Mandarmani beaches attract the beach-lovers and travelers of India and abroad. Bengal's most religious places are the Kali temple at Kalighat, Tarapith, and Dakshineshwar; St. Paul's Cathedral and St. James' Church; Furfura Sharif, Nakhoda Masjid, and Imambara are the greatest places of worship of different religious pilgrims. The lord Shiva temple of Tarakeshwar is a holy place to Shiva devotees. The people of different caste, races, and colors all live in perfect harmony here and celebrate all festivals together like the Id, the Christmas, the Durga Puja, the Holi, Diwali, etc. Bengal's film industry at Tollygunge, Satyajit Ray film institution, houses of Netaji Subhas Chandra Bose at Kolkata and Rabindranath Tagore's at Shantiniketan, Hazarduari at Murshidabad, Rajbari at Cooch Behar, ISCON Temple at Mayapur, Chaitanya Deb's birthplace at Nabadwip, Ramkrishna Deb and Sarada Ma's birthplaces at Kamarpukur and Joirambati, and Ramakrishna Math at Belur, etc are attractive places to indigenous and foreign tourists.[9] These are major places of attraction. This is just a sample, the entire West Bengal is now a place of attraction to the visitors of India and abroad.

Figure: 3.4 Arrival of foreign tourists

Source: Paschim Banga, Year 50, Vol. 1-3, May-July, 2017, p.VII.

It is learned from the report of India Tourism Statistics, 2019, Government of India, that a total number of 8,56,57,365 domestic visitors, as well as 16,17,105 foreign visitors, have visited West Bengal during 2018, which was a growth of 7.57 percent for domestic visitors and 2.68 percent for international visitors in comparison to the total number of visitors in 2017.[10] While Lakshadweep topped the list with both foreign (35) and domestic (36) tourists, West Bengal remained satisfied with merely 7 (domestic) and 6 (international) ranks in 2018.[11] But in terms of percentage share of top 10 States/UTs in domestic tourist visits in 2018, Tamil Nadu topped the list with 20.8% share while West Bengal stood at the 7th position with total 4.6% domestic tourists. On the other hand, West Bengal held the 6th position, and its share in the top 10 States/UTs in several international tourist visits in 2018 was 5.6 %. Bengal's hotels and service industry are congenial for foreign as well as domestic tourists. From the report of the India Tourism Statistics, 2019 it has come to light that, West Bengal has a total of 27 hotels including 5 numbers of 5-star Deluxe; 4 numbers of 5-Star; 3 numbers of 4-Star, 11 numbers of 3-Star; 2 numbers of 2-Star; and 2 Guest Houses. And the number of rooms available in the hotels and guests are 2703.[12]

Figure: 3.5 Arrival of foreign tourists

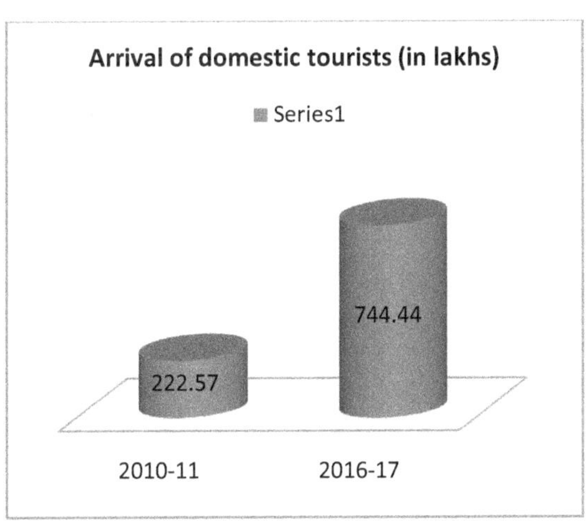

Source: Paschim Banga, Year 50, Vol. 1-3, May-July, 2017, p. VII.

Industrial Growth

Now West Bengal is the safe and favorite destination of businessmen and industrialists from across the world. Since its inception, the state has so far organized five big State Business Summits (SDGs). The greatest success was received in 2015 and 2016 SBG when the state received a proposal of 4.93 thousand crores and the business proposals. Those proposals were at different stages of implementation. The GBS of 2017 was well attended by 29 foreign delegates, which received a business proposal of Rs. 2.36 thousand crores and progress is going on in different stages. A large delegation led by the Chief Minister has already visited Bhutan, Singapore, Germany, and Great Britain for attracting investors. The state has been successful in creating a congenial atmosphere of investment in the state. Several MoUs were signed with many investors during these foreign visits. In 2017 North Bengal was selected for Business Summit to introduce the investors with the northern districts of the state where about 1000 crore investment proposals were received by the state. Further, it came to light that, for Bengal's Global Business Summit in 2019, already Rs. 71,646 crore was under implementation. The employment generated through these investments was to the tune of 28 lakh already.[13]

In terms of Micro, Small, and Medium Enterprises (MSME), the state has advanced a lot. "About 89 Lakh MSMEs of the State contribute nearly 14% of the total MSMEs of the country. MSMEs have grown at 11% CAGR in the last 9 years."[14] In this sector, the amount of loans given to different enterprises is the highest in the country. In the last 5 years, the total amount of the loan was Rs.1.22 lakh crores. The state has given importance to improving the skills of the entrepreneurs and assisted them in growing their production and sending the products to the market. For this purpose, the state has created various clusters. More than 300 such clusters have so far been created in the state. Namrata Acharya wrote in the Business Standard[15] that, since May 2011, the state received investment proposals of Rs. 1.12 lakh crore, with the potential to create 314,000 jobs. But in actuality, the implementation of the projects was nowhere near the proposed investments. The year 2012 was particularly rugged in the industrial front for West Bengal. The state saw projects worth Rs. 312 crore being implemented, which was a fall of nearly 85% over the previous year, and 97% over 2010-the last year of Left Front rule in the state.

Only because of the strict and uncompromising attitude of the Chief Minister with the strikes and hartals, not a single working day has been wasted in the state. This has resulted in a better work atmosphere, which created a healthy and happy atmosphere for both the existing investors and would-be investors and industrialists. As a result, the state of West Bengal has witnessed healthy investment proposals and some big-ticket project formalization during the pandemic-hit year, 2020. The total investment proposal as per records of the West Bengal Industrial Development Corporation (WBIDC) was Rs. 4,064 from January to December 2020. IT sector also could push the figure up Rs. 3,000 crore to the Rs. 7,064 crore and total employment were expected to be over 39,000. The project proposals came across sectors including manufacturing, iron & steel, food processing, construction, chemicals, Information Technology (IT), gems & jewelry, and logistics. The Government has already cleared the Tajpur port project, where the proposed investment would be Rs. 15,000 crore and it might create the employment opportunity for 25,000 youths of Bengal. The iron & steel industry around Kharagpur and the exports of iron and steel from Purulia, Burdwan, and Bankura will get a boost. Wipro's investment proposal of Rs. 500 crore for setting up a second campus will employ about 10,000 IT professionals. Also, the proposal of 20 companies for an investment of Rs. 3,000 crore with an estimated employment opportunity of 9,000 IT professionals is refreshing news for Bengal's job seekers. In addition to that, the investment proposal of Amazon (Rs. 200 crores) and Flipcart (Rs. 150 – 200 crore) at Uluberia will expand employment opportunities for 5,400 people. Star cement has also proposed an investment of Rs. 450 crore in Siliguri to set up a Greenfield cement grinding plant.[16] Thus, it is found that West Bengal is turning gradually from a moron to a smart state in terms of industrialization.

The number of factories in Bengal increased from 8,322 in 2010 to 9,534 (15%) in 2020, with average factory worker earnings rising from Rs.1.3 Lakh to Rs. 2.3 Lakh (77%). Bengal Silicon Valley Project is a great achievement of the Trinamool Congress Government. More than 100 acres of land has been allotted to over 20 organizations attracting an investment of around Rs. 11,317 Crore. Deocha Panchami is the world's second-largest coal block with an estimated reserve of 2.1 billion tonnes. More than one lakh jobs might be created once the Deocha Pachami coal block in Birbhum district gets operationalized."[17]

Agriculture and Allied Sectors

Agriculture is the essence of livelihood for around 58 percent population in India. West Bengal is the largest food grain-producing state in India. It is known for its rice production. In West Bengal, rice's total production is 146.05 lakh tons on 2600 kilograms per hectare yield. The state is now truly the leading state in agriculture production. In the last six years from 2010-11 to 2016-17, the growth in agriculture and allied sectors have increased many folds. In agriculture, the growth of investment has increased more than 5 times, while expenditure on planned projects has been increased to four times. Agricultural infrastructure has been increased to three and a half times and investment in creating permanent assets has been increased to seven-folds.

The Government expenditure in agriculture and allied sector activities has increased in the last 10 years by 6.1 times as compared to 2011; it grew from Rs.3,029.39 Crore in 2010-11 to Rs.18,603 Crore in 2019-20. Foodgrains production has increased from 148.10 LMT in 2010-11 to 198.65 LMT in 2019-20, total rice production has increased from 133.9 LMT in 2010-11 to 165.03 LMT in 2019-20, the productivity of Maize remarkably increased from 4.60 ton/Ha in 2016-17 to 6.80

Figure: 3.6 Growth in agriculture and allied sectors

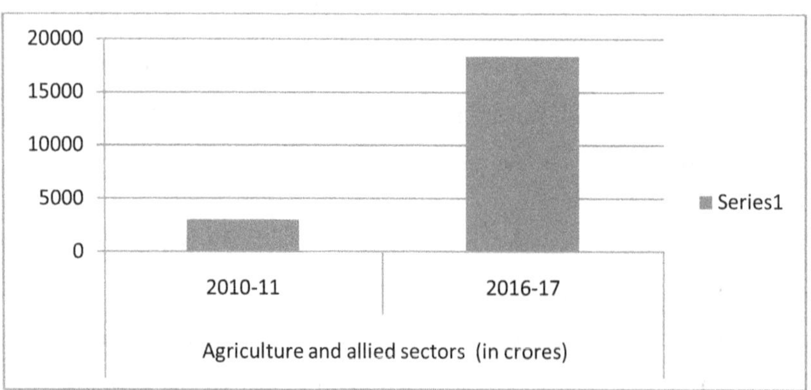

Source: Paschim Banga, Year 50, Vol. 1-3, May-July, 2017, p. III.

ton/Ha and production of pulses has increased from 1.77 LMT in 2010-11 to 3.93 LMT in 2019-20. During 2020-21, 12.90 LMT of fish and 24,875 million fish seeds have been produced in West Bengal up to December 2020. In the past nine years, egg production has increased by 143.31%, meat production increased by 56.50%, and milk production increased by 33.45%.

West Bengal, for the past 6th consecutive year, has been awarded the "Krishi Karman Award" for the best performance in coarse cereals production during the year 2017-18. Under Krishak Bandhu, Rs.2,647.89 Crore has been disbursed benefitting 46.76 Lakh farmers. 186 Kisan Mandis have been constructed with a storage facility to ease the selling of the produce for the local farmers. Amar Fasal Amar Gola project has been initiated by the Government. To prevent post-harvest losses and to enhance farm level value addition, one-time assistance is provided through 'Amar Fasal Amar Gola' at Rs.17,975 for constructing a Farm Family level paddy processing yard (Gola) to sundry parboiled paddy and/or Rs.5,000 for constructing an improved low-cost paddy and grain storage structures. The Government has also increased its distribution of Kisan Credit Cards - from 20 lakhs in 2011 to 70 Lakh Kisan Credit cards till 2020. Under the Farmers' Old Age Pension Scheme, a monthly pension of Rs.1,000 is being provided to nearly 1 lakh farmers.

Under the fully State-funded crop insurance 'Bangla Shasya Bima' scheme, 64 Lakh farmers have been insured under this scheme covering 22.55 LHa, during Kharif 2020. Another project - Matir Shristi – under this program the Government endeavored to make productive use of fallow land in 6 western Districts viz. Birbhum, Bankura, Purulia, Paschim Medinipur, Jhargram & Paschim Bardhaman. Last year, the project was launched on 13,000-acre land in 1,942 sites. This year another 14,000-acre land will be converted, creating huge employment opportunities in agriculture, horticulture, pisciculture, animal husbandry, etc. Under the Watershed Development program, a fund of Rs.409.36 Crores has been released. With a view to increasing the agriculture production, 31,285 Ha of the additional area has been brought under irrigation providing benefit to 2,21,127 farmers. Moreover, 14,472 Ha of agricultural land benefitting 30,845 farmers were covered under Micro Irrigation by the installation of Sprinkler and Drip

Irrigation. Electronic delivery systems have been made operational to enable services like the leasing, mutation, and conversion of land. 21.45 Lakh farmers have registered for the e-paddy procurement system. West Bengal State Agricultural Marketing Board has introduced an online integrated electronic single platform permit (e-Permit) system for fast and hassle-free transactions of agricultural produce in the State.[18]

Health and family welfare

The government of West Bengal has taken up the policy of better health and better hygiene for all. Not only that, healthcare facilities with affordable prices have become the motto of the government. The government has set up 112 new fair-price medicine shops and 95 fair-price diagnostic centers in government hospitals in Bengal that have supplied medicine, artificial limbs, and diagnostic service among the rural people. Out of 42, 34 new multi-specialty hospitals have started service for the improvement of health for the people of Bengal. The number of beds has also been increased to 27,000 by the present government.

Further, it came to light that the number of hospital beds has been increased in the State. "In the last 10 years, government hospital beds increased from 58,647 to 85,627 marking an increase of 46%. Bengal has the highest number of government hospital beds in the country. Even the number of doctors has been increased from 4,800 to 15,338 and the number of nurses has increased from 37,366 to 56,589. The honorarium of Accredited Social Health Activist (ASHA) has been increased from a maximum of just Rs.1,500 in 2011 to around Rs.6,500 per month now.[19]

More than 70 CCU/AHDU/ICCU service of Critical care management has been added to the state health service. These facilities were not available before 2011 in rural hospitals. 370 Sick Newborn Stabilization Units (SNSU) have been newly introduced in West Bengal, while there was not a single SNUC in any government hospitals before 2011. Moreover, 65 special SNUCs have been introduced in the state. Prior to 2011, there were only 6 SNCUs in the state. Six modern mother and child welfare facilities and services have been introduced in the state, more 7 were expected to be set up and start operation. The total proposed number of mother and child welfare hubs was 16 in the state.[20]

In 2010 total number of institutional deaths was only 65 percent, while this number has been increased to 93 percent in 2016. This indicates the great improvement in institutional deliveries in Bengal.

Figure: 3.7 Institutional deliveries

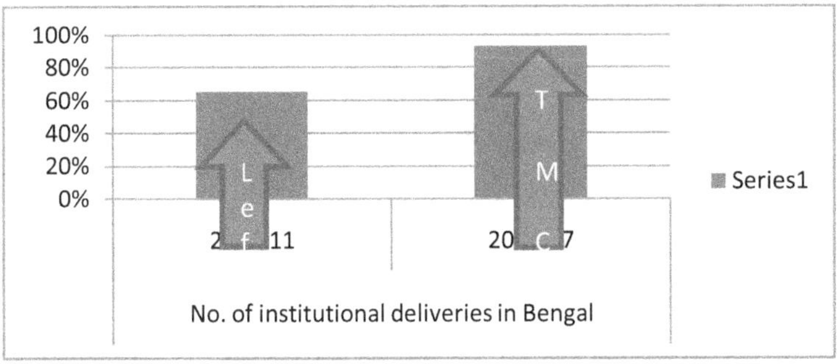

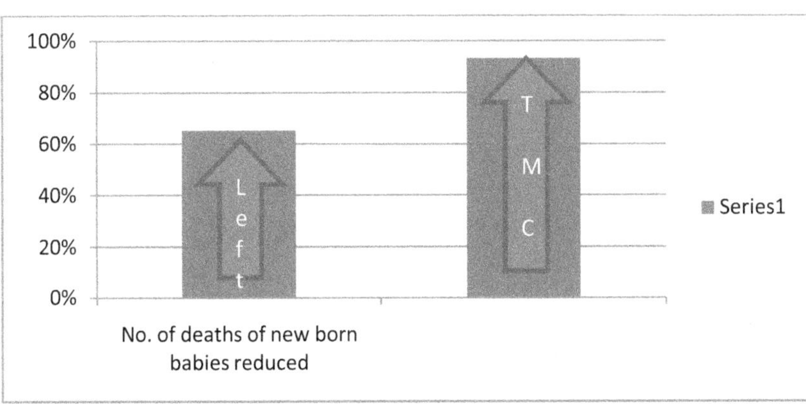

Source: Paschim Banga, Year 50, Vol. 1-3, May-July, 2017, p. VI.

Similarly in 2011 total number of deaths of newborn babies was 32 per 1000 births, but this number of deaths of newborn babies also increased to a great extent (93/1000). All these have been possible for the initiatives taken by the TMC government. Moreover, due to the lack of physicians in the state, the retirement age of existing doctors has been increased from 60 to 65 years.

Figure: 3.8 Deaths of new born babies

Source: Paschim Banga, Year 50, Vol. 1-3, May-July, 2017, p. VI.

The scheme was officially launched by Hon'ble Chief Minister of West Bengal on 30th December 2016.

Inclusive health for all

Swasthya Sathi scheme, officially launched by Hon'ble Chief Minister of West Bengal on 30th December 2016 that provides annual health insurance of Rs. 5 Lakh, has been made a universal covering over 1.94 Crore families (Nearly 10 crore people). The basic health covers for secondary and tertiary care up to Rs. 5 lakh per annum per family. It is paperless, cashless, and Smart Card bases. There is no cap on the family size and parents from both the spouse are included. All dependent physically challenged persons in the family are also covered. The entire premium is borne by the State Government and no contribution is required from the beneficiary.[21] The health and family welfare budget increased by more than 3-times, from Rs. 3,442 Crore in 2010 to Rs.12, 561 Crore in 2021-22. Rs.1,000 advanced Matri Yan ambulances have been started for the transportation of pregnant mothers and newborn babies. Up to March 2021, the government has created 102 dedicated COVID-19 hospitals with 13,588 oxygen beds and 2,523 CCU/HDU beds and also requisitioned 57 private hospitals. At present, the State has 41 units of fully functional super-specialty hospitals and 72 critical care facilities with more than 1,90,000 people have received quality critical care treatment. It has 152 High-end Fair Price Diagnostic and Dialysis Centers with over 96.44 Lakh patients availing the free services from the centers. Five separate health districts have been organized and structured in Basirhat, Diamond Harbour, Rampurhat, Bishnupur, and Nandigram, and under the Shishu Sathi Prakalpa, free heart operation is arranged for children.[22]

Welfare Schemes of the State Government

West Bengal Government is globally renowned for its illustrious pro-poor, pro-student, and pro-people schemes and programs. In the wonderful land of Bengal, nay in India, Mamata Banerjee and coruscation are synonymous. Since her inception at the Writers' Buildings, she has remained in the center stage of cardinal attraction. Her introduction of welfare schemes one after another, some are her own brainchild while others are duplicate and simulating from the Centre, have touched the life and work of almost every section, every community, and every age-group people in Bengal. In the following part, some significant and most discussed developmental schemes and vote-centric programs are delineated, which will explain why she was voted to power for the third time in 2021.

Schemes and Benefits

1. **Sufal Bangla – 2014:** Sufal Bangla scheme has been launched for the benefit of the people to ensure fresh vegetables at a reasonable price at their doorstep. The project also aims to provide benefits to the farmers through an arrangement of procurement by the Government. It seeks to help farmers get a premium prices and have a rational share in consumer's prices. Another aspect of this initiative is to provide employment opportunities to the unemployed who would be associated with this program.

The state government is committed to fair play in agricultural marketing practices in order to safeguard the interests of both the growers and the consumers, thus paving the way for Sufal Bangla. At present, the state has 47 static counters and 97 mobile counters. Kolkata has the highest concentration of these counters; the city has 24 static counters and 92 mobile counters out of the total 144 counters. These counters are located all across the city. [23]

2. **Shilpa Sathi – 2019:** With a view to assisting the investors in setting up industries in West Bengal, the Government of West Bengal has launched Shilpa Sathi where an investor can submit a Common Application Form in the Single Window Cell at WBIDC.[24]

Silpa Sathi Kiosks are available at 23 Industry Facilitation Centres (IFCs) located in every district of the State. In short, Shilpa Sathi is Bengal's call for business to ride in growth in the industry, commerce, and enterprises in the state across micro, small and medium, and large sectors.[25]

3. **Shilpa Disha - 2019:** This is a mobile app to reach the highest authority of MSME Department, Government of West Bengal. This is a grievance redressal app prepared for convenient meaningful solutions to the issues, problems, and hardships if any faced by entrepreneurs. This app is run by the Micro, Small & Medium Enterprises and Textile (MSME &T) Department.

4. **Sech Bandhu – 2014:** This is a farmer-friendly project offering 46,000 new pump sets with power connectivity to farmers to boost irrigation in the state. The West Bengal cabinet cleared this project on September 13, 2014, to boost irrigation in the state.[26] This was meant to help the farmers in a big way and keep them away from illegal power consumption. It sought to reduce power theft and improve regularized power supply in rural Bengal.

5. **Samajik Mukti – 2017:** The government issued 'Samajik Mukti' (Social Freedom) cards to unorganized sector workers of the State for Provident Fund & Other Social Benefit scheme. The new and consolidated Samajik Suraksha Yojana for unorganized workers was notified on April 3, 2017. Initially, 25 lakhs beneficiaries were proposed to be given the card under the State assisted scheme of Provident Fund for Unorganized Workers (SASPFUW). The objective of the project was to realize the following: (i) Bringing a maximum number of Workers under the welfare schemes, (ii) Smooth and Speedy delivery of Welfare benefits under the three schemes, and (iii) Effective and Transparent management and utilization of the funds available.[27]

6. **Pran Dhara – 2014:** The West Bengal Government has ventured to produce bottled drinking water Pran Dhara with 8 bottling plants across the state. The Public Health & Engineering Department is responsible for supplying safe drinking water to all the people of the state. Water pouches are produced through Mobile Treatment Units (MTU) for easy distribution of drinking water to the people. The Public Health Engineering Department (PHED) introduced bottled water named Pran Dhara. For the first time, this type of Package Drinking Water Plant was installed at Dakshin Roypur Water Treatment Plant Complex in the year 2012-13 in accordance with BIS Specifications. The capacity of this plant is 3600 Bottles of 1000 ml. or 500 ml. per hour. After the successful

commissioning of the Plant, another 7 (Seven) Packaged Drinking Water Plants have been installed in different locations of West Bengal.

7. **Patha Sathi:** With a view to facilitating the people, especially the women, toilets were constructed at every 50 kilometers of National Highway, State Highway, and other important roads throughout the state. Pathasathi consists of pay & use toilet, waiting room, night shelter, and restaurant under one roof. The Housing Directorate also executes and maintains rental housing schemes for different income groups with emphasis on the Economically Weaker Sections (EWS), quarters for State Government employees, and integrated housing estates for industrial workers and maintain those buildings in West Bengal. Apart from these, hostel accommodation for working women and night shelters for waiting of the passengers at Bus Terminus and patient parties at hospitals was also included in the activity of the Directorate. [28]

8. **Nijo Griha Nijo Bhumi Prakalpa – 2011:** The Scheme was was launched on 18th October 2011 by the Govt. of West Bengal for providing 5 decimal of land to each identified eligible beneficiary family i.e. to all landless homestead less agricultural laborers, village artisans, and fishermen in rural areas towards a world of self-respect, dignity, and peace. Pattas were distributed either in the name of women who were the head of the family or jointly both in the name of the wife & husband. Priorities were also given to the eligible beneficiaries of the weakest section of the society. All the benefitted families received pattas, record-of-rights, and possession of the land on spot.

9. **Mukti Dhara – 2013:** This project was launched in Purulia district on March 7, 2013, under the administrative control and patronage of the SHG & SE Department. The objective was to create and maintain the sustainable livelihood of SHG members. The project is being implemented in association with NABARD. The Project is aimed at providing sustainable livelihood to the Self Help Groups on their selected livelihood activities viz. - homestead garden, poultry, goatery, vegetable cultivation, etc. Society for Self Employment of Unemployed Youth, W.B. has been entrusted to execute the Scheme.

10. **Jal Dharo Jal Bharo – 2011-12:** This program was launched during 2011-12 with the aim of preserving precious water resources by large scale harvesting of rainwater as well as arresting runoff of surface water to improve and availability of precious water resources through the construction and management of Minor Irrigation structures. 'Jal Dharo-Jal Bharo Program' also aims towards building citizen's awareness for rainwater conservation and efficient water use in irrigation.

As of December 2014, 1,18,557 nos water bodies/ retention structures have been created out of which 32,851 pond equivalent has been created by WRI&DD, 85,423 nos have been created in convergence with P&RD Deptt and 283 nos tanks have been created by WRI&DD under MGNREGS.[29]

11. **Matir Katha -2013:** 'Matir Katha' is an agriculture-based portal, launched in October 2013, for empowering the farmers of the state that involves 5 Departments which are Agriculture, Agricultural Marketing, Animal Husbandry, Fisheries, and Horticulture. The range of information covered in this portal includes name and kind of seeds, availability, price and quality control of seeds, suggestions for Season / Area / Crop/variety wise cropping (based on crop calendar), different information related to Soil and Fertilizer, Cultivation Technique of different crops, crop diseases and their remedies, Agro-Climatic Zones and Schemes for the cultivation of different crops.

12. **Madhur Sneha – 2013:** Mamata Banerjee launched Eastern India's first and country's most modernized "Human Milk Bank" in SSKM Hospital in August 2013. It is equipped with pasteurization and the most advanced milk collection, screening, processing, testing, and storage facilities. The project is named "Madhur Sneha". Babies who are prematurely born, or are of very low birth weight or those babies whose mothers are unable to feed directly can be recipients of banked milk from "Madhur Sneha".[30]

13. **Karma Sathi Prokolpa – 2021:** Anyone between the ages of 18 and 50 in the state will get financial assistance from the state government to set up their own company. Soft loan up to a maximum of Rs. 2 lakh is given. [31]

14. **Karma Tirtha:** With a view to promoting sustainable entrepreneurship and generating employment, the West Bengal government has set up 'Karmatirtha' - a one-stop shop allowing entrepreneurs to market their products directly to buyers. 'Karmatirtha' is a scheme to strike a synergy between the abundance of natural resources and the availability of a skilled workforce and thereby move toward sustainable entrepreneurship. The State government is providing the requisite infrastructure support including training and finance, allowing individuals, self-help groups, cooperative enterprises, artisans, and weavers to avail of the benefits of the scheme. The objective is to set up at least one 'Karmatirtha' in every block of the State.[32]

15. **Amar Fasal Amar Gola & Amar Fasal Amar Gari Scheme – 2013:** Amar Fasal Amar Global project seeks to provide financial assistance to marginal farmers of the State so that they can have their own storehouses and vending carts. A subsidy varying between Rs. 5,000 and Rs. 25,000 are provided for the warehouses. Though there are 24 lakh small and marginal farmers in the State, only around 10,000 such farmers were covered initially under two schemes. In the case of the Amar Fasal Amar Gari project, the rate of subsidy was Rs.10,000 flat. This project facilitated those farmers who wished to directly sell their products to end-users. The subsidies would be directly credited to the bank accounts of those farmers who own Kisan Credit Cards.[33]

16. **Housing Scheme "Akanksha" for State Govt. Employees – 2014:** Considering the hardship faced by the State Government employees for construction of their own houses/ flats for their own accommodation, the Government has introduced a new scheme of House Building Loan to the State Government Employees named "Akanksha" with a provision of 100 crore rupees. The benefit of the scheme may be applicable to all Government Servants as defined in W.B.S.R. except those Government Employees who have their own separate housing scheme such as the Housing Scheme called 'Pratyasha' for policemen. The Government will provide land free of cost to the Housing Department for the construction of flats. The Housing Corporation will charge only the cost of construction and infrastructure development from the buyer and the exercise will be done on no profit no loss basis. The flats will be distributed to the applicants by lottery on a random selection basis.[34]

17. **Sajubshree – 2016:** In 2016, the chief minister has devised a new strategy to raise awareness about the environment and also the need to save the girl child. The government has decided to gift saplings to the families of every newborn girl child in the state. The aim of the scheme is to achieve two goals at the same time - create awareness about the environment and also teach the importance of planting trees to nurture the environment just as they nurture their girl child.[35]

18. **Sabooj Sathi -2013:** Under the scheme, about 70 lakh bicycles were distributed to target group students – both boys and girls - of class IX to XII. This scheme has helped students to continue their studies, enjoy easy transportation, and protect the environment. Moreover, free books, exercise books, and shoes are given by the state government to all the students in schools.

19. **Khadya Sathi – 2016:** Through the Khadya Sathi Scheme the State Government is ensuring food security for the people of the state, the hallmark of the scheme is giving 5 kilograms (kg) of rice or wheat per family member per month at Rs.2 per kg. There are special arrangements under this scheme for those below the poverty line, affected by the Cyclone Aila, working in tea gardens, living in the Jangalmahal region, those in Singur whose farmlands were snatched away for setting up industries by the Left Front Government, and a few other categories. Nearly 8.66 crore people, comprising about 90.6 percent of the state's population, have been covered under this scheme.

20. **Shikshashree – 2014:** Shikshashree is a scholarship scheme for scheduled caste (SC) category students from classes V to VIII. The scholarship is being paid directly into the bank accounts of the students. During financial years 2014-17, almost 38 lakh students were covered under this scheme.

21. **Aikyashree Scholarship:** West Bengal minority development and finance Corporation (MDFC) has started a scholarship scheme called Aikyashree for the poor and meritorious students of minority communities comprising Muslims, Sikhs, Buddhists, Jains, Christians, and Parsees in West Bengal. Under this scholarship scheme financial assistance is provided to deserving students at both college and school levels. Through

this scholarship scheme, the government provides social-economic benefits and educational opportunities to minority students. Through this scholarship, students can avail financial assistance from class 1 to Ph.D. level. Also, the MDFC seeks to provide Education Loans for poor and meritorious students for their studies; promote training programs for development and up-gradation of skill; provide training for various competitive exams, and undertake programs for the empowerment of minority women.[36]

22. **Gatidhara – 2014:** Through the scheme the government provides loans of up to Rs. 10 lakh on an easy installment basis to enable people to buy cars, small trucks, etc. for commercial use, with a subsidy of 30 percent or up to Rs.1 lakh over the sanctioned loan while repaying the loan. Families with a monthly income of Rs. 25,000 or less qualify for financial support under this scheme. As of March 2017, the total number of beneficiaries covered was 13,393 and the amount of subsidy disbursed was Rs.125 crore.

23. **Gitanjali – 2011, and Amar Thikana – 2014:** Gitanjali is a housing scheme, introduced in 2011, meant for providing shelter to people belonging to economically weaker sections (EWS). A grant of Rs. 70,000 is provided to a beneficiary in the plains whereas Rs 75,000 is provided to a beneficiary from the Hills region, the Sundarbans, and Jangalmahal. Another scheme named Amar Thikana is also being implemented by the Panchayat and Rural Development Department at a unit cost of Rs. 70,000/- for the plains and Rs. 75,000/- in Hills, difficult and coastal areas. Till March 2017, benefits have been extended to 2 lakh 98 thousand 745 families.

24. **Lok Prasar Prakalpa – 2014:** The scheme, Lok Prasar Prakalpa was started in 2014 to rejuvenate the folk arts of Bengal coupled with the aim of disseminating social messages and information on the various developmental schemes run by the State Government. Folk artists between 18 and 60 years of age receive a retainer ship fee of Rs. 1,000.00 and in addition an opportunity for four performances per month, with Rs.1,000.00 paid for each. Senior artistes, that is, those above 60, receive a similar sum as a monthly pension. As of March 2017, benefits have been extended to nearly 1.94 lakh folk artists.

25. **Fair Price Medicine Shops -2012:** The purpose of Fair Price Medicine Shops (FPMS) or (in Bengali) 'Najyamuller Aushadher Dokan', was introduced by the government to ensure round-the-clock availability of quality medicines, consumables, surgical items, implants, etc. at pre-approved discounted rates over the maximum retail price (MRP), to enable people from all economic backgrounds to buy them. These types of medicine shops are located at State Government-run hospitals and medical college-cum-hospitals.

Till March 2017, 112 Fair Price Medicine Shops have been set up, selling goods at discounts of 48 to 78 percent on the MRP. As of December 2016, the total sales have been Rs. 1,331 crore and patients availed of discounts worth Rs. 829 crore, with 2.93 crore prescriptions being served from these facilities.

26. **Shishu Sathi – 2013:** Shishu Sathi Prakalpa is a program that was launched for providing free-of-cost operations for children up to the age of 18 years, covering the treatment of congenital cardiac diseases, cleft lip/palate, and club foot. It is available at all State Government hospitals having pediatric facilities and at three private hospitals, namely, RN Tagore International Institute of Cardiac Sciences, BM Birla Heart Research Centre (both in Kolkata), and Durgapur Mission hospital. About 12,000 children have received treatment through this scheme, so far.

27. **Shishu Aloy – 2012:** Shishu Aloys are a type of advanced Anganwadi Centres, aimed at making children ready for school at the age of 6 years. Children are prepared here for schools in every possible way and they are provided with nutritious food; they also get medical assistance.

As of March 2017, 2,000 Shishu Aloys were developed across all districts and two more at the Dum Dum and Alipore Correctional Homes to facilitate children of inmates. On November 25, 2017, which is celebrated by the State Government as Shishu Aloy Dibas, 10,000 more Shishu Aloys were inaugurated across Bengal.

28. **Swasthya Sathi – 2016:** Swasthya Sathi is a cashless group health insurance scheme (that is, including families) for all those employed by the State Government's

departments, both permanently and part-time. It is meant for various categories of employees like panchayat functionaries, para-workers like ASHAs, Anganwadi workers and civic police volunteers, contractual, part-time, and daily wage earners under various departments, teachers and non-teaching staff of primary schools, secondary schools, and government-aided madrasas, and others.

The scheme covers secondary and tertiary care up to Rs. 5 lakh per annum per family. All pre-existing diseases are covered in it. There is no cap on the family size and Parents from both the spouse are included. All dependent physically challenged persons in the family are also covered. The entire premium is borne by the State Government and no contribution from the beneficiary.

As of 31st March 2021, the total population covered was 10 crore. 2245 hospitals were included under the scheme, where service will be available. Total of 18,10,000 patients have received hospitalization facilities so far.37

29. **Sabala – 2011:** Sabla is a scheme for adolescent girls, which aims to improve the nutritional and health status of girls between 11 to 18 years of age and equip them with life skills training and knowledge on family welfare, health and hygiene, and information and guidance on existing public services. It is being implemented on a pilot basis in seven districts namely, Cooch Behar, Jalpaiguri, Alipurduar, Malda, Nadia, Kolkata, and Purulia through 29,444 Anganwadi Centres from 141 ICDS projects. The benefits of the Sabla Scheme have reached 12.72 lakh girls between the ages of 11 and 18 years.

30. **Anandadhara – 2012:** The Anandadhara Scheme is an anti-poverty program for the rural poor, implemented through women's self-help groups (SHG). The number of blocks involved in the program has increased from 32 during the financial year 2012-13 to 158 during 2016-17, and consequently, the number of SHGs has increased from 3.18 lakh to 4.58 lakh respectively. During 2016-17, the credit accessed from banks was Rs.3,329.81 lakh.

31. **Yuvashree – 2013:** This scheme was introduced to extend financial assistance of Rs.1,500 per month to 1 lakh job seekers who registered in the employment bank portal.

The beneficiaries were selected on the basis of criteria like education (those who have passed at least the eighth standard) and fall in the age group of 18 to 45 years. The recipients of the allowance are required to use it for training, vocational or otherwise, which will make them fit for employment.

32. **Samabyathi and Baitarani – 2016:** This scheme was made for paying money to the next of kin of poor people in rural regions for organizing their funerals. Rupees 2,000 are paid per funeral.

33. **Swabalamban:** Swabalamban is a scheme implemented through NGOs and companies for imparting vocational training to socially marginalized and distressed women, victims of trafficking, sex workers, the transgender community, and women in mortal danger, in the age group of 18 to 35 years; if necessary, the upper age limit for such category of women is relaxed up to 45 years. Beneficiaries successfully placed at renowned outlets like Wow Momo, Pantaloons, Kothari, Au Bon Pain, and others.

34. **Khelashree – 2017:** The Khelashree Scheme is a developmental initiative to encourage sporting activities. As per the scheme, Madhyamik and Higher Secondary schools, High Madrasahs, colleges, universities, all clubs from the first to the fifth divisions of the Kolkata League, and all clubs and sports institutions which have been getting annual financial aids from the State Government, would be given five footballs each.

35. **Safe Drive Save Life – 2016:** The Safe Drive Save Life program was started in 2016 to bring down road accidents in the State. As a result of the program, the number of road accidents in the state has been reduced by 19.52 percent. Consequently, the numbers of deaths and cases of injury have also come down by 11.5 percent and 14 percent, respectively.

36. **Mission Nirmal Bangla:** In 2013, Nadia became the first ODF district in India. The state reported 21,324 villages as 'Declared ODF', covering 1,929 Gram Panchayats, till May 17, 2017, which is the highest in the country. This initiative of the State Government achieved international recognition when it was selected as the first place winner for the

2015 United Nations Public Service Award in the category of 'Improving the Delivery of Public Services.' [38]

In addition to the above schemes, Mamata Banerjee surprised the people with her declaration of distribution of Tablets for all the Class XII students of Higher Secondary schools. The number of students covered under the scheme was over 9.5 lakh, many of whom were going to vote in the 2021 assembly elections.

Secondly, she launched *Didi Ke Bolo* Program. Through the program, the government wanted to connect with the people of the state. This grievance redress mechanism, launched in July 2019, was held around 14 key policy programs being rolled out. This program was a huge success with more than 28 lakh complaints and 80 lakh calls to find solutions of their grievances.

This helped to strategize the future course of action for the TMC. The complaints were analyzed and mapped to a particular issue or pattern. For example, a nature of grievance appeared to be around the pay disparities among state and central employees. The state has accepted the Sixth Pay Commission recommendations and implemented it from January 1, 2020.

However, nearly 10-lakh odd complaints were local in nature, including road repairs, drainage, water issues, classrooms, and even culverts. The 'Paray Samadhan' scheme gave financial powers to the local administration to do the work, easing the red tape.[39] Further, the West Bengal government launched a massive outreach program called "*Duare Sarkar*" program on December 1, 2020, for doorstep delivery of government schemes. It came to news that "90 lakh people across West Bengal received different kinds of services. This included 60 lakh beneficiaries under Swasthya Sathi, 7 lakh beneficiaries who received SC/ST/OBC certificates, and 4 lakh beneficiaries who received assistance under *Krishak Bandhu*. The second phase of the scheme was launched in January 2021.[40]

After the huge success of the *Duare Sarkar*, the West Bengal government announced a new initiative 'Paray Paray Samadhan', under which local neighborhood grievances were redressed. The program continued from January 2 to February 15. This program, though not addressed major infrastructural gaps, addressed municipal, local or service gaps through specific mission modes to reach out to the neighborhood. This was supplementary to 'Duare Sarkar' which has reached out to crores of people. A separate task force comprising a principal secretary and a secretary were appointed for 'Paray Paray Samadhan.'[41]

'Paray Paray Samadhan' also resolved local issues such as constructing culverts, adding a schoolroom or even repairing water pipelines. West Bengal chief secretary Alapan Bandyopadhyay said while the 'Duare Sarkar' scheme was for individuals and families; 'Paray Paray Samadhan' was more community-centric. Bengal's 'Duare Sarkar' scheme has already had over 1.5 crore people enlisting for state schemes in 573 camps state-wide. The third round of 'Duare Sarkar' camps was held from January 2-12. The outreach effort was ended on January 25. Caste certificates were distributed by holding camps in localities where SC/ST people lived in large numbers.[42]

Benefits through budgetary allocation

Through the latest budget (2020-21) document the state government provided some additional benefit schemes to the people of the state to woo the voters. To mention a few, at first comes the Pension scheme for SCs and STs. The scheme highlights that, persons belonging to the Scheduled Castes (SCs) and Scheduled Tribes (STs), who are more than 60 years of age and not covered under any pension scheme, will be provided a monthly pension of one thousand rupees. The new pension scheme is expected to benefit 25 lakh persons. An amount of Rs 3,000 crore has been allocated for the proposed scheme for 2020-21. Another new scheme has been proposed to provide free electricity to poor domestic consumers. Under the scheme, no electricity charge will be levied on those poor domestic consumers whose quarterly consumption of electricity is up to 75 units (lifeline consumers). The scheme is expected to benefit 35 lakh poor families. Rupees 200 crore has been allocated for the proposed scheme for 2020-21.[43]

The budget analysis indicates that, total expenditure in 2020-21 is targeted at Rs. 2,55,677 crore. This is 3.1% higher than the revised estimate of 2019-20. This expenditure is proposed to be met through receipts (other than borrowings) of Rs. 1,79,905 crore (69%) and borrowings of Rs. 79,465 crore (31%). Total receipt (other than borrowings) in 2020-21 is expected to be 9.9% higher than the revised estimate of 2019-20. Borrowings, on the other hand, are estimated to decrease by 2.6% in 2020-21, as compared to the revised estimate of 2019-20.44

Conclusions

From the above discussion it can be remarked without any hesitation that, the schemes and programs that the Mamata Banerjee government initiated and implemented in Bengal since the very beginning of her chief ministership were transformative and adjuvant to the people of the state. But a close comparison of the State Schemes with that of the Centre's will clearly demonstrate that duplicity and rip-off have been done by the state government while implemented the schemes with renaming many of those Central schemes. Also, it is true that the ratio of contribution by the Centre and State is 60:40. Hence, instead of declaring exclusively one's own, credit should be given according to their level of contribution. But the propaganda and management of the schemes by a bunch of efficient officers, and below the level officials at the local level brought about remarkable dividends in the TMC baskets. Another remarkable observation is that majority of the developmental schemes are being made with borrowed money as it was evidenced in the end of this chapter. On this background, the 2021 legislative assembly elections were held in Bengal. Now, let us examine the elections of 202, and the general perception of respondents about the performance of the Trinamool Congress Government in the following two chapters.

Chapter – IV

The Legislative Assembly Elections - 2021

"Government of the people, by the people, for the people, shall not perish from the Earth."

-   Abraham Lincoln

Introduction

The Preamble to the Constitution of India ushered with the words: 'We, the People of India' and it 'resolved to constitute India into a Sovereign Socialist Secular Democratic Republic'. Also, the Constitution makers wanted "to secure to all its citizen: Justice, social, economic and political; Liberty of thought, expression, belief, faith and worship; Equality of status and of opportunity; and to promote among them all Fraternity assuring the dignity of the individual and the unity and integrity of the Nation" (The Constitution of India). The Constitution of India is the supreme law of India. The most important ingredient of democracy is regular elections of all its decision-making and law-making bodies. And India, the world's largest, is renowned for holding elections in regular intervals. In the months of March & April 2021 West Bengal, along with some other States and the Union Territory of Puducherry, conducted its general elections to the Legislative Assembly. One striking fact is that every year West Bengal surpasses its own record of violence in elections, may it be local body elections or legislative assembly elections. Consequently, it is pertinent to discuss the nature and extent of violence taking place in elections. The following chapter delineates the nature and extent of violence held in both pre and post-election periods in Bengal. Also, it argues if it is necessary to resort to violent means to capture or retain power. Prior to that, the district-wise reports of various incidents and facts relating to elections have been analyzed to have a proper picture of the phase-wise elections, voters' turns out, and votes polled in this State. The election and political participation of people are two major features of democracy. Robert A. Dahl in his epoch-making work On Democracy expressed that, large-scale democracy requires: 1. Elected officials, 2. Free, fair, and frequent elections, 3. Freedom of expression, 4. Alternative sources of information, 5. Associational autonomy, and 6. Inclusion citizenship.[1] We will examine how free and fair was election to the legislative assembly of West Bengal was in the following part.

The Election Commission of India and its dynamic role

The Election Commission of India (ECI) is primarily responsible for conducting elections to the Lok Sabha, Rajya Sabha, State Legislative Assemblies and Councils, and the President and Vice President of the country. The ECI is a permanent and independent body established by the Constitution of India under Article 324 to ensure free and fair elections to the above-mentioned bodies and persons. Also, it functions with both autonomy and freedom along with other independent Constitutional bodies such as the Supreme Court, the Union Public Service Commission, and the Comptroller and Auditor General of India. In India generally, elections of Lok Sabha, Rajya Sabha, Legislative Assembly, and Local Government Bodies (LGBs) are held after every five years. The term of office begins and ends at different years and months in different states. In 2021 the term of office in five States and Union Territories was supposed to be ended. Hence, elections in these States and Union Territory were a compulsory task before the ECI.

How did the ECI prepare for elections?

The just-concluded election was the highest voltage election in West Bengal. The ECI had taken all precautionary measures with the deployment of central forces to deter any untoward incidents. The first phase of the election was held on 27th March 2021. Around 600 companies of central forces arrived before March 25. Even prior to that, 125 companies of central forces had reached Bengal and another 169 companies were scheduled to arrive prior to the beginning of the elections. In comparison to the 2016 assembly elections and 2019 Lok Sabha polls, this deployment was much higher. The highest deployment of central forces in Bengal to date had been during the 2019 Lok Sabha polls when 842 companies of central forces were stationed. The central forces included Border Security Force (BSF), Indo-Tibetan Border Police (ITBP), Service Selection Board (SSB), Central Industrial Security Force (CISF), and Central Reserve Police Force (CRPF), etc.

The first and second phases of elections were held in West and East Midnapore, Jhargram, Bankura, and South 24 Parganas. Except for South 24 Parganas and East Midnapore, other districts were dens of Maoist activities. These are known as Maoist hotbeds. Hence, additional precautionary measures were needed in these areas. Therefore, around 43 companies of central forces have been stationed in Maoist zones from earlier, so that people do not fear to come out to cast their votes. One company means a military unit, typically consisting of 80-250 soldiers and usually commanded by a major or a captain. Around 650 companies of central forces were deployed for the first phase of elections. The first phase elections were held in 10,288 booths spread across 30 assembly constituencies. This means more than six paramilitary personnel were deployed in each booth. However, the strategy of the ECI was to cover booths, dominate areas and perform other tasks: "The entire force will not be used for booth management. Some will also be used for area domination and as flying squads."[2]

When the elections were held in West Bengal, in the beginning, there was not so much high of the COVID-19 infections. But in the later phases, it started to spread rapidly. Hence India, along with the entire world, was reeling under the devastation of the COVID-19 pandemic while the elections were held in this state. Despite the fact, there was little option before the ECI other than conducting elections to keep on the smooth running of the state administrative machinery. Therefore, it was a great challenge before the ECI, but with its expertise and experience, the Election Commission of India conducted the elections with minimum casualties.

The ECI, like all the previously held elections in India, held a preparatory meeting with the general, police, and expenditure observers prior to the beginning of the legislative assembly polls 2021 held in four states viz. Assam, Kerala, Tamil Nadu, and West Bengal, and Union Territory of Puducherry. The election schedule was announced on

26th February 2021. The observers being the important torchbearers of Indian democracy played a very significant role in elections. Indian democracy lies in the fact that the so-called "Common Man" plays a decisive role in Government formation. The motto of the ECI was to ensure empowered, vigilant, well-informed, and safe voters. The ultimate aim of the ECI was to enable citizens to vote fearlessly. The ECI further reiterated that there should not be any lax in performing their duties, and there should not be any willful lapses by the ECI. A unique feature of this year's election was that the persons with disabilities, senior citizens, and women voters were given all facilities to cast their votes. In the elections in five states and union territory, more than 18 crore voters were supposed to exercise their right of franchise. Accounting for social distancing norms, more than 80,000 polling stations have been added. The great challenge before the ECI was to curb money and muscle power and control the vices of liquor and freebies. Hence, building the confidence of the electors was a priority work of the ECI. Therefore, it is required to play an important role in making these elections totally inducement-free. This year for the first time the ECI has extended the option of Postal Ballot facility to the electors who were marked as Persons with Disabilities (PwD), electors above the age of 80 years, electors employed in notified Essential services, and electors who were COVID- 19 positive/suspect as certified by the competent authority and were in quarantine (home/institutional).[3]

Restriction on media coverage

In regard to the general elections to the legislative assemblies of Assam, Kerala, Puducherry, Tamil Nadu & West Bengal, 2021, the ECI released a Press Note on media coverage during the period of elections referred in Section 126 of the Representation of People's Act, 1951. The said prohibits displaying any election matter by means, inter alia, of television or similar apparatus, during the period of 48 hours before the hour fixed for conclusion of poll in a constituency. Section 126 prohibits public meetings during a period of forty-eight hours ending with an hour fixed for the conclusion of the poll, and no person shall display to the public any election matter by means of cinematograph, television, or other similar apparatus in any polling area during the period of forty-eight hours ending with the hour fixed for the conclusion of the poll for any election in the polling area.

Further, it said that, any person who contravenes the provisions of sub-section (1) shall be punishable with imprisonment for a term which may extend to two years, or with fine, or with both. In this Section, the expression "election matter" means any matter intended or calculated to influence or affect the result of an election. (2). During elections, there are sometimes allegations of violation of the provisions of the above Section 126 of the Representation of the People Act, 1951 by TV channels in the telecast of their panel discussions/debates and other news and current affairs programs. The Commission has clarified in the past that the said Section 126 prohibits displaying any election matter by means, inter alia, of television or similar apparatus, during the period of 48 hours ending with the hour fixed for conclusion of poll in a constituency. "Election matter" has been defined in that Section as any matter intended or calculated to influence or affect the result of an election. Violation of the aforesaid provisions of Section 126 is punishable with imprisonment up to a period of two years, or with a fine, or both.[4]

Poll schedule

The West Bengal Legislative Assembly elections started on March 27, Saturday, and the entire elections were completed by April 29, 2021. The voting timing was extended this time. It started at 7.00 A.M. and ended at 6.00 P.M. In West Bengal total numbers of assembly seats are 294, of which 68 are reserved or Scheduled Castes and 16 for the Scheduled Tribes. The seats are scattered in total of 23 districts of the State. West Bengal has a total of 42 Lok Sabha seats. In the general election of 2019, the TMC was reduced to 22 from its previous 34. While the BJP won 18 seats in the left bastion.

The schedule for holding the General Election to the Legislative Assemblies of Assam, Kerala, Puducherry, Tamil Nadu, West Bengal, 2021 was announced on 26.02.2021. Polls in the states were held as per the schedule given below.

Table: 4.1 State-wise election schedule

Name of State/UT	Phase & Poll date

Assam	Three phases – 27/03/2021, 01/04/2021 & 06/04/2021
Puducherry, Kerala & Tamil Nadu	Single phase – 06/04/2021
West Bengal	Eight Phases - 27/03/2021, 01/04/2021, 06/04/2021, 10/04/2021, 17/04/2021, 22/04/2021, 26/04/2021 & 29/04/2021

Source: The Election Commission of India

The entire elections were planned to be concluded by the Election Commission of India in total 8 phases in the state of West Bengal. This was an exceptional decision for which the ECI had to face severe criticism from different quarters, and particularly from the opposition parties. Now let us see the district-wise poll schedule in West Bengal.

Table: 4.2 Details of W.B. legislative assembly election-2021

Phase	Date of Poll	Districts covered	Total Seats	Name of Legislative Assembly Seats
1st	27.03.2021	**Total = 5** Paschim Midnapore Part-I, Purba Midnapore Part-I, Bankura, Jhargram, and Purulia	30	1. Patashpur, 2.Kanthi Uttar, 3. Bhagabanpur, 4.Khejuri, 5.Kanthi Dakshin, 6. Ramnagar, 7. Egra Purba, 8. Dantan Paschim, 9. Nayagram, 10. Gopiballavpur, 11. Jhargram, 12. Keshiary, 13. Kharagpur Paschim, 14. Garbeta Paschim 15. Salboni, 16. Paschim Medinipur 17. Paschim Binpur, 18. Bandwan, 19. Balarampur, 20. Baghmundi, 21. Joypur, 22. Purulia, 23. Manbazar, 24. Kashipur, 25. Para, 26. Raghunathpur, 27. Saltora, 28. Chhatna, 29. Ranibandh, 30. Raipur
2nd	01.04.2021	**Total = 4** South 24 Parganas Part-I, Bankura Part-II, Paschim Midnapore Part-2 and Purba	30	1. Gosaba, 2. Patharpratima, 3. Kakdwip, 4. Sagar, 5. Tamluk, 6.Panskura (204), 7. Panskura (205), 8. Moyna, 9. Nandakumar, 10. Mahisadal, 11.Haldia, 12. Nandigram, 13. Chandipur, 14. Kharagpur Sadar, 15.

		Midnapore		Narayangarh Paschim, 16. Sabang Paschim, 17. Pingla Paschim, 18. Debra Paschim, 19. Daspur Paschim, 20. Ghatal Paschim, 21. Chandrakona Paschim, 22. Keshpur Paschim, 23. Taldangra, 24. Bankura, 25. Barjora, 26. Onda, 27. Bishnupur, 28. Katulpur, 29. Indas, 30. Sonamukhi
3rd	06.04.2021	**Total = 3** Howrah, Hooghly, and South 24 Paraganas	31	1. Basanti, 2. Kultali, 3. Kulpi, 4. Raidighi, 5. Mandirbazar, 6. Jaynagar, 7. Baruipur , 8. Purba Canning, 9. Paschim Canning, 10. Purba Baruipur, 11. Paschim Magrahat, 12. Purba Magrahat, 13. Paschim Diamond Harbour, 14. Falta, 15. Satgachhia, 16. Bishnupur, 17. Uluberia Uttar, 18. Uluberia Dakshin, 19. Shyampur, 20. Bagnan, 21. Amta, 22.Udaynarayanpur, 23. Jagatballavpur, 24. Jangipara, 25. Haripal, 26. Dhanekhali, 27. Tarakeswar, 28. Pursurah, 29. Arambag, 30. Goghat, 31. Khanakul
4th	10.04.2021	**Total = 5** Howrah Part-II, South 24 Parganas Part-III, Hooghly Part-II, Allipurduar (all five constituencies) and Cooch Behar (all 9 constituencies)	44	1. Mekliganj, 2. Mathabhanga, 3. Cooch Behar (Uttar), 4. Cooch Behar (Dakshin), 5. Sitalkuchi, 6. Sitai, 7. Dinhata, 8. Natabari, 9. Tufanganj, 10. Kumargram, 11. Kalchini, 12. Alipurudar, 13. Falakata, 14. Madarihat, 15. Sonarpur Dakshin, 16. Bhangar, 17. Kasba, 18. Jadavpur, 19. Sonarpur Uttar, 20. Tollyganj, 21. Behala Purba, 22. Behala Paschim, 23. Maheshtala, 24. Budge Budge, 25. Metiaburuz, 26. 169 Bally, 27. Howrah Uttar, 28. Howrah Madhya, 29. Shibpur, 30. Howrah Dakshin, 31. Sankrail, 32. Panchla, 33. Uluberia Purba, 34. Domjur, 35. Uttarpara, 36. Sreerampur, 37. Champdani, 38. Singur, 39. Chandannagar, 40. Chunchura, 41. Balagarh, 42. Pandua, 43.

				Saptagram, 44. Chanditala
5th	17.04.2021	**Total = 4** Nadia (Part 1), Bardhaman (Part 1), Darjeeling, and Jalpaiguri.	45	1. Dhupguri, 2. Maynaguri, 3. Jalpaiguri, 4. Rajganj, 5. Dabgram-Phulbari, 6. Mal Jalpaiguri ST, 7. Nagrakata, 8. Kalimpong, 9. Darjeeling, 10. Kurseong, 11. Matigara-Naxalbari, 12. Siliguri, 13. Phansidewa, 14. Shantipur, 15. Ranaghat, 16. Uttar Paschim, 17. Krishnaganj, 18. Ranaghat Uttar Purba, 19. Ranaghat Dakshin, 20. Chakdaha, 21. Kalyani, 22. Haringhata, 23. Panihati, 24. Kamarhati, 25. Baranagar, 26. Dum Dum, 27. Rajarhat New Town, 28. Bidhannagar, 29. Rajarhat Gopalpur, Madhyamgram, 30. Barasat, 31. Deganga, 32. Haroa, 33. Minakhan, 34. Sandeshkhali, 35. Basirhat Dakshin, 36. Basirhat Uttar, 37. Hingalganj, 38. Khandaghosh, 39. Bardhaman Dakshin, 40. Raina, 41. Jamalpur, 42. Manteswar, 43. Kalna, 44. Memari, 45. Bardhaman Uttar
6th	22.04.2021	**Total = 4** North Pargana (Part-II), Purbo Bardhaman (Part-2), Nadia (Part-3), Uttar Dinajpur.	43	1. Chopra, 2. Islampur, 3. Goalpokhar, 4. Chakulia, 5. Karandighi, 6. Hemtabad, 7. Kaliaganj, 8. Raiganj, 9. Itahar, 10. Karimpur, 11. Tehatta, 12. Palashipara, 13. Kaliganj, 14. Nakashipara, 15. Chapra, 16. Krishnanagar Uttar, 17. Nabadwip, Krishnanagar, 18. Bagda, 19. Bangaon Uttar SC, 20. Bangaon Dakshin SC, 21. Gaighata, 22. Swarupnagar, 23. Baduria, 24. Habra, 25. Ashoknagar, 26. Amdanga, 27. Bijpur, 28. Naihati, 29. Bhatpara, 30. Jagatdal, 31 Noapara, 32. Barrackpur, 33. Khardaha, 34. Dum Dum Uttar, 35. Bhatar, 36. Purbasthali , 37. Dakshin, 38. Purbasthali Uttar, 39. Katwa, 40.

				Ketugram, 41. Mangalkot, 42. Ausgram, 43.Galsi
7th	26.04.2021	**Total = 5** Dakshin Dinajpur, Kolkata South, Malda (Part-1), Murshidabad (Part-1), and Paschim Bardhman.	36	1. Kushmandi, 2. Kumarganj, 3. Balurghat, 4. Tapan, 5. Gangarampur, 6. Harirampur, 7. Habibpur, 8. Gazole, 9. Chanchal, 10. Harishchandrapur, 11. Malatipur, 12. Ratua, 13. Farakka, 14. Samserganj, 15. Suti, 16. Jangipur, 17. Raghunathganj, 18. Sagardighi, 19. Lalgola, 20. Bhagabangola, 21. Raninagar, 22. Murshidabad, 23. Nabagram, 24. Kolkata Port, 25. Bhabanipur, 26. Rashbehari, 27. Ballygunge, 28. Pandaveswar, 29. Durgapur Purba, 30. Durgapur Paschim, 31. Raniganj, 32. Jamuria, 33. Asansol Dakshin, 34. Asansol Uttar Paschim, 35. Kulti Paschim, 36. Barabani Paschim
8th	29.04.2021	**Total = 4** Malda (Part-II), Birbhum, Murshidabad, and Kolkata North	35	1. Manikchak, 2. Maldah, 3. English Bazar, 4. Mothabari Sujapur, 5. Baisnabnagar, 6. Khargram, 7. Burwan, 8. Kandi, 9. Bharatpur, 10. Rejinagar, 11. Beldanga, 11. Baharampur, 13. Hariharpara, 14. Naoda, 15. Domkal, 16. Jalangi, 17. Chowranghee, 18. Entally, 19. Beleghata, 20. Jorasanko, 21. Shyampukur, 22. Maniktala, 23. Kashipur Belgachhia, 24.Dubrajpur, 25. Suri, 26. Bolpur, 27. Birbhum, 28. Nanoor, 29. Labpur, 30. Sainthia, 31.Mayureswar, 32. Rampurhat, 33. Hansan, 34 Nalhati 35. Murarai

Source: Compiled from various places

The 1st phase of elections

In the first phase of the West Bengal elections, a total of five districts were covered. These districts were Paschim Medinipur Part-I, Purba Medinipur Part-II, Bankura,

Jhargram, and Purulia. There were a total of 30 seats. The date of notification for this phase was March, 2 and the last date of nomination was March 9, Scrutiny of nomination was scheduled to be completed by March 30 and the last date of withdrawal of candidature was March 12, while the date of the poll was on March 27.

The 2nd phase of elections

In the second phase of the Bengal elections, a total of four districts were covered. These districts were Paschim Medinipur Part-II, South 24 Parganas Part-I, Bankura Part-II, Purba Medinipur. There were a total of 30 seats. The date of notification for this phase was March 5, and the last date of nomination was March 12, Scrutiny of nomination was scheduled to be completed by March 15 and the last date of withdrawal of candidature was March 17, while the date of the poll was on April 1.

The 3rd phase of elections

The phase three elections in West Bengal elections were held in total 3 districts. These districts were Howrah, Hooghly, and South 24 Parganas. There was a total of 31 seats. The date of notification for this phase was March, 12 and the last date of nomination was March 19, Last date of withdrawal was March 22, while the date of the poll was on April, 06. The Election Commission of India on 06.04.2021 released a Press Note to inform that, polling in Kerala, Tamil Nadu, and Puducherry and for Phase 3 assembly constituencies in Assam and West Bengal was conducted peacefully. Voting was held in total of 1,53,538 polling stations spreading across 475 assembly constituencies. The number of polling stations has increased in view of the fact that the number of voters per polling station has been reduced from 1500 to 1000 keeping social distancing norms. In West Bengal total number of electors was 78,52,425 including a total of 80+ electors of 1,26,177 persons.[5]

The 4th phase of elections

In the fourth phase of elections, a total of five districts was covered. These districts were Howrah Part-II, South 24 Parganas Part-III, Hooghly Part-II, Allipurduar (all five constituencies), and Cooch Behar (all 9 constituencies). There was a total of 44 seats. The date of notification for this phase was March 16, and the last date of nomination was March 23, Scrutiny of nomination was scheduled to be completed by March 24 and the last date of withdrawal of candidature was March 26, while the voting date was on April 10.

The Election Commission of India in a Press Note[6] declared that under Article 324 it will reduce the timing of campaigning. The COVID-19 infection rate was increasing rapidly. As a result, by exercising its power mentioned under Article 324 the ECI intended to "(1) curtail the timing of campaign up to 7 PM. There shall not be any campaign between 7 PM and 10 AM on campaign day and to (2) extend the silence period from 48 hours to 72 hours in each of the remaining three phases."

The Commission further directed all the political parties to adhere to the COVID norms/instructions. It has directed all the candidates and political parties to ensure absolute adherence to Covid guidelines in letter and spirit. It said that violations, if any, shall be sternly dealt with and action, including criminal action, might be taken as per extant legal framework. Also, the ECI notified that it shall be the responsibility of the organizers of public meetings, rallies, etc. to provide masks and sanitizers to every person attending these meetings, rallies, etc at their cost which shall also ensure proper usage of masks, sanitizers, and also be responsible for maintaining minimum social distance by everyone. Another important declaration of the ECI was that the star campaigners/political leaders/candidates/aspiring policymakers shall demonstrate by their personal example and nudge all supporters at the beginning of the rally, meeting, and any other event during the campaign to wear mask, use sanitizers and maintain social distance and put in place such crowd control measures as were necessary for the observance of extant guidelines. District Election Officers and Returning Officers were asked to take strict measures to enforce Covid guidelines during the campaign. Also, they shall be instructed to cancel public meetings, rallies, etc. if any violations were observed, in addition to invoking penal sections. It further directed the Special Observers and General, Police, and Expenditure Observers to strictly monitor compliance of covid norms during the campaign. Above all, the Commission has directed that Chief Secretary, West Bengal, CEO, West Bengal, all DEOs, and Ros of the remaining three phases shall ensure strict compliance of this order and enforcement of extant guidelines. Special observers and other districts/ constituency(ies) level observers shall regularly monitor compliance.[7]

The 5th phase of elections

The fifth phase elections were held in total four districts such as Nadia Part-I, Bardhaman – Part I, Darjeeling, and Jalpaiguri. There was a total of 45 seats. The date of notification for this phase was March 16, and the last date of nomination was March 23, Scrutiny of nomination was scheduled to be completed by March 24 and the last date of withdrawal of candidature was April 07, while the voting date was on April 22.

After the fifth phase of polling, the ECI released a press note in the evening that said peaceful polling was held in 15,789 polling stations spread across 45 assembly constituencies in Phase V WB Elections. Voter turnout (at 5 PM) for Phase VII West Bengal Election was 78.36%. The ECI thanked all voters for following Covid protocol. However, polling in 56-Samserganj and 58 Jangipur Assembly constituencies in West Bengal was adjourned. In the 5th phase, total polling stations monitored through webcasting were 8,266 out of 15,789. Also, the police administration's time seizure of bombs and arms ensured secured and peaceful elections.[8]

Polling at 56-Samserganj Assembly Constituency & 58-Jangipur Assembly Constituency West Bengal scheduled on 26 April stands adjourned due to death of Indian National Congress candidate and Revolutionary Socialist Party candidate respectively. More interesting reports were revealed by the Election Commission of India. In Phase V of West Bengal Assembly Elections, the total number of PwD electors and 80+ electors are 60,198 and 1,79,634 respectively. A total of 15,789 Ballot Units (BUs), 15,789 Control Units(CUs), and 15,789 VVPATs were used in West Bengal during this phase. 8266 (52.35%) out of 15789 polling stations were monitored live through webcasting. During the ongoing elections till this phase in West Bengal, a record seizure of Rs.310.50 Crores has already been reported to date. The seizure figure, which includes seizure of cash, liquor, narcotics, freebies, etc., is 7 times the total seizure of Rs. 44.33 Crores in GE LA 2016. The progressive seizure of all five States/UT where assembly elections have been/are being held, as of date is Rs.1013.1 Crore (this includes seizures of Rs.12.11 Crore in by-elections also).[9]

The 6th phase of elections

In the sixth phase elections to total numbers of districts covered were North 24 Parganas Part-III, Purba Bardhaman Part –II, Nadia Part-III, and Uttar Dinajpur. There was a total of 43 seats. The date of notification for this phase was March 26, and the last date of nomination was April 3, Scrutiny of nomination was scheduled to be completed by April 5, and the last date of withdrawal of candidature was March 26, while the voting date was on April 10. In the VI phase of elections held in 14,480 polling stations spreading across 43 assembly constituencies, the voters' turnout (at 5. PM) was 79.09 percent.[10] The Election Commission of India invited the attention of all political parties to abide by the Covid protocol during their campaigns. Webcasting was done in 7466 polling stations, where live monitoring was done through drones to keep watch over vote proceedings.

The 7th phase of elections

The 7th phase of assembly elections in West Bengal was held in a total of 5 districts. These districts were Dakshin Dinajpur, Kolkata South, Malda Part-I, and Paschim Bardhaman. The total numbers of seats were 36. The date of notification for this phase was March 31 and the last date of nomination was April 07. The scrutiny of nomination was April 8, and the last date of withdrawal was April 12, while the date of the poll was on April 26. After every phase of polling, the ECI released a press note in the evening. The Press Note[11] dated 26th April, 2021 said that peaceful polling was held in 11,376 polling stations spread across 34 assembly constituencies in Phase VII WB Elections. Voter turnout (at 5 PM) for Phase VII West Bengal Election was 75.06%. Not only that the voters in all booths scrupulously followed Covid's appropriate behavior i.e. wore masks, kept physical distancing of 5 meters each. The ECI reiterated that instructions to District authorities to take action under extant rules against Covid protocol violators. In the 7th phase, total polling stations monitored through webcasting were 5982 out of 11,376. Also, the police administration's time seizure of bombs and arms ensured secured and peaceful elections.[12]

The last phase of elections

The last phase of the poll was held in 35 seats on April 29, 2021, in the districts of Malda Part-II, Birbhum, Murshidabad, and Kolkata North. The date of notification was March 31, the last date of nomination was April 7, scrutiny of nomination was April 18 and the last day of withdrawal was April 22.[13] At the end of the last phase of elections in Bengal, the Election Commission of India in a Press Note stated that peaceful polling concluded across 11,860 polling stations in 35 assembly constituencies of West Bengal. Also, re-polling in Amtali Madhyamik Sikha Kendra polling station in 5-Sitalkuchi (SC) assembly constituency was conducted with the last phase of elections.[14] We come to know from the said Press Note that, strict preventive measures and timely seizures of bombs and arms ensured violence-free peaceful elections. Voters abided by Covid protocols at all the polling booths. Up to 5.00 PM, voter turnout for the VIII phase of the West Bengal election was 76.07%.

Now we will have a look at the consolidated factsheet through the following table (Table 4.3). This factsheet shows the phase-wise elections in total 292 assembly constituencies; a number of polling stations; registered electors, and a number of contesting candidates in all 8 phases. In addition to these, also we find the number of general poll observers deployed in every phase of elections; the number of police observers, and the number of expenditure observers engaged in conducting free, fair, and corruption-free elections in all assembly seats in West Bengal.

Table: 4.3 Factsheet for West Bengal

State	Phase -I	Phase - II	Phase - III	Phase - IV	Phase -V	Phase - VI	Phase - VII	Phase - VIII	Total Up to Phase - VIII
Assembly constituency	30	30	31	44	45	43	34	35	292
No. of polling stations	10,228	10,620	10,871	15,940	15,789	14,480	11,376	11,860	101224
Registered electors	7380942	7594549	7852425	11581022	11347344	103877 9 1	818890 7	847827 4	728112 5 4
Total number	191	171	205	373	319	306	368	283	2116

of contesting candidates									
No. of general observers deployed	20	23	22	35	33	26	26	24	209
No. of police observers deployed	7	6	9	9	12	13	10	9	75
No. of expenditure observers deployed	9	9	7	10	16	13	9	10	85
% of voting till 5 PM	84.63 (final VTR)	86.11 (final VTR)	84.61 (final VTR)	79.90 (final VTR)	82.49 (final VTR)	82 (final VTR)	76.90 (final VTR)	76.07 (final VTR)	-

Source: The Election Commission of India, Press Note No. ECI/PN/58/2021 dt. 29th April, 2021.

Measures of ECI to curb the money power in elections

Money power, muscle power, intimidation, consumption of alcohol, and distribution of freebies and cash to the vulnerable electors to buy votes are some of the common features of Indian elections, may it be Panchayat or Legislative Assembly, or Lok Sabha elections. Considering the above problems in the pre-election period and during election days the ECI sought to curb the distribution of money, liquor, and valuable gifts during ongoing elections in the States of Assam, West Bengal, Tamil Nadu, Kerala, and Union Territory of Puducherry. In a Press Note on 17th March, the ECI declared that it had seized a record quantity of things worth Rs. 331 crores from the States that were going to the polls in the first quarter of 2021. This amount of seizures till 16th March, in the middle of elections in West Bengal, already surpassed the total seizures made in assembly elections to these State/UT held in 2016 (Rs. 225.77 crores), and the most significant point is that record seizures have been made only when the polls were not yet started. The following table (Table 4.4) highlights the state-wise confiscation of cash, liquor, drugs, freebies, and precious metals by the Election Commission prior to the elections in state assemblies.

Table: 4.4 State-wise seizures before elections 2021

States	Cash	Liquor (worth Rs crores)	Drugs (worth Rs crores)	Freebies	Precious Metals	Total
Assam	11.73	17.25	27.09	4.87	2.82	**63.75**
Puducherry	2.32	0.26	0.15	0.14	2.85	**5.72**
Tamil Nadu	50.86	1.32	0.35	14.06	61.04	**127.64**
Kerala	5.46	0.38	0.68	0.04	15.23	**21.77**
West Bengal	19.11	9.72	47.40	29.42	6.93	**112.59**
Total	**89.48**	**28.93**	**75.67**	**48.52**	**88.87**	**331.47**

Source: The Election of Commission of India

The ECI had deployed a total of 295 Expenditure Observers for effectively monitoring to curb black money in the general election to the legislative assemblies of Assam, West Bengal, Tamil Nadu, Kerala, and Union Territory of Puducherry. The Election Commission of India had also appointed five Special Expenditure Observers. Being experienced and having their formidable domain expertise and impeccable track record the Observers were deputed for monitoring election expenditure more effectively. After the due assessment, 259 Assembly Constituencies in the four States and one Union Territory have been marked as Expenditure Sensitive Constituencies and more focused vigil was done on those areas.

During the entire electoral process, the distribution of cash and gifts is not permitted under the law. Thus, it is completely illegal to distribute money, liquor, or any other item to the electors with the intent to influence the voters. This expenditure comes under the definition of "bribery" which is an offense both under 171B of IPC and under the R.P. Act, 1951. The expenditure on such items is illegal.[15] Despite having all the rules and laws, the contending parties mostly try to influence the electors with money, liquor, and other gifts.

Confiscation of illegal items during election days

The ECI was very active in seizing prohibitory items such as cash, liquors, and other kinds that might have been used for bribe purposes. During the ongoing elections till the 3rd phase, the ECI had seized Rs. 947.98 crore from the five states went to the polls till April 6, 2021. The seizure figure, which included the seizure of cash, liquor, narcotics, freebies, etc., was more than 4.198 times higher than the total combined seizure of Rs. 225.77 Crore in the legislative assembly elections of 2016. The Commission has laid specific emphasis on inducement of free elections and curbed the malaise of undue money power, liquor, and freebies. For effective monitoring a total of 4606 Flying Squads (FS) and 4670 Static Surveillance Teams (SST) were operationalized to check movement of cash, liquor, drugs & freebies in the five states/UT closely supervised by DEOs, Expenditure observers in Districts and Special observers. A total of 19 Air Intelligence Units (AIU) of IT Departments was also set at different stations in Assam, West Bengal, Kerala, Tamil Nadu, and Puducherry. The detailed seizure items were as following:

Table: 4.5 State wise and item wise break-up of seizure report (till 06.04.2021 Forenoon)

States	Cash (in Rs. Crore)	Precious metal (in Rs. Crore)	Drugs/Nargcotics		Other items/freebies	Liquor		Total In Rs. crore	Total seizure in 2016 (in Rs. Crore)	Percentage change over LA 2016
			Quantity (in kg.)	*Worth (in Rs. crore)*	*Worth (in Rs. crore)*	*Quantity (in ltrs.)*	*Worth (in Rs. crore)*			
Kerala	22.64	49.21	812.01	4.05	1.94	67542.7	5.01	82.84	26.13	+317.03%
Tamil Nadu	236.51	176.22	-	2.22	25.64	289618.27	5.24	445.81	130.99	+340.33%
Puducherry	5.45	27.42	27644.82	95	0.25	3.06	0.7	36.89	7.74	+476.61%
Assam	26.69	3.69	6940.95	34.4	15.18	2044249.33	39.34	119.29	16.58	+719.48%
West Bengal	40.27	10.28	255.41	115.89	73.21	1935455.18	23.52	263.15	44.33	+593.61%
Total	331.56	266.82	8103.37	156.81	119.03	4364510.3	73.81	947.98	225.77	+419.88%

Source: The Election Commission of India, Press Note No. ECI/PN/45/2021 dt. 6th April, 2021.

West Bengal recently became notorious for its paranormal violence in elections, booth capturing, proxy votes by ruling party goons, intimidation to voters, and use of cash, gifts, freebies, and other illegal things by both ruling and opposition parties. And this trend is galloping. From the following table (Table 4.5) it came to light that, only in West Bengal total cash seized by police till the forenoon of the last day of elections was Rs. 55.59 crores and precious metal confiscated has amounted to Rs. 13.52 crore. On the other hand, drugs and narcotics, supposed to be used for election purposes, were caught with the worth of Rs. 129.99 crore, while other items/freebies held amounting to Rs. 100.82 crore. The use of alcohol in elections has become common in this state. Shockingly, police seized a total of 33,17,970 liters of liquor with a worth of Rs. 39.53 crore. It is surprising to note that, the price of total seized items including cash was only Rs. 44.33 crore during the elections of 2016, but this year's (2021) seizure increased to +776% (Worth Rs. 339.45 crore).

Table: 4.5 break up of seizure report as till 29.04.2021 Forenoon

States	Cash (in Rs. Crore)	Precious metal (in Rs. Crore)	Drugs/Nargcotics	Other items/freebies	Liquor		Total In Rs. crore	Total seizure in 2016 (in Rs. Crore)	Percentage change over LA 2016
			Worth (in Rs. crore)	*Worth (in Rs. crore)*	*Quantity (in ltrs.)*	*Worth (in Rs. crore)*			
West Bengal	55.59	13.52	129.99	100.82	3314970	39.53	339.45	44.33	+766.00 %

Source: The Election Commission of India, Press Note No. ECI/PN/58/2021 dt. 29th April, 2021.

Violation of model code of conduct

The Election Commission of India tried its level best to control the use of cash, liquor, and other items in elections. It introduced the cVIGIL App, a citizen-centric mobile application that empowered people to report cases of MCC violations on a real-time basis, with auto populated details of location and responded within 100 minutes after verification at field level. A total number of about 28,054 cases of Model Code of Conduct violations for West Bengal were reported through the cVIGIL app out of which 28,012 cases were disposed of as of today (4:00 PM).[16]

Model Code of Conduct for the Political Parties and Candidates

Indian politicians are either ignorant of the Model Code of Conduct or they have grown a habit of violating those. Only the issues of code of conduct come prior to the elections and, the politicians, mostly being lowly educated, repeatedly violate the norms. Like the previous ones, this year also the Election Commission of India issued a notice detailing the model code of conduct for the guidance of political parties and candidates. The guidelines are given hereunder for the general readers and political aspirants. Let us learn first the lessons on the general Code of Conduct.

I. General conduct

1.   No party or candidate shall include in any activity which may aggravate existing differences or create mutual hatred or cause tension between different castes and communities, religious or linguistic.

2.   Criticism of other political parties, when made, shall be confined to their policies and program, past record, and work. Parties and Candidates shall refrain from criticism of all aspects of private life, not connected with the public activities of the leaders or workers of other parties. Criticism of other parties or their workers based on unverified allegations or distortion shall be avoided.

3.   There shall be no appeal to caste or communal feelings for securing votes. Mosques, Churches, Temples, or other places of worship shall not be used as forums for election propaganda.

4.   All parties and candidates shall avoid scrupulously all activities which are "corrupt practices" and offenses under the election law, such as bribing of voters, intimidation of voters, impersonation of voters, canvassing within 100 meters of polling

stations, holding public meetings during the period of 48 hours ending with the hour fixed for the close of the poll, and the transport and conveyance of voters to and from the polling station.

5.   The right of every individual for peaceful and undisturbed home-life shall be respected, however much the political parties or candidates may resent his political opinions or activities. Organizing demonstrations or picketing before the houses of individuals by way of protesting against their opinions or activities shall not be resorted to under any circumstances.

6.   No political party or candidate shall permit its or his followers to make use of any individual's land, building, compound wall, etc., without his permission for erecting flag-staffs, suspending banners, pasting notices, writing slogans, etc.

7.   Political parties and candidates shall ensure that their supporters do not create obstructions in or break up meetings and processions organized by other parties. Workers or sympathizers of one political party shall not create disturbances at public meetings organized by another political party by putting questions orally or in writing or by distributing leaflets of their own party. Processions shall not be taken out by one party along places at which meetings are held by another party. Posters issued by one party shall not be removed by workers of another party.

II. Regarding the meetings

1.   The party or candidate shall inform the local police authorities of the venue and time of any proposed meeting well in time so as to enable the police to make necessary arrangements for controlling traffic and maintaining peace and order.

2.   A Party or candidate shall ascertain in advance if there is any restrictive or prohibitory order in force in the place proposed for the meeting if such orders exist, they shall be followed strictly. If any exemption is required from such orders, it shall be applied for and obtained well in time.

3.   If permission or license is to be obtained for the use of loudspeakers or any other facility in connection with any proposed meeting, the party or candidate shall apply to the authority concerned well in advance and obtain such permission or license.

4.   Organizers of a meeting shall invariably seek the assistance of the police on duty for dealing with persons disturbing a meeting or otherwise attempting to create disorder. Organizers themselves shall not take action against such persons.

III. Regarding procession

1.   A Party or candidate organizing a procession shall decide beforehand the time and place of the starting of the procession, the route to be followed, and the time and place at which the procession will terminate. There shall ordinarily be no deviation from the program.

2.   The organizers shall give advance intimation to the local police authorities of the program so as to enable the latter to make the necessary arrangements.

3.   The organizers shall ascertain if any restrictive orders are in force in the localities through which the procession has to pass, and shall comply with the restrictions unless exempted specially by the competent authority. Any traffic regulations or restrictions shall also be carefully adhered to.

4.   The organizers shall take steps in advance to arrange for passage of the procession so that there is no block or hindrance to traffic. If the procession is very long, it shall be organized in segments of suitable lengths, so that at convenient intervals, especially at points where the procession has to pass road junctions, the passage of held-up traffic could be allowed by stages thus avoiding heavy traffic congestion.

5.   Processions shall be so regulated as to keep as much to the right of the road as possible and the direction and advice of the police on duty shall be strictly complied with.

6.   If two or more political parties or candidates propose to take processions over the same route or parts thereof at about the same time, the organizers shall establish contact

well in advance and decide upon the measures to be taken to see that the processions do not clash or cause hindrance to traffic. The assistance of the local police shall be availed of for arriving at a satisfactory arrangement. For this purpose, the parties shall contact the police at the earliest opportunity.

7.   The political parties or candidates shall exercise control to the maximum extent possible in the matter of processionists carrying articles which may be put to misuse by undesirable elements especially in moments of excitement.

8.   The carrying of effigies purporting to represent members of other political parties or their leaders, burning such effigies in public, and such other forms of demonstration shall not be countenanced by any political party or candidate.

IV. On polling day

All Political parties and candidates shall –

1.   co-operate with the officers on election duty to ensure peaceful and orderly polling and complete freedom to the voters to exercise their franchise without being subjected to any annoyance or obstruction;

2.   supply to their authorized workers' suitable badges or identity cards;

3.   agree that the identity slip supplied by them to voters shall be on plain (white) paper and shall not contain any symbol, name of the candidate, or the name of the party;

4.   refrain from serving or distributing liquor on polling day and during the forty-eight hours preceding it;

5.   not allow the unnecessary crowd to be collected near the camps set up by the political parties and candidates near the polling booths so as to avoid confrontation and tension among workers and sympathizers of the parties and the candidate;

6.   ensure that the candidate's camps shall be simple. They shall not display any posters, flags, symbols, or any other propaganda material. No eatable shall be served or crowd allowed at the camps and

7.   co-operate with the authorities in complying with the restrictions to be imposed on the plying of vehicles on the polling day and obtain permits for them which should be displayed prominently on those vehicles.

V. In the polling booth

Excepting the voters, no one without a valid pass from the Election Commission shall enter the polling booths.

VI. For observers

The Election Commission appointed Observers. If the candidates or their agents have any specific complaint or problem regarding the conduct of elections they may bring the same to the notice of the Observer.

VII. Party in power

The party in power whether at the Centre or in the State or States concerned shall ensure that no cause is given for any complaint that it has used its official position for the purposes of its election campaign and in particular –

1.   (a) The Ministers shall not combine their official visit with electioneering work and shall not also make use of official machinery or personnel during the electioneering work.

(b) Government transport including official air-crafts, vehicles, machinery, and personnel shall not be used for the furtherance of the interest of the party in power;

2.   Public places such as maidens etc., for holding election meetings, and use of helipads for air-flights in connection with elections shall not be monopolized by itself.

Other parties and candidates shall be allowed the use of such places and facilities on the same terms and conditions on which they are used by the party in power;

3.   Rest houses, dak bungalows or other Government accommodation shall not be monopolized by the party in power or its candidates and such accommodation shall be allowed to be used by other parties and candidates in a fair manner but no party or candidate shall use or be allowed to use such accommodation (including premises appertaining thereto) as a campaign office or for holding any public meeting for the purposes of election propaganda;

4.   Issue of advertisement at the cost of public exchequer in the newspapers and other media and the misuse of official mass media during the election period for partisan coverage of political news and publicity regarding achievements with a view to furthering the prospects of the party in power shall be scrupulously avoided.

5.   Ministers and other authorities shall not sanction grants/payments out of discretionary funds from the time elections are announced by the Commission; and

6.   From the time elections are announced by Commission, Ministers and other authorities shall not –

(a) announce any financial grants in any form or promises thereof; or

(b) (except civil servants) lay foundation stones etc. of projects or schemes of any kind; or

(c) make any promise of construction of roads, provision of drinking water facilities, etc.; or

(d) make any ad-hoc appointments in Government, Public Undertakings, etc. which may have the effect of influencing the voters in favor of the party in power.

It is to be noted that, the Commission shall announce the date of any election which shall be a date ordinarily not more than three weeks prior to the date on which the notification is likely to be issued in respect of such elections.

7.   Ministers of Central or State Government shall not enter any polling station or place of counting except in their capacity as a candidate or voter or authorized agent.17

Conclusions

From the above discussion, it comes to light that, unlike the other states West Bengal elections were held in eight phases. Despite taking all measures by the Election Commission of India to curb and control the expenditure in elections; prevent violence in pre-election or during the election days; stop the use of money, freebies, gifts, liquor, etc. to the voters, the latest assembly elections in four states and one Union Territory witnessed the record number and amount of seizures of cash, gifts, liquors, drugs and other items intended to use for election purposes. A great number of election observers, expenditure observers, and police observers were deployed by the ECI. In the fourth phase of elections, there was a shooting by CRPF Jawans at Sitalkuchi that took away four young lives causing massive criticism of the Election Commission as well as the Central BJP leadership including the Prime Minister. The last three phases of the elections were conducted when the COVID-19 pandemic situation was grave and the daily infection rate was abnormally high. It was a challenge before the ECI to conduct elections without with least casualties. Therefore, the ECI had to invent various elector-friendly measures for the safety and security of the voters. At the same time, the life, security, and safety of the election officers and others were at stake. Many officers and general workers, who mostly were the government employees of various departments including teachers, headmasters, and others, had to sacrifice their life in conducting the elections in 2021. A large gathering in delivery centers (DCs) and Receiving Counters (RCs) made many officers ill, infected with COVID-19 while many lost their lives. Many civil society members and ruling Trinamool Congress party leaders demanded clubbing the last three phases of elections together, but the ECI turned a deaf year. The most striking fact in the election was that the use of money, muscle power, and violence in the pre-election and during the election days was havoc. Not only is that, but the after-poll violence in the state was also heart-rending. Therefore, it is pertinent to discuss the nature and extent of violence that took place in the State in relation to legislative assembly elections in Bengal. Consequently, the following chapter seeks to discuss the violence that had taken place in the pre and post-election period in West Bengal.

Chapter – V

Violence in Pre and Post-Poll Bengal

"Violent rulers are ghouls, and they are transient too."

– Keshavananda Bharati

Introduction

West Bengal, the pioneer of Indian freedom movement, continued its image as a state of movements and agitations even after attaining Independence long back. The new millennium too broke up with widespread violent movements, demonstrations, processions, shouting slogans and what not. The election periods in Bengal are the most fertile time of violent activities. The debate is going on without any interruption even after the four months of publication of poll results. The arguments of the Opposition party is that rampant violence took place in the pre-election, post-election and during the election time, while the counter-argement of the ruling party is there was no any violence, and people are living here peacefully. The ruling party, as usual, thinks that the people are fool and they can neither see nor feel the heat of violence in their family or neighborhood. How people were beaten, how people were evicted, how the houses and cars were ransacked, how the human rights of people were violated. Therefore, the High Court had to intervene in the matter where recently (August 19, 2021) a five-judge bench of the Calcutta directed the formation of a Special Investigating Team (SIT) to look into the other offences to the reports of violence in parts of West Bengal following declaration of Assembly election results. The CBI and SIT probe into the alleged post-poll violence will also be monitored by the Calcutta High Court. Not only that, the High Court has directed the central agency to file a report on its investigation in the next six weeks.

Professor Ash Amin[1] the former Foreign Secretary and Vice-President of the British Academy wrote in the Preface of the Violence and Democracy that, "It is not unusual to suppose that democracy opposes rule by violence, taking the step beyond and resorting to aggression only to defend itself against its detractors and enemies. Yet this supposition may not hold in all parts of the world or indeed even among members of a democratic society used to other forms of customary rule that might not exclude violence." Thus it is not the fact that violence and democracy are two completely distinct phenomena, and majority democratic societies are free from all violent activities. Rather, democratic societies often integrate, or even turn a blind eye to violence in their workings, ranging from intimidation to eviction including taking away lives of opposition with a view to exerting authority and influence. In India and particularly in the state of West Bengal since independence, even from the freedom movement era, political violence in its different forms and intensities are so intrinsic as though Bengal's electoral politics cannot sustain without violence.

The above observations allude to proximities and connections between violence and democracy, and it is very true to the politics of West Bengal. Hence, it is not possible to understand the politics of Bengal without knowing the roots and extent of violence. But, if violence and democracy are mutually constituted, or in other words they are interdependent, we must have to alter our concepts and hopes. Violence, in any form, cannot strengthen democracy. Hence, we have to devise such democratic values and norms that enlighten our democracy and save the valuable lives and property of our brethren. In this light, this chapter will be discussed.

I would like to begin with a pertinent question: Is violence in elections a new phenomenon in West Bengal elections? To answer this question we may take the assistance of history. Since independence, several hundreds of elections to Lok Sabha, Legislative Assemblies, and Local Government Bodies (LGBs) were held in Bengal. History demonstrates that murder, threatening, bombing, shooting, booth capturing, and evicting from home for not obeying the dictates of ruling party leaders are the most idiosyncratic characteristics in electoral politics in the state of West Bengal. In an article titled 'Violence, lower-caste politics and India's post-colonial democracy', Sohini Guha clearly mentioned that, "For it is precisely in order to win elections that political parties have engineered riots, murdered political opponents, courted corporations, and flouted spending norms. Violence has been in abundant display on the day of the vote itself; it has been developed to 'capture' polling booths, prevent people from casting the ballot, coerce them into voting in a particular way, and achieve a range of other objectives."[2] However, the most serious concern in recent time is that, in place of assuaging the violent incidents in elections; it is, rather, increasing year after year. Surprisingly, many of the state media – both electronic and print - are averse to publishing and airing the incidents of violence taking place almost regularly in the state. Hence, it is appropriate to explore the extent of violence that occurred during and after the state assembly elections in Bengal in 2021, and how the ruling party after winning a thumping majority maintained hegemony on the subaltern electors.

Roots of violence in Bengal

Apparently, the Bengalee people are gentle, modest, and soft-spoken 'bhadraloks' who prefer rice and fish with sandesh, rasogolla, chatni, papad in lunch, and adores Rabindra Sangeet (music of Rabindranath Tagore). They are argumentative too. At the same time, the Bengalees are mutinous; they do not instantly agree with any new concept or ideology, and accept new people as their rulers without testifying its veracity, utility and, of course, its beneficial effect on general people and particularly to the 'gentlemen' of this State. A very well-known example can be cited here - the rift between Mahatma Gandhi and Subhas Chandra Bose. Also, the birth of a number of revolutionaries such as Khudiram Bose, Prafulla Chaki, Kanailal Dutta, Masterda Surya Sen, Binay-Badal-Dinesh, and others who, with all their limitations and resources raised their voice and arms to fight against the British, rejecting the Gandhian concept of non-violence.

Sohini Guha, in one of her articles, wrote that "It is by now well-established that democracy does not look the same everywhere."[3] Further, Dominic Davies pointed out that, "Democracy must be violent, it was agreed because democracy requires and therefore creates a state; meanwhile, the very premise of a state (at least in its contemporary neoliberal incarnation) is the necessity of its monopoly on, and ability to wield, violence. There can, therefore, be no such thing as a non-violent state."[4] During the pre-independence period, Bengal was at the forefront of violent movements. Jawaharlal Nehru observed this trait of Bengal many years ago. He pointed out that, "The Bengali terrorist mentality of extreme emotionalism", and "colors the so-called Communist viewpoint that makes them look sometimes quite insane. There is violence and an intense hatred looking out of their eyes." The extremism found in the post-independence Bengal is well known to the world of scholars. History demonstrates that the "revolution" against the colonial rulers found expression even before the British left when the peasants of undivided Bengal rose against the landlords during the "*tebhaga*" movement, demanding a two-thirds share of the crops produced.[5] The period between the sixties and before the Left Front government resumed the political reign of Writers' Buildings, there was a significant level of political violence in the state. In the sixties and early 70's the last century witnessed ego clashes between the Governor and Ruling Parties. Even the clashes between political parties were often violent. Also, between the United Front coalition partners, there were political and ideological conflicts and frictions. It came to light that, over 700 political murders were reported in 1969, over 600 of them being acknowledged by the state Home Department.[6] By mid-1969, the CPI(M) had an organized 50,000 member strong volunteer force in West Bengal, a body the party thought of as an embryo of a future Liberation Army.[7]

Birth and fostering of violence in Bengal

To understand today's political violence in Bengal; we need to go back to the '60s and '70s of the previous century. The volume of violence was so large that it is quite implausible to describe in a book chapter. Consequently, a few uprisings and outrageous political alacrity of that time are merely discussed here. Within the communists, the CPI(ML) formed its own force earlier, and the RSP had also formed a paramilitary body of its own, the Inquilabi Fouj ('Revolutionary Army'), and the CPI also developed a fighting unit.[8] They initiated violent movements, and disruptions of property resorted to killing to the bourgeoise landlords, rich businessmen, and factory owners. Consequently, the wealthy landlords in resistance against the United Front parties and the Naxalites set up their own private paramilitaries.[9] We will discuss in detail in the following part the origin and proliferation of the violent politics in Bengal under the communists. However, what we saw in modern Darjeeling in 2009 was not new in Bengal. How Bimal Gurung formed his own force can be highlighted in the following report of The Times of India: "On a large tract of arid land, strewn with boulders and rocks, hundreds of young men and women stand in formation, practicing kicks, punches, and knee strikes. Hundreds more are in line to sign up. This patch of land in the upper Phagu valley near Gorubathan is the training ground of Bimal Gurung's army of volunteers' the so-called Gorkha Land Personnel of Gorkha Janmukti Morcha (GNM). Most of them are from very poor families, drawn here by Gurung's promise of Rs. 2,000 monthly stipend...."[10] It was in mid-2008 that Gurung had announced the formation of GLP a direct challenge to the authority of the state police. The training was conducted by 50 army veterans, headed by retired colonel Ramesh Alley. Almost at the same time at Junglemahal or Nandigram or Singur also witnessed such types of forces under the Maoist banner or in different names such as 'Bhumi Uchhed Pratirodh Committee' and others.

Mamata Banerjee's Banga Janani Bahini and Jai Hind Bahini can be cited as the replica of Gorkha Land Personnel of GNM. The DNA reported that "...for escalation of the fight with the BJP, West Bengal Chief Minister Mamata Banerjee asked the party leaders to recapture TMC offices allegedly "occupied" by the saffron party as early as possible. The TMC chief, who held an extended core committee meeting of the party, appointed her brother Kartik Banerjee and state minister Bratya Basu as the president and chairman respectively of the party's frontal 'Jai Hind Bahini'. TMC MP Kakoli Ghosh Dastidar was appointed the chairman of 'Banga Janani Bahini', another frontal organization. The two organizations, which she had launched, were meant to "counter the growth" of the RSS in the state."[11]

Let us turn back once again to trace out the origin of violent politics in Bengal. The CPI(M) was a partner of the United Front government in Bengal in 1967. The CPI(M) being in charge of the Home and Labour departments, police was instructed not to intervene against striking workers belonging to their party.[12] It seemed that gheraos were effectively legalized during the '60s when CPI(M) was a partner of the United Front government.[13] The CPI(M) was the originator and propagator of extremist politics in

Bengal in the post-independent West Bengal. The disruption of civic life caused both annoyance and anger so much so of the coalition chief minister Prafull Chandra Ghosh that he put his resignation from the post. The CPI(M) willfully formulated a 'program' as a partner of the United Front government in Bengal. The program of the Front in 1967 had promised to reorganize the police force, and not to interfere in democratic movements. A fundamental aspect of this was barring the police from taking action in labor disputes. In this regard, the United Front government issued a circular to the police, stating that police would not be able to interfere in gheraos (besieging blockades) unless having the permission of the Minister of Labour. Essentially, this resulted in a sharp rise in gheraos in connection to labor disputes. It comes to light that in May 1967, there were 151 gheraos in West Bengal.

The High Court vs. state government tussle

The Front government used power to legalize the politics of strikes and gheraos through legislative authority. But the law of the land cannot sit idle. As a result, the High Court intervened and nullified the circular of the government. The United Front government responded by issuing a new circular further on 12 June 1967. The new circular differentiated between 'legitimate' and 'unlawful' actions in labor conflicts, barring police from intervening in legitimate trade union activities. In the case of unlawful activities, the police would be able to intervene, but only after establishing factual grounds. The numbers of gheraos continued to increase, reaching 194 in September. The High Court intervened again, ordering the police force to ignore the circular of the state government in case of gheraos and act in accordance with the law. As a result of the gheraos, many industrial units were closed down. The Bangla Congress came under pressure from industry owners to stop the gheraos. The Industry and Labour ministries, run by Bangla Congress and SUCI respectively, were at loggerheads with each other.[14] In the first six months of the second United Front government there were 551 strikes and 73 lock-outs across the state, affecting some 570,000 workers.[15] This was the beginning of Bengal's degeneration. The hooliganism, frequent strikes, lockouts, besieging blockades, demonstrations, shouting loud slogans disrupted normal life and public property, and squeezed the freedom of the general people. Hence, we can conclude without any hesitation that, the Communist parties initiated and catalyzed the socio-economic downfall of Bengal through its dangerous and fierce political agenda.

Naxalite movements

North Bengal became notorious for its revolutionary activities in the sixties of the last century. The acid-spirited Marxists and Leninists in Bengal, being over-enthused with the revolutionary successes in Russia, Vietnam, Cuba, and other South American and East European countries, wished to bring about a similar change in political power through violent revolution. The then Communist Party of India (CPI-M) saw a rift among its party workers. Thus we found a further complication to the United Front government where an internal division within the CPI(M) came up. Radical elements, calling for immediate revolution, were present in the second-rank leadership of the party in West Bengal. In the northern parts of the state, Charu Majumder and Kanu Sanyal had built up a power base of their own inside the party ranks. In March 1967 peasants led by the Krishak Samiti, the CPI(M) peasants front, began occupying excess lands in Naxalbari. The revolt grew, and by June reports came that the rebels in Naxalbari had acquired firearms. Inside the United Front, differences arose over how to deal with the rebellion. The view of the CPI(M) was that social and economic problems were the cause behind the insurgency, whilst Bangla Congress wished to deal with the rebellion as a law and order problem.[16]

Thus, it becomes evident that Bengal was not been a peaceful and tranquil state for the last six decades. With all the above revolutionary acts and mainly with peasants' movements, the Left Front government came to power in 1977. Since 1977 the communists in the guise of rulers took control of the state machinery. It continued its uninterrupted rule without any big trouble up to 2007. But as a result of its own folly and haughty politics, its castle of power began to decay thereafter and was ultimately demolished in 2011 by the Trinamool Congress party led by Mamata Banerjee. The former ruling party is still alive within an insignificant number of supporters, sympathizers, and members. On the other hand, the Trinamool Congress party, after coming to power in 2011, began from the very place where the Left Front ended. One by one the gram panchayats, Zilla Parishads, and urban local bodies were brought under their complete control either by threatening or luring or by overpowering opposition members including MLAs. The last nail was hit directly in the coffin of the Communists in the assembly elections of 2021 by the electors. This election was notorious for abnormal violence in the pre-poll as well as during the poll periods. The violence continued even in the post-poll period also. Now, let us examine the nature and extent of violence that were eventuated in the latest elections in Bengal. At first, we will draw the attention of the readers to the reign of terror initiated by the ruling TMC on the erstwhile mighty CPI(M).

TMC's terror on CPI(M) from 2011-2021

In the pre-2011 election campaign the Trinamool Congress party promised to give good governance and its famous slogan – *Badla Noi, Badal Chai* - became very popular amongst the electors of Bengal. But after coming to power it sought to establish a totalitarian state. The Trinamool Congress party, after assuming power, began a reign of terror on one hand, and politics of wooing to the erstwhile Maoists from Jungle Mahal on the other hand. As part of its expansionist policy, the TMC won over the members, supporters, and sympathizers of Opposition parties. The people, who opposed, were faced dire consequences. The following table (Table 5.1) will highlight the level and extent of the tyranny of TMC on CPI(M). It is not that the Congress and the Left parties had widened the democratic avenues for opposition parties during their respective regimes. Subodh Verma, in an article, wrote that "This narrative turns a blind eye to the decade long reign of terror that the Trinamool Congress unleashed against the Left, physically decimating activists, displacing hundreds from villages, striking terror through rapes and assaults, extorting money from poor families, evicting bargadars and small landowners from their land, preventing the harvesting of crops, attacking students unions and cooperatives and other such atrocities."[17] The following table (Table 5.1) will substantiate the fact.

Table: 5.1 TMC atrocities against CPI(M)

Killed	225

Women assaulted/Molested	2351+
Minor/Teenaged torture	32+
Injured and hospitalized	12,211+
Evicted from homes	65,778+
Displaced from locality	20,000+
Shops/homes looted/burnt	37890+
Left offices attacked/captured	2865+
Not allowed to cultivate land or evicted	28,103+
Forced collection of money	11,265+
False police cases	Approx. 1 lakh +
Attacks on edu. Bodies and coops.	83
Attacks on election process in different orgns.	166+
Newspaper boards destroyed	446+

Source: CPI(M) West Bengal state and district committees, published in Subodh Verma, 'West Bengal elections: How TMC Violence against Left Opened Doors for the BJP', News Click, March 21, 2021.

Despite ruling Bengal for 34 years without any interruption, the CPI(M) had to lose 225 activists who were mostly killed brutally, like hanged or hacked with a scythe. The people being angered with the misrule of the Communist leaders and workers resorted to violence and retaliation. It is not that all the CPI(M) workers were heckled and tortured; only those who during their party's rule misbehaved with people stole government money and were involved in corruption only became prey in the hands of newly elected TMC party workers. It came to light from the report that at least 2,351 women, some of them teenagers, were sexually and physically assaulted after the debacle of the Left Front in 2011 till the elections in 2021. The numbers were more than likely to be much higher as many women did not want to be identified out of fear for their lives or for social stigma.

The CPI(M) workers lost property worth over Rs. 8.67 crore in the carnage. Even Rs. 3.59 crore was extorted by rampaging TMC supporters over the years, threatening the families with dire consequences if they did not pay up. A more pathetic fact was that over 65,000 workers and sympathizers of CPI(M) had to flee their homes and hide elsewhere, often for months. Over 20,000 families had to leave their villages and the localities they stayed in. More than one lakh supporters had fabricated criminal charges filed against them for which they were harassed intermittently by police persons and the very criminals who were terrorizing them. The newspaper boards used by the CPI(M) for a free reading of the Ganashakti (a newspaper of CPIM) were ransacked and vandalized, many party offices of Left parties were occupied by TMC members. Thousands of candidates could not file their nomination papers in the panchayat elections. In fact, in the local body elections, in thousands of villages, nobody except the TMC candidates was allowed to file their nominations.[18] If this is the fact after 2011, then peeping into the past one could find that the same fate was there for the then Opposition Congress and others in Bengal during the Left regime after 1977.

Violent Politics in Bengal During the TMC Regime

The politics of Bengal was rarely peaceful and non-violent as we read above. The continuation of the same tradition was more transparent and spectacular as we are witnessing before our eyes. Reading the literature of the past and seeing something before eyes are quite different. Let's see the latest situation in Bengal. There is the law for protecting public property. The Prevention of Damage to Public Property Act, 1984 sought to punish anyone "who commits mischief by doing any act in respect of any public property" with a jail term of up to five years and a fine or both. Provisions of this law can be coupled with those under the Indian Penal Code. Public property under this Act included "any building, installation or other property used in connection with the production, distribution or supply of water, light, power or energy; any oil installation; any sewage works; any mine or factory; any means of public transportation or of telecommunications, or any building, installation or other property used in connection therewith."[19]

Mamata Banerjee, though herself led many violent political activities including the vandalization of furniture of Writers' Buildings, turned against violent politics (in the post-2011 period) by the opposition parties – the CPI(M), the Indian National Congress, and the Bharatiya Janata Party. To prevent any violence in Bengal, her government brought about a law in line with the Central Act – The West Bengal Maintenance of Public Order (Amendment) Bill 2017 - to curb the tendency to destroy public and private properties during riots, unrest or violent political movements.[20] Interestingly the CPIM and Congress protested against the bill, and together walked out from the Assembly, while Abdul Mannan termed it a "Black Law." Did Congress and CPI(M) not bring the same type of law during their regime in the Centre and State? The Central Act, brought by Congress, had a provision of imprisonment but there was no compensation clause. The Tamil Nadu Public Property (Prevention of Damage and Loss) Act has a penal provision against offenders doing damage to companies other than public institutions including a compensation clause. But the chief minister Mamata Banerjee brought this stringent law, in the wake of an irate mob set the police vehicles on fire during a protest at Bhangar in South 24 Parganas, to curb the practice of damaging public and government property.[21]

What did the people of Bengal see in the month of December 2019 when people vandalized Government property in different districts of Bengal. In protest against Citizenship Amendment Act and a possible NRC exercise, a section of people vandalized and set fire to railway stations, and squatted on the railway tracks and highways, disrupting train services and vehicular movement. The most disgraceful act was found in the Murshidabad district. In Beldanga of the said district, a mob torched the station master's cabin and ransacked the ticket counter before setting it on fire. The protesters blocked the track, disrupted train movement between Lalgola and Krishnanagar. A large group of protesters obstructed National Highway at Beldanga, burning tires and damaging vehicles, including an ambulance. The angry mob also barged into the Uluberia station under South Eastern Railway and vandalized its premises as also a couple of trains. Not only that, the protesters threw stones at the railway employees where a driver and railway personnel were injured by their stones. Both Howrah and Kharagpur train movements were halted for several hours due to the agitation. That was not all. The Howrah-Coromondol Express and the Howrah-Digha Kandari Express were damaged in the attack. Eleven suburban trains were stranded in and around various stations.[22] What a targeted attack on the Central properties! The assets of the Central government located within the geographical areas of State government, where the law and order are under the control of State police, were vandalized by a section of state people, while the state police remained as silent spectators.

When people of this state damaged railway stations, the State government did not apply the law it formulated to protect government property. Further, it can be highlighted that the present government is against all kinds of bandhs. It is praiseworthy, but the act of bearing the atrocities by mobs in the name of protest movements cannot be appreciated at all for any reason. The law for every citizen should be equally applied – for own party workers, members, and leaders as well as opposition party leaders, members, and supporters. The level of violence in Bengal is breaking its own record in every election time. This time also, with the highest numbers of security forces, the state broke all its past records in committing violence during election days, and in the pre and post-election periods. Let us have a look at violent incidents that took away many lives; drove away many Opposition political leaders, and supporters; evicted their families; and deserted thousands of Opposition party supporters and sympathizers alike.

Violence on BJP Workers by TMC in the Pre Poll Period

The name of West Bengal became infamous for murders, bombing, booth capturing, threatening, bribing to the electors, and use of alcohol, money, and muscle power during elections. As a whole, the political atmosphere was vitiated in the state. During the Left Front rule, violence was mainly heard in Uttar Pradesh and Bihar assembly elections, and panchayats elections were mainly bloody and violent in Bengal. But recently the name of West Bengal has been tarnished to the Bengalees living out of this State for political violence during and after the elections – from Panchayat to Lok Sabha. Interestingly, unlike Kashmir, in West Bengal, nobody claims the responsibility for the murders which are passed off as gang rivalry, factionalism, suicide, and so on. On October 5, journalist-turned BJP leader Swapan Dasgupta cited numbers of murders of 110 BJP workers, but at the end of October, West Bengal BJP's general secretary Sayantan Basu cited as many as 123 BJP workers had been killed in the state since 2013. Earlier in July 2020, the BJP gave out the names of 93 slain party workers. A booklet released by BJP state president Dilip Ghosh listed 93 BJP workers, including five women, who fell victim to political violence in the state during the last seven years. The first name in the list was that of Bapi Ghosh, a BJP worker of Nadia, Krishnanagar, who was murdered on July 15, 2020, while the last name was of Nripen Mandal, who was killed in Malda district on June 16, 2013.

According to the booklet, during the seven years (from June 16, 2013, to July 17, 2020), the maximum number of killings of the BJP workers (33 total) took place in 2018. Most of those killings were on account of the violence that was unleashed in the wake of the panchayat elections held in the state in 2018.[23] But the number of murders of BJP workers increased with the passage of time and with the approach of legislative assembly elections of 2021. The Hindustan Times[24] reported that more than 300 Dharatiya Janata Party (BJP) workers have been killed in West Bengal till December 20, 2020. The Home Minister alleged that "Political violence in the state is at its peak. More than 300 BJP workers have been killed. Investigation in those cases hasn't moved an inch." It was alleged by Bengal's ruling party that, many BJP workers were killed because of infighting within the party. Even death by suicides was being passed off as political killings. Since 1998, 1,027 TMC workers were killed in political rivalry. At least 116 of BJP's Lok Sabha MPs have criminal records. [25]

One political party member murdered every 2 days

A horrible report was published in the Sunday Guardian that pointed out, in 34 days, 16 people from either the BJP or the Trinamool Congress have been killed allegedly by the other party. This indicates that nearly one political party worker has lost life every two days in West Bengal between 27 February and 1st April 2021. Without caring for the Model Code of Conduct declared by the Election Commission of India on 26 February, political violence and killings going on in the state on the eve of elections in 294 assembly seats in West Bengal. In the violence, BJP has lost 11 of its party workers who have allegedly been killed by the TMC, while the TMC claimed to have lost five of its political workers in political violence by the BJP workers.

We can highlight a few more incidents of such brutal murders, hangings, and severe political violence in West Bengal. On the second phase of polling on 1st April the body of a BJP worker, Uday Dubey was found hanging at his home in the Nandigram constituency of West Bengal. It was alleged that the TMC workers killed and later hanged Dubey. His death on the day of the high-profile election contest in Nandigram created huge tension in the area where villagers alleged that Dubey had been under "tremendous pressure" from the local TMC leaders for being tilted to the BJP.

Another BJP worker was also allegedly killed on the eve of the second phase of polling in Bengal. On the intervening night of 31 March and 1 April at Purba Medinipur district's Chandipur Vidhan Sabha, a BJP worker Gurupada Pradhan was allegedly beaten up brutally by TMC workers and he had succumbed to his injuries on the spot. The other nine BJP workers who have been allegedly killed by TMC in Bengal over the above-mentioned 34 days included Amit Sarkar, BJP's Mondal President from Dinhata in the Cooch Behar district. His body was found hanging at a nearby Veterinary Hospital on 24 March. His death had come just 72 hours before the first phase of polling in Bengal.

During this period, in another incident, the body of Akhil Biswas, a BJP karyakarta from Uttar Dinajpur district, was found hanging from a tree in a nearby forest on 28 March. His family members claimed that he had gone missing since 26 March and despite searching for him in the local vicinity, he was nowhere to be found. Later on, his "wounded body" was recovered from a tree. The BJP claimed that he was "murdered" and later hanged by the TMC goons. Further, in the wee hours of 27 March, when Bengal was going for the first phase of polls, the body of Mangal Soren was recovered from a nearby field. Soren was a BJP worker from Keshiyari village in Kharagpur Subdivision, his family claimed that he was killed by TMC goons.

Another incident took place just a day earlier (of the first phase of the vote) on 26 March, when a BJP booth secretary from Medinipur assembly, Lal Mohan Soren's body was found hanging from a tree in the nearby forest in Shalboni. The BJP alleged that he was killed by TMC for just being a BJP worker. Even on 25 March, two bodies of BJP workers were found with injury marks that might have been caused by sharp weapons. Pratap Barman and Dipankar Biswas, both BJP workers, were allegedly attacked and killed with sharp weapons in the Shantipur area of Nadia district. The BJP claimed that it was done by TMC goons. On 17 March, the BJP claimed that two of their party workers were killed in two different places in West Bengal. Vikas Naskar, a BJP booth worker from the Sonarpur area of South 24 Parganas, and a 24-year-old BJP worker Bapi Naskar from Illambazar were allegedly killed by TMC goons. On 7 March, a BJP worker Shoban Debnath from Gosaba of South 24 Parganas district was killed after a bomb went off at his house while he was eating his lunch.

TMC workers also murdered

The TMC also lost its workers. It was learned that a TMC member was killed on the day of the second phase of polling on 1 April. TMC claimed that the 48-year-old TMC worker Uttam Dolui from Kehspur in Paschim Medinipur was chased by several BJP workers and was allegedly stabbed to death. On 25 March, a TMC worker Shraban Choudhury was killed in a bomb blast in Ranigunj's Beniadhi Village in Paschim Burdwan, and on the same day, another TMC worker Ruhul Amin Middye had succumbed to his injuries after he was brutally injured in a clash between the TMC and Abbas Siddiqui-led ISF workers in South 24 Pargana's Baruipur area.

Another TMC worker Durga Soren was allegedly killed by BJP workers at the Netura Bus Stand in Jhargram. Even on 10 March, the TMC claimed to have lost one of their party workers allegedly in the hands of BJP workers. The TMC claimed that one of its workers Masood Anwar from Hooghly was brutally attacked and killed by BJP workers and his body was recovered from a nearby field. Apart from the political killings, reports of political violence and clashes were reported every day from different places of the state. [26]

Violence during the elections

Almost everyday newspaper reports and television channels in West Bengal showed pictures of violence and incidents of austere political clashes across the districts of Bengal. This started from the beginning of poll declaration day and continued till the publication of results that extended in the post-poll period too. It is not possible to write all the incidents of heartrending political vendetta that were being reported regularly in a book chapter like this. Therefore, only a few such incidents reported in important newspapers and television channels are enumerated hereunder.

The first phase of Bengal's assembly elections were held on 27 March and ended the day with ruling TMC lodging several complaints of muscle-flexing by the BJP. There were 30 assembly seats in five western districts of Purulia, Jhargaram, Bankura, West Midnapore, and East Midnapore which consisted of 10,288 booths, with more than 73 lakh registered voters, spread across the districts. The election was not peaceful at all. Complaints of violence were heard from television channels and newspapers. The Telegraph newspaper reported, "The violence included an alleged attack on Sushanta Ghosh, CPI(M) candidate from Salboni in West Midnapore, and the ransacking of a car belonging to Trinamool turncoat Soumendu Adhikari, brother of fellow Trinamool turncoat and BJP leader Suvendu Adhikari, in Contai South, East Midnapore.[27] Fortunately, Soumendu was not inside the car. But Sushanta Ghosh, once a very popular and stalwart leader in Paschim Medinipur, was attacked at Chhototara booth and his car was severely damaged. Also, he was physically assaulted as well. In the incident, two journalists were also injured and media vehicles damaged.

Further, it was reported in the same newspaper[28] (The Telegraph) on the page No. 5 that sporadic violence took place on day one of the elections. It came to light that a polling agent of the BJP was allegedly hit on the head in a fight between BJP and Trinamool workers at Begumpur booth, a sequel reportedly to the discovery of the body of BJP worker Mangal Soren near his home with the BJP claiming it a planned murder by Trinamool. In another incident, crude bombs were hurled in Trinamool – BJP clashes near the Birbandar booth after a Trinamool worker was allegedly beaten up at 9.00 am. Trinamool candidate from Bankura's Chhatna Subhasish Batabyal has allegedly pushed around and forced out of a polling station after Batabyal was involved in an argument over why the polling agents were not allowed inside the booth.

On 31st March, the Telegraph reported that a person named Rabin Manna was grievously injured and admitted to a government hospital in Calcutta. Rabin was allegedly beaten up by a group of BJP supporters outside his house in Balarampur, apparently, because he was a sympathizer to the Trinamool Congress party.[29] It was alleged that the BJP had made their lives troublesome and hellish. Also, the BJP had been giving them all kinds of threats. They were helpless, and they beat the man to death. The chief minister arrived at their house to be with them and console the family members.

On the last day of March, a piece of very shocking news was published in The Telegraph on Jalpaiguri, where a BJP supporter's car was slashed allegedly by Trinamool supporters on 30 March night in the town while the two rival parties clashed at Jalpaiguri Sadar block. Trouble started when BJP supporter Subas Roy forcibly smeared color on a Trinamool supporter and shouted 'Jai Shri Ram' in Padri Kutir on the outskirts of Jalpaiguri. Soon, some 100 Trinamool supporters reached the local BJP office, ransacked it and attacked Roy with a sharp weapon, and slashed his left ear. They also hit him in his head. He was hospitalized immediately in a critical condition. In another incident, the supporters of both parties clashed on 30 March night in the Dhapganj area when BJP supporters were putting up flags. BJP supporter Rabi Roy was injured and hospitalized.[30]

From Nandigram, wherefrom the chief minister was contesting against her one-time lieutenant Suvendu Adhikary, more news of violence came to the fore. In three separate incidents, two BJP candidates – Dr. Harekrishna Bera and Ashok Dinda – and party supporters accompanying CPM's Nandigram candidate Minakshi Mukherjee were attacked and injured in East Midnapore. In the first incident, Dr. Harekrishna Bera, the BJP candidate from Tamluk, was allegedly attacked by Trinamool supporters outside Tamluk police station around 1.30 AM. On the other hand, in Moyna, the BJP candidate and cricketer Ashoke Dinda's car was attacked when he was returning home around 4.00 PM. Minakshi Mukherjee and her supporters were also allegedly attacked by Trinamool backed goons in Bhutamore area of her constituency.[31]

On the Election Day, there was a bombing at Ketugram in Purba Bardhaman. Seven persons were arrested and they were sent to police custody. Again, in Falta, the BJP candidate Bidhan Parui was attacked by TMC supporters, and he was admitted to the district hospital of Diamond Harbour. When he entered to campaign at Mallickpur panchayat a group of youths informed him that no campaigning could be done there. This resulted in arguments and counterarguments. Soon a group of TMC workers attacked the procession with stones and sticks.[32]

Clashes and killings in 2nd phase of elections

The newspapers wrote many articles and published many photos of clashes, while television channels also showed debates on incidents of violence in the second round of polls in Bengal. In total, the Election Commission received 1,605 complaints, where at least 28 people were arrested and several others detained as a preventive measure. Hours before the voting began on April 1, a 37-year-old TMC worker, Uttam Dolui, was stabbed to death in Keshpur in Paschim Medinipur. He was attacked with a sharp weapon by some miscreants near a club at Hariharpur, In another incident, a BJP worker Uday Shankar Dubey, aged 52, was found hanging at his home at Nandigram's Bhekutia area in Purba Medinipur. He, being a polling agent of BJP candidate, was threatened by TMC backed miscreants for the last few days and asked him to steer clear of politics. BJP's Keshpur candidate Pritish Ranjan Konar and five others were injured in the attack around noon. Four vehicles were vandalized. On the same day, an unidentified group of people attacked Dilip Ghosh and his vehicle with bricks and bamboo sticks, and also vandalized cars of media personnel. Another BJP leader Tammay Ghosh's car was vandalized by some miscreants. Not only that, TMC candidate and actor Soham Chakraborty was attacked and his car was also vandalized at Chandipur in Pruba Medinipur.[33]

BJP's candidates were attacked

This election saw some unprecedented incidents of violence on candidates. BJP's Diamond Harbour candidate Dipak Halder and his supporters were thrashed allegedly by TMC supporters during their election campaign. Dipak Halder, who was originally a TMC MLA, changed his allegiance to BJP and was contesting the election as a candidate of BJP. When he was campaigning in the Haridebpur area his supporters had an altercation with a few people, and he was attacked brutally in the end. His injury was so much that he had to be admitted to a hospital.[34]

Violence in the 3rd phase of elections

Newspaper reports and television channels highlighted as many incidents as possible with their limited resources. The Indian Express reported on 5 April that, a TMC worker and three other BJP workers were injured in separate incidents of violence two days before the third phase of the assembly elections. TMC worker Barik Mollah was injured in firing at his home at Minakhan in North 24 Parganas district's Basirhat area. He was shot in the leg and ribs and was admitted to NRS Hospital in Kolkata. On the other hand, three BJP activists in the Pursurah assembly constituency in Hooghly district were injured after allegedly being assaulted by unidentified men. The incidents occurred in the areas of Harinkhola and Serampore. The three were admitted to the Arambagh Sub-divisional hospital for treatment. At Kalna in Purba Bardhaman district, TMC-turned BJP-leader Biswajit Kundu was attacked allegedly by a group of workers of the ruling party prior to the third phase of polls. Even a low-intensity blast shook the village of Atpara in Purba Bardhaman district's Galsi area on the same night of 5 April.[35]

Attacks held on other candidates

Unlike earlier, the latest elections saw attacks on candidates. The level of the courage of common people increased to such an extent that the supporters and workers of political parties did not spare the candidates. It came to light that, six candidates, including four from the ruling Trinamool Congress, were roughed up by rival party activists as Bengal entered the third phase of the assembly elections. Though violence during elections was not an uncommon phenomenon, rarely have so many poll candidates have been attacked simultaneously, raising the specter of more phases of the elections that have witnessed unprecedented pent-up tensions. Most of the attacks took place when the candidates arrived to protest alleged instances of electoral malpractice.

Let us reminisce about those candidates who were attacked in the third phase of the elections. Sujata Mondal (Khan) an SC candidate has inflicted a serious injury while she was visiting a booth. Television channels showed that she was even chased out of the Arandi South Primary School polling station in the constituency by a stick-wielding mob.

She and her personal security officer were allegedly hit on the head with sticks. She was running through the middle of the empty field to save her life. It was alleged that she twisted the arm of a BJP supporter during an argument. The woman suffered a fracture, the BJP alleged. She also abused and assaulted the villagers that prompted the rural people to chase her with sticks while she tried to flee in her car.

Again, Trinamool's Khanakul (Hooghly) candidate Najibul Karim ran into protests when he arrived at Gaurangachowk to prove allegations that his party's election agents had been driven out by the BJP. After reinstating the polling agents and encouraging Trinamool voters to return to the queues, Karim was about to leave when a group of alleged BJP workers armed with sticks thrashed him and his personal security officer. Both suffered multiple injuries. As the candidate himself was beaten up and taken away for hospitalization, the Trinamool polling agents once again ran away in fear. In neighboring Howrah's Uluberia North constituency, Trinamool candidate Nirmal Majhi, a minister of state, had arrived at a booth in Muktir Chowk following allegations of BJP-backed malpractice when he faced demonstrations by the Opposition party's activists who refused to let him enter. When Majhi refused to relent, the BJP group allegedly started hurling bricks at him. His security personnel immediately gave him a helmet, but the police and his security officer got hit in the head. He needed several stitches.

Again, in the neighboring constituency of Ulubeia South, BJP candidate Papiya Adhikari had been touring the constituency when she found out that a party worker had been attacked and admitted to Uluberia State General Hospital. She immediately rushed to the hospital around noon when local Trinamool leader Akbar Sheikh and his supporters blocked her way before assaulting her physically and verbally. Everyone saw her tearful eyes on the television screen. The people watched the television reports on various channels that she was slapped and pushed physically and abused too. In another incident at Falta in South 24 Parganas, BJP candidate Bidhan Parui faced demonstrations by Trinamool activists at the Bellsinha High School polling station. He was slapped and people threw bricks at him. In Canning East, Trinamool candidate Saokat Molla accused central forces personnel and ISF supporters of heckling and assaulting him.36 Madhavi Adak, the mother of BJP worker Piru Adak, died early after goons allegedly belonging to the Trinamool Congress had beat her up at Goghat on 6 April night.[37] Further, the TMC candidate from the Mathabhanga Assembly seat Girindranath Burman received head injuries and his car was ransacked in an attack allegedly by BJP supporters. This happened just one day after miscreants ransacked BJP state president Dilip Ghosh's car at Sitalkuchi in the district. When the Mathabhanga candidate was returning from Ghoksadanga, around 9 PM towards home, miscreants attacked him and his car.[38]

It is not that political violence was happening in rural Bengal only. It took place in Kolkata also. We found that a clash broke out between members of the Trinamool Congress and the BJP at Chetla, considered to be the bastion of senior state minister Firhad Hakim, after posters of saffron party candidate Rudranil Ghosh were found torn in the locality. The two sides hurled stones at each other leaving a few persons injured around April 9 at midnight when Ghosh along with BJP workers was going to Chetla police station to lodge a complaint regarding the tearing of posters. Several vehicles were also ransacked during the incident.[39] It is not that the BJP alone knocked on the door of the Election Commission. The CPM also knocked on the door of the Election Commission for taking stern action against those behind the violence in West Bengal. Blaming the ruling Trinamool Congress and the BJP for the violence. The party complained that "The goons of the TMC are now divided between the party and the BJP. The leaders of these political parties are saying things such as '*khela Hobe* (the game is on]', *Dekhe Nebo* [we will see what happens]'. All are basically instigating violence. The Election Commission should take proper steps against them."[40]

The fourth phase of elections and violence at Cooch Behar

The election debate in West Bengal reached its zenith when four young men were killed in CISF firing at a Cooch Behar booth on 10 April 2021, bloodying the fourth phase of the Bengal polls that raised uncomfortable questions for the Election Commission that had deployed 77,000 central force personnel and 35,000 state police to ensure peaceful voting. The four dead men from Jorpatki in Sitalkuchi constituency – Nur Alam Mian (20), Maniruzzaman Mian (28), Samiul Haque (21), and Hamidul Mian (31) – belonged to poor families and they all were supporters of Trinamool Congress Party. It came to light from The Telegraph that mentioned a report of Special observers Ajay Nayak and Vivek Dube who had sent their report to the EC at 5.12 PM that stated, "…that recourse to open fire by the CISF personnel became absolutely necessary in order to save the lives of the voters lined up at the polling booth, those of other polling personnel and their own lives as the mob had attempted snatching their weapons."

As a result of the firing and killing of four fresh young voters, Sitalkuchi became a focal point of attention on 10 April, which was considered the most violent phase of elections in Bengal. Consequently, violence continued to happen in different places in Cooch Behar. Pranesh Sarkar reported in The Telegraph newspaper[41] that the day started with the death of Ananda Barman, an 18-year-old first-time voter. Barman died on the spot soon after casting his vote in the morning at a booth (5/285) in Cooch Behar's Sitalkuchi after some unknown goons had opened fire. In another incident, Amal Das, who claimed to be a BJP supporter, was found hanging in Patlakhawa in Cooch Behar.

Was the gunshot genocide or the consequences of instigation?

Bengal politics turned intensely hot with debates for or against the CISF firing on the villagers at Sitalkuchi that took away four lives. The Indian Express[42] highlighted the war of words between TMC and BJP leaders. When CISF personnel opened fire at a mob that tried to snatch their weapons outside a polling station in West Bengal's Cooch Behar, the Union home minister blamed it as 'Mamata Banerjee's provocative comments for the attack on central forces; but the chief minister described the incident as 'genocide'. It was reported earlier that in several election meetings the chief minister "Mamata Banerjee had advised the people to gherao Central forces". When there was another death on the following day i.e. on 11 April, the Union home minister accused the chief minister of indulging in "appeasement politics" by being selective in paying tributes. It came to light that Amit Shah blamed the chief minister for her appeasement politics in the following words: "Mamata Banerjee had paid tributes to four persons who were killed in the CISF firing but did not condole the death of Anand Barman as he is from the Rajbongshi community and is not suited for her vote bank. It is very unfortunate to see appeasement politics even in the case of deaths. This is not Bengal's culture."

In this phase also, some candidates were manhandled in and outside of Kolkata. The BJP candidate from Kasba, Kolkata Indranil Ghosh was injured when a group of people heckled him in front of a booth. In another incident, the BJP candidate from Chinsurah, Locket Chatterjee, was also heckled by a group of people allegedly backed by the Trinamool. During the scuffle, the car she was traveling in was damaged. She alleged that some people deployed to distribute hand sanitizers and gloves to the voters were influencing voters inside the booth to vote for the Trinamool Congress. The car of another BJP candidate, Payel Sarkar, from Behala (East) was also ransacked at Haridevpur when she visited a booth. A car in the convoy of BJP's Bally candidate, Baishali Dalmia, was ransacked near a booth in Liluah in Howrah. The car of a CPI(M) candidate, Mohd. Salim was also attacked by alleged Trinamool goons at Chanditala in Hooghly. Salim was on his way to visit a polling station in his constituency when a group of Trinamool supporters rushed towards his car and slammed on its body.[43]

Tension increased in Cooch Behar after bombs recovered

Bomb blasts were very common affairs during election days in the state. The Indian Express published a report by its express news service pointing out that, tension gripped Gopalpur Gram Panchayat of Mathabhanga in Cooch Behar after "a bucket of crude bombs" was recovered from roadside on 11 April 2021. Local people claimed that the bucket contained 12-13 bombs. The recovery prompted police and other security agencies to increase their vigilance in the area with more check posts. In another incident, police recovered bombs, bomb-making equipment, gun powder, and bullets at the Madral Joychanditala area of Bhatpara on the same night. In Cooch Behar, incidents of violence remained unabated for quite some time. Another hotbed of the political feud was Bhatpara in North 24 Parganas. Further, at the Dubrajpur Assembly constituency, the BJP candidate Anup Saha claimed that his car was vandalized by a TMC group raising "*Khela Hobe*" slogans when he was campaigning at Bhadulia village. Two BJP workers were injured in the attack. In another incident, Congress's Manikchak candidate Md Mottakin Alam was allegedly attacked by miscreants during campaigning in the area on 11 April. The vehicle of Congress MP Abu Hashem Khan Chowdhury who was accompanying Md. Mottakin Alam was also vandalized. The Congress accused TMC supporters of staging the attack, and quite naturally the charge was denied by the ruling party officials.[44]

Violence in the fifth phase of elections

It was revealed from a report of India Today (March 18, 2021) that ahead of the West Bengal Assembly election, 725 companies of central forces were deployed in the state for pre-poll duties. This was done with a view to curb poll-related violence in the State. West Bengal witnessed country-made bomb factories that were making crude bombs. Why the bombs were made? Were those made to love the people during elections? No, and never. Those were always used either to kill people or to threaten or disperse the voters during elections. The role of Central forces was not very satisfactory here. It came to light that the West Bengal assembly election was a hotbed and a matter of tension to all the officials engaged in the elections process. Further, the Election Commission of India had deployed 1,071 companies of Central forces for polling in 45 assembly seats across six districts of West Bengal in the 5th Phase of elections.[45] Despite all those Central Forces, violence continued in different booths and constituencies in Bengal.

It is to be noted that, the Election Commission prohibited political leaders from entering Cooch Behar district for the next 72 hours from the time of the election in the fifth phase of the poll. The silence period for the fifth period of polling on April 17 had been extended from 48 hours to 72 hours. The sad incident took place at Booth 5/126 at the Amtali Madhyamik Siksha Kendra.[46]

Malda also came to the news for violence during the poll period. Newspapers reported and television channels of Bengal highlighted the murder of BJP's Malda candidate Gopal Chandra Saha, who was allegedly shot at while he was returning from campaigning on 18 April. After attending a party workers' meeting at Sahapur Gram Panchayat, when he was getting in his car, some miscreants shot at him. He received a bullet injury in his neck and was immediately taken to Malda Medical Hospital where he underwent an operation. In another incident, the body of BJP worker Dilip Kirtaniya, aged 31, was found under mysterious circumstances in front of his house at Mandalpara under Chakdah police station in Nadia district. It came to light that after the fifth phase poll, Kirtaniya was called by some local TMC workers. He left his home and never returned alive at home. Later his body was found lying in his home yard.[47]

Exorbitant violence in 6th phase elections

Are violence and elections synonymous in Bengal? While watching television on 22nd April, the G-24 Ghanta television news channel reported that excessive violence erupted at Bijpur in Kancharapara where Trinamool Congress workers were attacking the BJP workers. The television channel showed at around 10.00 AM on 22nd April 2021 that the TMC workers attacked with lathi, bombs, and guns on BJP supporters. While the electorates of Hematabad boycotted votes in protest of the non-keeping of promises of the construction of a bridge.48 On the other hand, at Pratappur of Aushgram one Trinamool Congress leader, threatened two police constables. He said, *"Amake dhamkaben na chamkaben na* after… a few days when we will form government we will see you."* When the police told the TMC leader to move away from the place as he has already cast his vote, the TMC leader told this in reply to the words of the police. The TMC leader also cited "Do you want to repeat Sitalkuchi?" In another incident at Bamundi booth numbers 92 and 93 in Ketugram, there were comprehensive bombings and shooting by hooligans.

At Halisahar word No. 12 in North 24 Parganas, the house of a BJP leader was bombed and his mother and brother were attacked with lathi and bombs (News Bangla, 22nd April, 11.00 a.m.). When the elderly mother came to save her son, the elderly mother of the BJP leader was also beaten with lathi, and bloodstains were splattered on the floor of the house of the leader – such was the brutality. It was a very pathetic and inhuman act of TMC workers. In Nimta also, the BJP worker's mother Sova Majumber was badly beaten and she died after a few days ultimately. In Ketugram, the criminals were freely roaming with sharp arms and swords. In a television channel discussion Professor Biswanath Chakraborty of Rabindra Bharati University commented that "Within one kilometer when there is section 144, and when the TMC leader threatened the police, he should be immediately arrested by police." The news channels were showing about the bombing at Galsi, and threatening to the news reporters there.[49]

In recent years Barrackpore, Jagatdal, Bhatpara, Halishahar, and some other parts of North Parganas turned notorious for lawlessness and criminal activities. Another report of violence[50] was published in various newspapers during the fifth phase of polls from Jagatdal in West Bengal. It was revealed that three people, including a child, were injured in a crude bomb attack at multiple locations in West Bengal's North 24 Parganas district and particularly at Jagatdal, which was not too far from the residence of Barrackpore BJP MP Arjun Singh. The bombs were hurled at 15 places in the city and the accused also broke CCTV cameras at various spots. It was alleged by BJP leaders that, "An atmosphere of fear is being created so that the people cannot cast their vote.

Violence in the 7th phase of elections

One after another the BJP candidates, party workers, supporters, and leaders were attacked and threatened by TMC workers and leaders. The opposite was not an exception. The TMC candidates and workers also became prey in the hands of BJP workers, but the numbers were negligible. On 25 April there was political violence at Ward No. 14 of Ukilpara under Raiganj town. In that incident, the councilor of Trinamool Congress and other five persons were injured. The most visible and most prominent two opponent groups were the TMC and the BJP. The booth president of the said Ward, Subhas Gupta, was seriously injured and taken to Raigunj Medical College Hospital. One Trinamool Congress leader alleged that when some TMC workers were coming back home at night, a group of BJP workers attacked them, even they hit them with some sharp arms, and even one round of gunshot was fired by a BJP worker.[51]

The news on violence became a headline in Anandabazar Patrika. It came to news that, at Aushgram and Bhatar in Burdwan, one BJP worker was beaten by Trinamool Congress leaders. On the evening of 24 April, the BJP worker Lambudhar Pal, as his wife Rupa Pal became a booth agent of BJP candidate Kalita Maji in Aushgram, was beaten by Nabakumar and Anchal President of TMC Madhab Roy. On the other hand, at Bhatar houses of two BJP workers were ransacked and they were threatened too.[52] Thus, various tactics were adopted by TMC leaders to threaten the voters and office bearers of BJP to leave the company of BJP. Also, by creating an atmosphere of terror, the TMC succeeded to keep BJP supporters away from voting in favor of the BJP.

Pompous nomination procession marred by gunshot

A new tradition has arisen in Bengal as various candidates go to file their nomination papers in a pompous procession. These also became a symbol of showing strength to the Opponent candidates as well as Parties. Often clashes were found between two main rival groups when they arrive to fill up nomination forms at the office of the Sub Divisional Officer. In such a case, there was a firing during a clash between alleged workers of the Trinamool Congress and BJP at Barrackpore in North 24 Parganas when the BJP's Bijpur candidate Subhrangshu Roy, son of Mukul Roy, went to file his nomination papers for the Assembly polls. A person was arrested in connection with the clash and a firearm was seized by police.[53]

Firing during the sixth phase of elections

At least two persons were injured when state police allegedly opened fire to control violent BJP supporters outside the polling station No. 35 at Ranaghat in the Badgah constituency of North 24-Parganas district. It happened in the 6th phase of Bengal's assembly polls. It was learned that police had to resort to a lathi charge to disperse a mob gathered to protest the vandalism of their tent. However, the police later opened fire when the villagers turned mob allegedly became violent. This act of police created panic among the voters. In another incident, two Trinamool supporters were injured when a group of armed miscreants with suspected Trinamool link hurled bombs and fired indiscriminately outside Tangra Buniyadi Vidyalaya polling premises (polling station No. 79, 79A, 80, and 80A) of Ashok Nagar constituency in North-24 Parganas. The reports said that tension flared up when BJP candidate Tanuja Chakraborty arrived near the booth. The miscreants ransacked a number of police vehicles and hurled a dozen of crude bombs close to the polling station, unleashing panic in the area. Not only had that, firing continued after the polls too. A group of miscreants allegedly backed by Trinamool fired pellets at the house of an election agent of the BJP at Nangtagach in the Chopra Assembly constituency of North Dijanpur in which two women and a man of the agent's family had suffered injuries and had been rushed to the block health center in Dalua.[54]

Miscreants kept bombs hiding in different secret places only to be used as and when it was demanded by party leaders. We found that just a day ahead of the voting for the sixth phase of assembly elections, one person was killed and another was seriously injured in a crude bomb explosion inside an abandoned house near Tigagarh railway station in North 24 Parganas district. Also, there were reports of bombs being thrown near BJP MP Arjun Singh's house in Jagatdal and Kanchrapara in North 24 Parganas.[55] The district of North 24 Parganas and particularly Barrackpore, Titagarh, Halishahar became notorious for the frequent bombing, shooting, and violent activities by both ruling TMC workers and Opposition BJP workers led by Arjun Singh.

Violence in the 8th phase of elections

Birbhum, the workplace of Novel Laureate Rabindranath Tagore and home of another Nobel laureate Professor Amartya Sen, turned to be famous or notorious for the district president of the Trinamool Congress since the party came to power in 2011. Earlier also during the Left Front rule, Birbhum came to news for its unbridled political violence at Nanoor and some other pockets. Again, Nanoor became the headline of The Telegraph newspaper. It was reported that during the poll period a Trinamool leader at Nanoor allegedly tried to stop sitting MLA and CPM candidate Shyamali Pradhan from campaigning and threatened that hands of those daring to vote for the CPM would be chopped off. Nanoor was scheduled to vote on the last phase of elections on 29 April (2021) where the CPM workers when campaigning for their candidate had been threatened. The ruling TMC was creating an environment of fear in the run-up to the polls. It is to be mentioned here that, Birbhum is one of the districts where most of the gram panchayats were won uncontested by Trinamool Congress.[56] So, the level of threat and intimidation to the electors and Opposition party candidates can easily be comprehended from the result the TMC candidates, who won majority seats without any contest in local body elections held in 2018.

Post-poll violence in West Bengal

Violence continued in the post-poll period. The winner party i.e. the TMC swam into action to teach a lesson to the workers of BJP who dared to come out to campaign, write walls and posters and participate in the meetings, processions, and finally ventured to cast their votes for BJP. The BJP was defeated badly in the assembly elections went inside the doors immediately after the declaration of results on May 2. However, it came to news that within just two days of coming out of results at least six of BJP's party workers were killed across the state. The BJP also alleged that a few hundred party offices and houses of BJP workers were ransacked across the state as the counting progressed, and the trends of winning of TMC became clearer. On the result day, one of the offices of BJP's Hooghly district was set on fire and some of its leaders, including Suvendu Abdhikary, were harassed by TMC activists in other parts of the state. The TMC supporters hurled stones and broke the window screen of Suvendu Adhikary's car near a counting center in Haldia. The BJP office at Arambagh in Hooghly was attacked and arsoned in a bid to avenge the defeat of TMC's candidate. The Home Ministry sought a report on the 3rd May, the next day of publishing the results because the post-election violence targeted only the opposition political workers in the state. The Governor also summoned the Director-General of Police and sought a report on the ongoing violence across the state ever since the poll results were declared.[57]

The brutality in the post-poll period

Media reports were flooded with the violence in Bengal since the beginning of assembly elections in Bengal. Dr. Rakesh Sinha has nicely articulated his views in The Indian Express: "The magnitude and brutality of the post–poll violence in West Bengal is an indicator of the extent of partisan polarization, so much so that rivals are considered enemies." This is a dangerous trend in Indian democracy. It indicated the absence of complete collapse of law and order in the State. Also, these acts of violence and political clashes describe the symptoms of a decline of democracy. Political violence cannot take place without the support of political parties, and the political patronage of violence by the ruling party betrays the principles and conventions of Indian democracy. Lack of mutual respect, lower awareness of Constitutional rights and duties of voters, and minimum level of tolerance are diminishing and destroying the political culture in Bengal.

The recent killings of BJP-RSS workers, looting and plundering of homes and shops, and even alleged attacks on women in Bengal give a picture of the horrendous state of affairs. They show how democracy dies through elected leaders in the State. Three years ago in 2018, the Supreme Court raised alarm bells when more than 20,000 out of around 58,000 candidates in the panchayat elections in West Bengal were elected "unopposed". What does all this mean for Indian democracy? We find here the repetition of Leftist political culture during the rule of the TMC government too.

Contemporary politics in West Bengal negates the state's progressive legacy. In the early 20th century, Bengal witnessed symbiotic relations between art, literature, social reforms, and politics. This was one of the reasons that compelled the colonial rulers to annul the partition of Bengal based on communal considerations in just six years, in 1911. But the Bengalee fraternity was destroyed by the communal virus. The same Bengal suffered Direct Action Day and communal madness in 1946. It seems that we have not learned any lessons from the dark pages of history. The politics of Bengal today reflects this.

Dr. Rakesh Sinha, further, pointed out that once Mamata Banerjee battled with Marxist hegemonic politics and earned fame for her bravery. But she herself has been increasingly undermining democratic values since the initial days of her rule. She knows the strength of the symbiotic relationship between culture and politics, which is a route for the expansion of the BJP. Her politics does not allow the "other" to express, expand and emerge. Therefore, the politics in the state — once known for its rich intellectual legacy — rejected a battle of ideas and preferred a battle of swords. History is replete with instances that show that politically, Bengal responds slowly but decisively. Hindutva's march in state politics is not about numbers. Banerjee is not afraid of the

BJP's 70-plus MLAs but of inconvenient questions, she is not in a position to answer. The truth of the moment is the weakening of institutional buffers, of both democracy and federalism.[58]

Conclusions

From the above discussion, it came to light that in West Bengal almost every day there was news of violence during poll days, and the unfortunate trend continued post-election periods too. This sent a very bad signal to the people of this State living abroad or in the other States of India. Many complained in private that their heads bowed down in shame for the use of words, and use of hands, frequent dropping of bombs and gunshots. This tarnished the image of Bengal – once known for its heritage, and babu culture. From the very first day, nay even prior to that, every day all leading newspapers reported on violence, and political clashes between rival Trinamool Congress and Bharatiya Janata Party. The CPI(M), ISF, and INC, being insignificant, were not much in news, because neither media nor TMC and BJP gave importance to the 'blank alliance'. The elections were fought mainly between two prominent rival parties – the TMC and the BJP. As a result of political clashes and non-stop violence, a section of people of this state were annoyed with the way of presentation of television news and newspaper reports, and definitely with the political leaders who were engaged in such [criminal] offenses. What did the children, the future electors of this State, learn from this massive violence and the politics of terror? The sons and daughters living outside this state were worried about the safety and security of their elderly parents and grandparents. But, all this news of assault, chasing, murder, threatening, eviction from home, and damaging property and others were a part of the whole story of violence. How many press reporters were there in one newspaper office? How many television news reporters and cameramen were there that they could cover all the incidents, clashes, and acts of violence? It proved that only a small fraction of violence was reflected in the papers and television news, the actual numbers of incidents were much more, and the level of oppression and suppression was manyfold more. Can Bengal elections not be free from political violence? I feel sorry for the disgusting violence continuing since the sixties. Let us take an oath to stop all kinds of violence in the pre & post-election periods in India and particularly in West Bengal.

Let our voters be more aware of their rights as well as duties. Let the ruling party and its workers be tolerant always and in every place of India including this State. Remember, one swallow does not make a summer. Today's rulers are tomorrow's opposition party and vice versa. However, we need total violence-free elections in the days to come in our State so that no mother losses her son; no wife becomes widow; and no sister losses her brother.

Chapter - VI

Perception Regarding the TMC Government

"You can fool all the people some of the time, and some of the people all the time, but you cannot fool all the people all the time."

- *Abraham Lincoln*

In the pre-election campaigning period, the ruling Trinamool Congress party in West Bengal has repeatedly beaten its drum in favor of development calling it robust and stupendous. The election contest is truly a war of words. The demagogue leaders often win the race. Prior to the elections, all the political parties endeavor to woo the electors through various tactics, and the most common route is campaigning. Voters eagerly listen to the promises made by main rival parties. This year the two major warring parties were the Trinamool Congress and the Bharatiya Janata Party. The third power of the war was a front made by the CPI(M), INC, and ISF. But, the entire attention of the voters was fixed on the simple but forceful speeches of Mamata-Abhishek on the one hand; and Modi-Shah-Nadda-'*Dada*'-Irani & others on the other. A lot of issues came up prior to the elections; and it must be pointed out here that as this survey was conducted about six months prior to the elections, a few monumental matters such as CBI/ED notices to coal mafias of opposition political leaders, transfer of DMs/SPs prior to the elections, leg fracture of CM, joining of turncoat leaders in BJP, etc. remained out of the plate. Apart from these, there were some serious issues, which were presented before the respondents through the questionnaire for getting their perceptions. Interestingly, a large section of general voters in the state with or without putting their seal for the thumping demands of the ruling party exercised their freedom of speech and expression on multiple issues that affected their life, livelihood, career, dignity, and holistic development of the state as a whole. The researcher asked a few burning questions to the respondents that raged the political, social, and economic atmosphere in Bengal prior to the state assembly elections. The opinions of the voters have been highlighted in tabular form.

The state government witnessed bluish development in the length and breadth of its territory. The color of blue with white beautified the cities, towns, and even walls of bridges and buildings even in semi-urban localities of the state. The infrastructural development of the state is no doubt praiseworthy and eye-catching, but the question of quality and their longevity hover in the minds of a large number of electors in the state. Who does not want the development of infrastructure? But at the same time it is important to know if the said development will be sustainable, and if it was accomplished with the hard-earned money of the state government, or it was done from the borrowed money.

The Business Standard[1] in an article in 2018 reported that "West Bengal's debt burden rose by a whooping Rs.1.16 lakh crore in the last five years. This year alone, so far the state government has raised close to Rs.26,000 crore, the second-highest among states, the Reserve Bank of India (RBI) data showed….At the end of 2013-14, West Bengal's total debt outstanding was close to Rs.2.50 lakh crore, which is expected to rise to Rs.3.66 lakh crore by the end of this financial year…." Further, Pinak Ghosh in another article published in The Telegraph (04.02.2019) in the following year highlighted a more bitter fact that, "Bengal's public debt is set to balloon to Rs.4,31,928 crore — more than twice the sum it inherited from the Left Front government. The revised estimate of the outstanding loan in 2018-19 was Rs.3,95,322.57 crore. The burden of past debt is forcing the state government to raise its market borrowings to Rs. 53,774 crore from Rs. 47,854 crore last year as the state plans to pay off Rs.56,183.16 crore of past debts, which include Rs.25,032 crore of the principal amount and Rs.31,151.16 crore as interest."

In the current year, though the exact figure is not available at hand yet, it is estimated that the loan of the amount of the state government has crossed to five lakh crore. So, the entire story of development and the politics of dole was done with the cost of the common taxpayer's money. When asked the question to the respondents: "Are you satisfied with the TMC government's policy of development with borrowed money?"

Only 8.60 percent of respondents said "Yes" while 213 respondents comprising 57.25 percent respondents did not approve the government's programs of development with borrowed money. In this matter, 10.75 percent of respondents said "maybe", while 23.38 percent of respondents remained silent.

Table: 6.1 Are you satisfied with the TMC government's policy of development with borrowed money?

Opinion	Number of respondents	%
Yes	32	8.60
No	213	57.25
Maybe	40	10.75
Non respondents	87	23.38
Total	372	100

Source: Survey data

The state government has distributed government money among thousands of clubs in the pretext of developing sporting infrastructure amid questions on whether the largesse was justified without proper monitoring. In an article of The Telegraph[2] it was reported in 2018 that more than Rs.600 crore was so far spent on helping the clubs since 2011. Rs.2 lakh each was given to 4,300 clubs. Rs.1 lakh each was provided to 10,648 clubs, which had received Rs.2 lakh earlier. The TMC government started this practice since it came to power in 2011 to give Rs.2 lakh in the first year and Rs.1 lakh each in the next three years. Thus a club got Rs.5 lakh in a period of four years. Though the clubs were asked to submit utilization certificates and audit reports for the money received from the government, many of the clubs only submitted an undertaking that funds were used properly. It was further reported in the newspaper (online The Telegraph dt. 25.01.2018) with a unanimous official statement saying, "The sports department has received several complaints that clubs, which have only registration numbers, are being given money as they have the recommendation from some ruling party MLAs. Most clubs don't have any infrastructure like a sports ground or a land parcel. This has to be stopped and a proper inspection at the district level needs to be carried out before allotting funds to the clubs."

However, let us examine the public opinion for the distribution of doles to the clubs by the state government with public money. The people were asked, "Are you satisfied with the present government's policy of distribution of money to the clubs?" The majority of the respondents 66.66 percent disapproved of the action of the state government. On the other hand, only a handful of people (5.57%) supported government action, and 4.30 percent of respondents said: "maybe." But, 23.64 percent of respondents did not like to make any comment at all.

Table: 6.2 Are you satisfied with the present government's policy of distributing money to the clubs?

Opinion	Number of respondents	%
Yes	20	5.37
No	248	66.66
Maybe	16	4.30
Non respondents	88	23.64
Total	372	100

Source: Survey data

Similarly, the state government distributed doles to the Durga puja committees in Bengal. The Hindu[3] reported with the headline "Mamata Banerjee doubles dole to the Durga puja committees" prior to the Durga puja in 2020. The chief minister on the eve of the 2020 Durga puja announced her plan to double the financial assistance of Rs. 50,000 to each club. The 37,000 community Durga Pujas organized by local clubs would get financial aid, up from last year's Rs. 25,000, which will cost the exchequer Rs.185 crore. Apart from the direct aid to the puja committees, they were given free access to all civic and fire facilities from Civic and Fire Departments of the government. Besides, the government arranged for a 50% rebate on the electricity consumed by the puja committees during the festival. But, the common citizens in West Bengal were afraid to air their grievances and speak against the government decision; only we found criticism from the Opposition political parties like the Communist Party of India (Marxist) and the Bharatiya Janata Party.

One respondent in the survey said that the government has no right to pay government money to the clubs. Another respondent, hiding his personal identity, said that the people or party in government must return the public money to the bank accounts of residents of the state. The present state government is the torch-bearer in the introduction of communal politics in Bengal. Since independence, no government in India has ever introduced "allowance to Imams and Muezzins". Almost nine years back in 2012, the TMC government announced for the first time an honorarium for Imams and Muezzins which was struck down by the Calcutta High Court. But the government arranged to give the monthly allowance through the Wakf Board. Again, considering the grudge of the Hindu priests prior to the 2021 elections, the government announced an honorarium of Rs.1000 each to nearly 8,000 Hindu priests in the state. It came to light from a report of The Federal[4] that, non-Brahmins were also included in the list of beneficiaries at the behest of local TMC leaders. The report alleged "Among others, the name of the husband of a TMC Zila Parishad member, Tina Saha, was also included in the beneficiaries list…." And added the statement of Sridhar Mishra, state secretary of the Paschim Banga Rajya Sanatan Brahman Trust, the apex body of the state's estimated 2.73 lakh Hindu priests, who said, "We have been receiving hundreds of complaints about such anomalies from across the state."

Regarding the announcement of dole to the Hindu priests, Frontline[5] published an article in this regard. The article said, "With the West Bengal Assembly election of 2021 drawing near and the Bharatiya Janata Party (BJP) poised to offer a serious challenge, Chief Minister Mamata Banerjee and her Trinamool Congress government appear to be pulling no stops to try and win back some of the Hindu support it has lost to the BJP." On September 11, 2020, the CM announced that her government would be paying Rs.1000.00 to the Hindu priests as an honorarium and for building houses under the Bangla Avaash Yojana for those who have no house of their own.

How do the people of West Bengal view the decision of the government? With a view to judging the public perception, a simple question is asked in this regard. But only a negligible number of 8 respondents (2.15%) nobody supported the action of the state government. The majority of respondents (68.71%) did not approve of the present government's policy of distributing money to religious priests. On the other hand, 9.94 percent of respondents said "maybe", and 19.07 percent of respondents did not like to say anything on this issue.

Table: 6.3 Do you like the present government's policy of distributing dole to the religious priests?

Opinion	Number of respondents	%
Yes	8	2.15
No	256	68.71
Maybe	37	9.94
Non respondents	71	19.07
Total	372	100

Source: Survey data

Anyone traveling in Kolkata and districts of West Bengal would find active and visible Civic Volunteers standing beside the West Bengal Police or Kolkata Police personnel. In April 2013 the state cabinet passed four proposals of the Home Department of the West Bengal Government. The state cabinet nodded to need-based recruitment of 1.3 lakh civic police volunteers for West Bengal Police, and additional 1000 such volunteers for the Siliguri police force. But there were reports of corruption in the recruitment process. In this regard, a court case can be cited to understand the recruitment process at least to some extent. The case named Chandra Kanta Ganguli vs The State of West Bengal and Others dated 20 May 2016 which was heard in the High Court at Calcutta Constitutional Writ Jurisdiction Appellate Side vide WP 6371 (W) of 2016, and the hearing concluded on May 18, 2016, before Sanjib Banerjee, Judge. Some clauses of the said judgment can be mentioned for understanding the inappropriate recruitment process of civic police volunteers. Clause 5 of the said judgment said:

"The petitioners claim that in terms of the relevant government orders, applications were invited for civic police volunteers all over the State including in Bankura. The applications were to be submitted to the local police stations. According to the petitioners, they were told that there would be a physical efficiency test and a physical measurement test followed by an interview, and a final list of chosen volunteers would be published thereafter. The petitioners allege that no efficiency or measurement tests were conducted, but the petitioners received call letters to appear before an interview board.

Clause 6 pointed out that, "The petitioners maintain that they were not subjected to an interview on the day that they were called therefor. The petitioners were not asked any questions but were required to submit photocopies of their identity cards and their call letters. According to the petitioners, later on, the same day on which their interviews were scheduled, lists were published containing the names of the successful candidates and the petitioners' names did not figure therein."

The said civic police volunteers were recruited at an honorarium of Rs. 141.80p per volunteer per day with a condition that such volunteers would be engaged for stretches not exceeding six months.

Clause 18 narrated that, "There is no evidence whether the engagements have been given on political or other extraneous considerations, but it is good enough to set aside a process which was designed to subvert due process."

Clause 19 stated that "Any person doing business with any government or seeking to obtain any funds from the government would know of the myriad formalities that need to be complied with to get even a rupee. There was a recruitment process that had the potential of costing the State revenue in excess of Rs.400 crore a year, with no checks in place to ensure that deserving candidates were selected. The entire scheme appears to have been framed for the choice of candidates to be made on extraneous and constitutionally immoral considerations."

Clause 23 stated that "It is completely unacceptable that there were no checks and balances put in place to ensure that a transparent process was followed, particularly when it costs the State exchequer an amount of about Rs.1.80 crore a day if all the civic volunteers envisaged being recruited are engaged."

Therefore, a question was asked to the respondents "Are you satisfied with the present government's policy of giving temporary jobs to the civic volunteers?" In reply to the question, more than a quarter of respondents (27.41%) replied that "Yes" they supported the action of the government, while a little less than half of the total respondents (44.08%) did not consider it proper to recruit civic volunteers with so little salary and with temporary nature. On the other hand, 9.67 percent of people said "Maybe" and another 18.8 percent of respondents completely avoided the question.

Table: 6.4 Are you satisfied with the present government's policy of giving temporary jobs to the civic volunteers?

Opinion	Number of respondents	%
Yes	102	27.41
No	164	44.08
Maybe	36	9.67
Non respondents	70	18.8
Total	372	100

Source: Survey data

In June 2020 the state government fixed salaries for guest lecturers in colleges, who were being paid earlier a fixed amount of Rs.3000 or Rs.3500 per month, or Rs.100/150 per class, and during vacation, they were not paid at all. In many colleges, they outnumbered regular employees. However, the government considered the demands of nearly 8,500 guest lecturers in the state. They have been recognized as State Aided College Teachers (SACT). Regarding the recruitment and recognization of the SACT, The Hindu[6] published a report that revealed: "As per the order, guest lecturers who have a Ph. D. or have qualified the NET/SET will earn Rs.36,000 monthly if they have put in more than10 years in an institution. Those with less than 10 years' experience will get Rs. 31,000. Those without a Ph. D. or who haven't qualified for the NET/SET will earn Rs.25,000 if they have 10 years of experience; while those with less experience will get Rs.20,000. They will all get a yearly 3% increment and will retire at 60, and upon retirement be given a sum of Rs.5 lakh." But this provision will hamper the interest of the fresh educated and qualified candidates who have already done research (M. Phil or Ph. D.) and got qualified in NET/SET (National Eligibility Test/State Eligibility Test). Moreover, the decision of the government is "arbitrary, irrational and politically motivated" as was complained by a section of job seekers in the state, because, the decision was taken in violation of the UGC norm of recruitment. Also, it came to light that, a large number of SACTs are lowly qualified, it was not held with proper notification and screening process and the whole recruitment process did not follow roster system (reservation of seats) of recruitment.

Hence, when a question in this regard was asked the majority of respondents (54.03%) did not support the government's action; while only 9.94 percent of people considered it proper. On the other hand, 8.60 percent of respondents said "Maybe" and 27.41 percent of the total respondents remained silent in the question.

Table: 6.5 Are you satisfied with the present government's policy of recruitment of guest lecturers in state-aided colleges?

Opinion	Number of respondents	%
Yes	37	9.94
No	201	54.03
Maybe	32	8.60
Non respondents	102	27.41
Total	372	100

Source: Survey data

The Indian Express[7] published an article in July (2020) with the heading – 'West Bengal didn't handle migrants issue properly: Bombay HC', which is self-explanatory. The article cited the judgment of the Bombay High Court which said the migrants' issue was not handled properly in West Bengal amid the COVID-19 pandemic, and the government there at one point of time even refused to permit laborers from other parts of the country to return to their homes. Around 56,000 laborers had stranded who wanted to travel back to their native states, and many of these laborers were from West Bengal. Many migrant laborers managed to travel at their own expense. Chief Justice Dipankar Datta mentioned the case of 30 laborers who were stranded in the Ratnagiri district of Maharashtra and ultimately arranged a bus on their own to travel back to West Bengal.

In another article[8] Shiv Sahay Singh, a reporter of The Hindu pointed out the plight of migrant workers after returning to Bengal. It came to light that, several laborers sought employment or earning opportunities from the state government. One Sekh Suraj Ali, a 25-year-old resident of Howrah's Udaynarayanpur block, used to earn Rs. 15,000 a month working as a tailor in Kerala. Days before the nationwide lockdown was announced, with COVID-19 cases rising in Kerala, he returned home and wrote a letter to the state government seeking reemployment, social security, and healthcare facilities. The chief minister indicated that over 10.5 lakh migrant workers have returned to the State by the first week of June; while a CITU leadership claimed that the figure was between 27 lakh and 30 lakh.

When asked to the respondents "Are you satisfied with the present government's handling of thousands of migrant workers?" the majority of respondents (52.68%) answered "No", though 16.96 percent of respondents replied affirmatively. Regarding this question, 7.52 percent of respondents said "Maybe", and 22.84 percent of people did not like to say anything.

Table: 6.6 Are you satisfied with the present government's handling of thousand of migrants workers?

Opinion	Number of respondents	%
Yes	63	16.96
No	196	52.68
Maybe	28	7.52
Non respondents	85	22.84
Total	372	100

Source: Survey data

A new term 'Syndicate Raj' came to the fore after the TMC government entered the Writers' Buildings in 2011. Though the term has become so popular to almost all the politically conscious electors of this state, it needs a little clarification as to how it operates, and by whom, and to what extent. In this regard, one article of India Today Magazine[9] can be highlighted here for understanding the whole affairs.

The article starts with "Give in or give up - that's the blatant and "dangerous" message of the 'syndicate raj' thriving under the Mamata Banerjee government. Patronized by Trinamool Congress councilors and members and some government officials, these syndicates have spread their tentacles from real estate to Durga Puja. These groups control the sale of land, construction, and building material and if the buyer seeks legit means, the syndicates make sure he succumbs to their demands." It is alleged that in most cases, the councilor, or a woman councilor's husband, and other active supporters of the party run the entire show. If one outsider wants to buy land, build a house, set up a restaurant or industry, he must have to pay 'protection money', and the building material materials should have to be purchased from them with a high price and lesser in quantity. And "If you protest, it will lead to a bigger problem and vandalism. They are very dangerous people. Their boss is a very big leader of West Bengal. He might become an MLA. He will have everything vandalized. Lockdown or shell out Rs.10 lakh," Soumen Banerjee, husband of Bidhannagar TMC councilor Swati Banerjee, blatantly mentions the 'muscle power' of syndicates when an India Today TV undercover reporter posing as a businessman approaches him regarding opening a 'restaurant' and asks why doesn't the police intervene?

The local members of the syndicate often ask the newcomers of the locality a huge amount as a Durga Puja subscription. It is often Rs.25,000 or more. Here, the TV undercover was asked Rs. 4.00 lakh from the reporter. Paying Rs.4.00 lakh to start a restaurant is nothing but extortion. That is how syndicates are thriving in the state, and their diktat is 'either pay up or suffer'. If a person disobeys the diktat, they will lock everything down and demand Rs.5-Rs.10 lakh. The work won't resume (if you don't pay up). This is the best example of the 'law of the jungle' in the 'syndicate raj' at the time of TMC ruling in West Bengal.

Basu's comment corroborates Banerjee's statement when he mentions how he has threatened a man who started construction in his area without donating to his club. "I have come to know that roofing is being done at a construction site in my area. When I told him clearly that my club hasn't got any donation and I will stop the construction, he started pleading and said that would consider it (the demand). Everything will be visible when I fix him up."

What is the root cause of this syndicate raj? Is it dire poverty or widespread unemployment in West Bengal? Or, is this a strategy of the ruling party to extract money from outsiders in the state? If this continues to happen for long how new industries will come in the State? How the Bengal's industrialists, scholars, professors who are living abroad will come to Bengal and settle? It is not that only the common people are having a similar experience. It happens with the big party leaders too, who are having exceptional academic and cultural backgrounds. Chandra Kumar Bose, a relative of Professor Sugata

Bose told that "Syndicates existed in Bengal earlier as well, but in the unorganized sector. Now, they are in the organized sector. I had given credit to Mamata Banerjee for being Chief Minister of a syndicate raj, not of West Bengal." Even the TMC leaders are not spared by syndicate raj. Chandra Kumar Bose lamented, "My cousin Sugata Bose, who is a TMC MP from Jadavpur constituency, was attacked. My aunt Krishna Bose, who is 90 years old, was attacked. Her family was threatened and was told that they could not repair their house unless they bought building material from the syndicate. TMC leaders are

Table: 6.7 Are you satisfied with the syndicate raj in West Bengal?

Opinion	Number of respondents	%
Yes	7	1.88
No	260	69.89
Maybe	18	4.83
Non respondents	87	23.38
Total	372	100.00

Source: Survey data

accepting [on camera] that there is syndicate raj." Prime Minister Narendra Modi also attacked Mamata Banerjee's government for "throttling democracy" and running a "syndicate raj."[10]

Not only did the media or Opposition politicians blame syndicate raj, but a section of academicians also expressed concern with the system of extortion in the state under the TMC government. 'Syndicate' has become a marker of corruption in the state – a sort of politician-contractor nexus that has a direct bearing on people who intend to build a house or buy a flat in Bengal. Syndicates are loose consortiums of people who operate as extortion agents in the real estate industry. An Assistant Professor of Presidency University expressed that, "Usually, if you want to build a house, you employ a promoter. The promoter – also the builder in most cases – is connected with the local syndicate which provides everything related to construction, from cement to bricks to even commission agents who register the house. Sometimes the transactions are business-as-usual, and sometimes it goes violently awry."[11]

Hence, a question was asked to the people, "Are you satisfied with the present government's policy of syndicate raj?" quite naturally the majority of respondents 69.89 percent told "No", while only 1.88 percent said "Yes". In reply to the question, 4.83 percent of respondents were not sure as they said "Maybe", while 23.38 percent of respondents kept themselves silent.

Like the syndicate raj, the allegation for collection of tolabaji tax is also leveled against some workers and leaders of the Trinamool Congress Party. Hitting out at the Chief Minister, prior to the Lok Sabha elections, the Prime Minister said repeatedly that she was not extending the social and developmental schemes of the Centre to the state and accused her government of imposing an 'extortion' tax - Trinamool Tolabaji Tax (TTT).[12]

Cut money was a vital issue that came up prior to the Lok Sabha elections in 2019, and this issue continued more vehemently up to the assembly elections in 2021. What is cut money? Cut-money is the cash political agents at the grassroots level allegedly take from beneficiaries to ensure the proper implementation of government schemes like MGNREGA, and housing initiatives, even widow pensions, and grants for funeral expenses. In all, there are nearly 100 social welfare schemes run by the state government and the Centre in West Bengal: While rural residents avail of them through panchayats, urban dwellers have to approach civic bodies.[13]

Between 18 June and 14 July, 2019 around Rs.25 lakh has been returned to beneficiaries in 15 cases in several districts including East Burdwan, Birbhum, North 24 Parganas, and Jalpaiguri. On 8 July (2019), for example, at a village in East Burdwan district, the panchayat pradhan and a TMC member returned close to Rs. 4 lakh to 142 villagers, who were charged the sum as a cut from their wages for 100 days' work. Meanwhile, protests went on as other beneficiaries demanded their money back, and looked unlikely to abate anytime soon. According to police sources, of the 278 protests between 18 June and 14

July, at least 50 were reported in East Burdwan and 42 in Hooghly. Bankura and Birbhum saw close to 30 such incidents.[14]

When asked the question "Are you satisfied with the culture of tolabaji of some leaders and close supporters of the present ruling party, only except for a small fraction of respondents (2.41%), the majority of them consisting 71.23 percent expressed their dissatisfaction with the cut money and tolabaji culture of a section of ruling party workers and leaders while 24.18 percent respondents did not respond at all.

Table: 6.8 Are you satisfied with the culture of tolabaji of some leaders and close supporters of the present ruling party?

Opinion	Number of respondents	%
Yes	9	2.41
No	265	71.23
Maybe	8	2.15
Non respondents	90	24.18
Total	372	100

Source: Survey data

The health infrastructure in West Bengal is shining outwardly and not internally. Behind the blue and white-colored big buildings there are many dark stories. The state witnessed 8 days' strikes in 2019 that brought many loopholes in front of the general public. Beating doctors and accusing them of a mishap during treatment has become common throughout the state. An examination of the root cause of this kind of dysfunctionality in hospital administration can be traced from the fact that in West Bengal although per capita expenditure on health has increased marginally from around Rs.552.00 in 2014-15 to Rs.643.00 in 2019-20 (BE) in 2012 prices, the rate of change in expenditure on health has fallen from 16 percent in 2015-16 to 0.4 percent in 2018-19 (RE). It even became negative thereafter in West Bengal.[15] While the state budget increased by 76% in the same period, the health budget increased only by 53 percent in the state.

The condition of public health infrastructure has remained very poor in West Bengal. Health centers all over the state are short of resources. The status of health infrastructure in rural areas is very poor. Nearly 12,310 sub-centers in West Bengal are currently running on a shortfall. As many as 1,870 sub-centers have been functioning out of rented buildings. There is a need for as many as 349 surgeons, 320 pediatricians, and 297 gynecologists at community health centers in Bengal. Doctor and bed population ratios were 1:10411 and 1: 1170 respectively in West Bengal, according to 2018 government data. Quite obviously, doctors are overburdened at public hospitals. In addition, they are not provided with modern equipment for facilitating services, and the security system is demonstrably not good enough to protect them from public outrage if anything goes wrong.

Mampi Bose, a policy analyst at the Centre for Budget and Governance Accountability, New Delhi in an article writes: "When one looks into the matter from a common person's perspective, it is not hard to understand the hassles an individual goes through while seeking treatment from public healthcare facilities. Long waiting times and poor quality of services (due to infrastructural bottlenecks and human resource shortages) are very common at public hospitals. Additionally, the introduction of user fees at public hospitals has worsened the situation. Most of the states have outsourced several services to the private sector. West Bengal has outsourced secondary and tertiary care, diagnostics, dialysis of patients, ambulance, catering, and laundry services to private partners. Private hospitals charge higher prices for render services. Healthcare no longer remains a publicly provided well. It becomes like any other commodity sold in the market and can be consumed only if the buyer has the willingness and ability to pay for it.[16] The poor, the unprivileged who are the majority in society have remained out of the purview of luxurious and better private healthcare facilities in the state. Moreover, the West Bengal government has neglected to spend on monitoring and evaluation. In most cases, the private profit-making nursing homes and hospitals remain out of the reach of the government's poor controlling mechanism.

A question was asked to the respondents - Are you satisfied with the health infrastructure of the present government? The majority of respondents totaling 198 persons (53.22%) answered negatively, and about one-fifth (21.23%) of participants in the survey expressed their satisfaction with the health infrastructure of the State. In reply to the question, 15.05

percent of respondents neither expressed satisfaction nor dissatisfaction, while 10.48 percent of respondents did not like to make any comment on the issue.

Table: 6.9 Are you satisfied with the health infrastructure of the present government?

Opinion	Number of respondents	%
Yes	79	21.23
No	198	53.22
May be	56	15.05
Non respondents	39	10.48
Total	372	100

Source: Survey data

Health and Family Welfare Department of the Government of West Bengal issued a notice on 22.04.2020 where it was said that "The requisitioned private hospitals will not charge any amount for the patients referred to them by the State/District authorities during the current period; the costs for such treatment shall be borne by the State Government."[17] Not only that the state government disbursed about Rs.100 crore to the requisitioned private hospitals for administering treatment of COVID-19 patients. It was revealed in the news that, to save people from Covid, the government has paid around Rs. 2 lakh for the 14-days treatment of each patient.[18]

Despite this fact, many private hospitals had charged exorbitant fees from the patients. It was reported that some were charging Rs.10 lakh while others were charging Rs.15 lakh for treatment of COVID-19 patients, while there was not medicine before 12 January 2021 when 83 carton-full COVISHIELD medicine arrived by plane for medical emergency service providers such as doctors, nurses, and other related staffs.

With a view to mitigating public grievances, and controlling the abrupt charges by most o the private hospitals and nursing homes, The West Bengal Clinical Establishment Regulatory Commission (WBCERC) directed health establishments including R-Fleming Hospitals, BP Poddar Hospital, Dum Dum ILS Hospital to refund money to patients or their family members for charging excessively. The Commission had even lodged a suo motu case against Desun Hospital for allegedly not admitting a 60-year-old Covid patient for failing to deposit Rs.3 lakh for admission and barred it from collecting advance from any patient at the time of admission besides directing to deposit Rs.10 lakh with the Commission.[19]

So, when a question was asked in relating to the free medical treatment theory of the State government, it came to light that about one-third of respondents (31.45%) consider that the free treatment of Covid-19 patients in the State was satisfactory, while 37.36 percent respondents were not satisfied with the government's free medical treatment arrangements to the Covid-19 patients. On the other hand, 12.08 percent of respondents remained silent.

Table: 6.10 Do you think that the government has provided free medical treatment to the COVID-19 patients?

Opinion	Number of respondents	%
Yes	117	31.45
No	139	37.36
Maybe	71	19.08
Non respondents	45	12.08
Total	372	100

Source: Survey data

West Bengal government introduced Swasthya Sathi Scheme in 2016. The government, further, declared the promotion of the insurance scheme to cover the entire population of the state from December 2020. The scheme intended to provide basic health cover for secondary and tertiary care up to Rs.5.00 lakh per annum per family. It became quite popular among rural and economically deprived sections of the population. The extension of the health insurance scheme is being seen as the first to outreach citizens of the state in the run-up to the 2021 state assembly elections. The annual expense which the state is going to bear for this scheme will be approximately Rs. 2,000 crore.

The health insurance scheme was much needed at the beginning of the COVID-19 pandemic situation. But the introduction of the health insurance scheme with taxpayers' money was planned to channelize to the insurance companies. Siddartha Gupta, associated with Shramajibi Swasthya Udyog, said: "When the state government implements a scheme that involves such a huge financial amount, it will definitely be taxpayers' money that will go into the pockets of private insurance companies. This scheme will not include the OPD treatment, on which a huge number of patients are dependent...... "There are chances that by upholding this kind of scheme, the government will stop building new health care facilities like health centers, government hospitals, etc. Private hospitals will largely benefit from this scheme and it will be easier for the government to evade responsibilities in providing health services. The only solution that can benefit all citizens of the state is direct free health care delivery for all."[20]

But how will the Swasthya Sathi scheme be implemented in the state? Prior to the introduction of the inclusive policy, the private hospitals, as well as many government hospitals, also were not accepting the Swasthya Sathi card and a large number of people could not avail of the service despite paying Rs.500.00 per month as the insurance premium which is deducted from the salary of the government-sponsored school teachers and non-teaching staffs and others. After the declaration of the diktat of the chief minister, representatives of private hospitals expressed their concerns over the rates for treatment of patients under the West Bengal government's Swasthya Sathi scheme.[21] Further, in a recent meeting (January 10, 2021) at Nabanna between the private health establishments and state health officials, all the private hospitals and nursing homes across the state have been asked by the government to get impaneled for the Swasthya Sathi scheme, failing which they will lose their clinical establishment license. They have also been asked to formulate an SOP for Swasthya Sathi patients.[22] This created anger and frustration among many private healthcare service providers in the state. When asked "Are you satisfied with the present government's policy of Swasthya Sathi Scheme? More than one-third (33.60%) of respondents answered in affirmative, while a little more respondents (38.70%) expressed their negative attitude, while 8.60 percent respondents said "Maybe' and 17.07 percent of respondents did not make any reply to the question.

Table: 6.11 Are you satisfied with the present government's policy of Swasthya Sathi Scheme?

Opinion	Number of respondents	%
Yes	125	33.60

No	144	38.70
Maybe	32	8.60
Non respondents	71	19.07
Total	372	100

Source: Survey data

During the rule of the Left Front government, School Service Commission (SSC) examinations were held regularly, and thousands of students were appointed in schools. But the TMC government took the first and the last SSC examination (upper primary level except for work education and physical education) in 2016. Still, the appointment process has not yet been completed till the month of January 2021. The College Service Commission held an examination for recruiting Principals in government degree colleges in 2013. West Bengal School Service Commission published an online advertisement for recruitment of Asst. Teachers for 465 vacancies with the last date 6th January 2021. Similarly, College Service Commission has also published an advertisement for the recruitment of an Assistant Professor in the month of January 2021, while most of the recruitments were taking place on a temporary basis. Besides, the government suffered frequently from court cases only because of its faulty recruitment process.

The majority of the educated but unemployed youths of the state were dissatisfied with the government's policy of recruitment. As a result, the majority of respondents (74.19%) in the survey data expressed that they were not satisfied with the present recruitment policy of the government in schools. On the other hand, only 8.87 percent of respondents stated their satisfaction with the recruitment policy of the government, while 12.62 percent of respondents did not respond at all.

Table: 6.12 Are you satisfied with the recruitment policy of government in schools?

Opinion	Number of respondents	%
Yes	33	8.87
No	276	74.19
May be	16	4.30
Non respondents	47	12. 62
Total	372	100

Source: Survey data

The government, again, has taken initiative for transferring the teachers, which has also been frequently been changed by the Education Department. There are several complaints against the transfer of teaching and non-Teaching staff. It is learned from newspaper reports that, some were transferred by following the proper procedure, while others were without doing so. The transfer policy was introduced at the end of the previous Left Front government. This was continued up to 2013 when the TMC government introduced a general transfer policy. But in 2015, that notification was modified to different categories such as general transfer, special transfer, and reallocation. Though it was notified that no application for transfer will be done in places less than 25 kilometers; in entire service period only two times one teacher can apply for the transfer – once for mutual transfer, and the other is general transfer; Unless a teacher completes five years in a post, he cannot apply for transfer. But these obligations are not being adhered to strictly.

So, when asked, "Are you satisfied with the government's policy of transfer of teachers in schools?" 18.54 percent of respondents expressed their satisfaction with the policy, while 38.44 percent were dissatisfied with the policy of the government. On the other hand, 17.20 percent of respondents answered "Maybe", and 25.79 percent of respondents did not reply at all.

Table: 6.13 Are you satisfied with the government's policy of transfer of teachers in schools?

Opinion	Number of respondents	%
Yes	69	18.54
No	143	38.44
Maybe	64	17.20
Non respondents	96	25.79
Total	372	100

Source: Survey data

Since long past, West Bengal has had a history of ideological and political clashes with the Union Government. When Jyoti Basu was the Chief Minister, the West Bengal government was blamed as "comrade raj' and "danger to democracy" for its disruptive politics. In 1987 Rajiv Gandhi came to West Bengal for campaigning and promised 10 lakh jobs to the youths, it comes to power and wanted to transform the backward state into a prosperous, pulsating "Natun (new) Bangla."[23] Though the Buddhadeb Bhattacharjee government had ideological animosity with the Congress, the CPI(M) extended issue-based support to the UPA-I. The Left front withdrew its support from the Indian National Congress-led UPA-I government. The Left Front said: "As you are aware, the Left parties had decided that if the government goes to the IAEA (International Atomic Energy Agency) board of governors, they will withdraw support. In view of the Prime Minister's announcement (of the government's decision to go to IAEA), that time has come."[24]

But the most notorious tussle was found between the TMC government in Bengal and the BJP-led Union government. The non-cooperative attitude of the TMC government was visible on different occasions - be it the implementation of NRC, or CAA in the State. The latest addition was the support of Rajiv Kumar, the Police Commissioner of Kolkata, who allegedly misled the Sarada Chit Fund investigation being a part of a Special Investigate Team set up by the state government. The Sarada Chit Fund Scam duped lakhs of people to the tune of Rs.2500 crore. Finally, the state government refused to send the police chief and chief secretary to the national capital to discuss the law and order situation in the state following the attack on the cavalcade of Bharatiya Janata Party president JP Nadda during his recent visit (December 9-10, 2020) to the state. During the incident, the cars of several BJP leaders, including national general secretary Kailash Vijayvargiya and West Bengal unit chief Dilip Ghosh, which were part of Nadda's convoy, were attacked and damaged. Not only that, but the Union Ministry of Home Affairs had also communicated to the West Bengal government to recall three IPS officers – Rajeev Kumar, Praveen Tripathi, and Bholanath Pandey to report on central deputation, which was turned down by the state government. Thus the present state government is continuously defying the Union government. It is necessary to remember that the Constitution bars states from "impeding" the Union's work and rightly requires them to comply with central laws. The state government did not implement the welfare schemes of the Union government such as "*Ayushman Bharat*" and "*PM-Kishan Samman Nidhi*" and deprived the poor people including farmers of the state. In such a situation how can the people of the State of West Bengal get support and big social and economic projects from the Central government? Ultimately, the people of Bengal are being the losers because of the non-cooperative politics of Bengal's present rulers.

When asked the question "Do you think the Bengal Government's dispute with the Central Government is lowering people's opportunity to have fruits of development?" the majority of respondents comprising 51.8 percent replied in affirmative, while 12.9 percent respondents did not think so. On the other hand, 18.27 percent of respondents said it might be, and 22.58 percent remained silent in the question.

Table: 6.14 Do you think the Bengal Government's dispute with the Central Government is lowering people's opportunity to have fruits of development?

Opinion	Number of respondents	%
Yes	176	47.31
No	44	11.82
Maybe	68	18.27
Non respondents	84	22.58
Total	372	100

Source: Survey data

The recruitment process in West Bengal got hindered on many occasions during the TMC rule. In 2017 West Bengal witnessed widespread protests in different parts of the State over the recruitment of 42,000 primary school teachers. Protests were held in Kolkata and Siliguri alongside the West Bengal Legislative Assembly where the MLAs of the Opposition parties blamed the State government over the irregularities in one of the biggest recruitment scams in the state. Discontent among the examiners started when the results of the recruitment were announced, but the merit list of successful candidates was not made public. Instead, the State government announced that successful examinees will be informed about their position through SMS or email. The confusion started to grow when candidates were asked to appear for counseling through text message. Many students who either have not completed their diploma in primary education or were working as para teachers got enlisted under 10 percent reservation fixed for para teachers. When they were asked for relevant documents they could not produce any leading to hiccups in their recruitment. Thus, the recruitment of primary teachers was "lack of transparency" and "flawed" as told by the former chairperson of West Bengal School

Service Commission Ranajit Basu and Left Legislative Party leader of CPI(M) respectively.[25]

Therefore, a question was asked to the respondents "Do you believe that there is corruption in recruitment of teachers?" more than half of respondents (55.91%) replied that they believe so, while 5.37 percent of respondents do not believe any such corruption in recruitment of teachers in the state. 13.97 percent of respondents said that there might be some corruption, while another 24.72 percent of people did not reply to the question.

Table: 6.15 Do you believe that there is corruption in recruitment of teachers?

Opinion	Number of respondents	%
Yes	208	55.91
No	20	5.37
Maybe	52	13.97
Non respondents	92	24.72
Total	372	100

Source: Survey data

The government, many of the leaders and supporters of TMC, and a section of the general public claim that women and girls are very safe in the State in comparison with other States. Let us examine the reports of some newspapers in different years during the present TMC government. Purnima Sah[26] writes in Gaon Connection that, "Uttar Pradesh tops the list with 59,853 reported cases in 2019. West Bengal and Assam, who make it to the top five states, are also not far behind at 30,394 and 30,025 reported cases of crime against women in 2019, respectively. Incidentally, West Bengal failed to provide its 2019 data for crime against women; hence its 2018 data had to be used in the 2019 report. Both the eastern states have women's helplines, but unlike Assam, which has a dedicated toll-free number, the toll-free helpline in West Bengal (1091) is still to function. For now, there are landline helpline numbers that work only during weekdays between 10 am and 5.30 pm. As per the Kolkata police website, on International Women's Day, 1091 was announced as the toll-free woman helpline number for the state. However, 1091 is not active yet. The situation is even worse at district levels. For instance, in Cooch Behar district, the post of protection officer for domestic violence has been lying vacant for almost a year now. The legal probation officer is doing both the jobs."

The Statesman[27] reported that "Are women safe in our city, Kolkata, also known as the 'cultural capital' of India? One would assume that the famed 'bhadralok' tag on the men who were known for their chivalrous demeanor, who would spring up to defend any woman in trouble, should have read in the affirmative. Unfortunately, the reality is quite the opposite. Even more shocking is that girls as young as six years of age have been molested, that too, in their school." Further, Snigdhendu Bhattacharya[28] reported that "West Bengal's capital Kolkata was one of the safest cities for women in the country but the state recorded the highest number of cases of domestic violence, the latest National Crime Records Bureau (NCRB) statistics for 2016 shows."

In line with the reports and articles published in different newspapers, when the researcher asked "Do you think women are safe and secured in Bengal?" 18.27 percent of respondents in the survey data said that women were safe and secured in the state while the opposite view was expressed by 44.35 percent of respondents. In this regard 18.01 percent of people said "Maybe", and 19.35 percent of respondents did not respond.

Table: 6.16 Do you think women are safe and secured in Bengal?

Opinion	Number of respondents	%
Yes	68	18.27
No	165	44.35
Maybe	67	18.01
Non respondents	72	19.35
Total	372	100

Source: Survey data

There is not a state in India where gender equality has been established. Not only that, except in a few Nordic countries such as Norway, Sweden, etc. equality of men and women is not found anywhere in the world. In the case of West Bengal, the majority of respondents (46.77%) in the present survey also believed that gender equality has not been established (46.77%), while about one-third of the respondents i.e. 29.03 percent people have expressed that there is gender equality in the state. On the other hand, 8.87 percent of respondents were not sure about the status of women, and 15.31 percent of respondents did not respond at all.

Table: 6.17 Do you think gender equality has been established here in Bengal?

Opinion	Number of respondents	%
Yes	108	29.03
No	174	46.77
Maybe	33	8.87
Non respondents	57	15.31
Total	372	100

Source: Survey data

The future of a nation lies in the strength and well-being of the students. Hence, the infrastructure of the schools, well-being of students as well as teachers depends largely on the valid managing committees of the schools. But after the formation of the managing committees in 2015, there are thousands of schools in the state where no new Managing Committees were formed or reformed, and even there neither the managing committees nor administrators to run the schools. The main work of the managing committee is to discuss and decide the implementation of all developmental schemes of the institutions; see the interests of the students such as providing uniforms; oversee the Mid-Day-Meal distribution, buy library books, repair school building, use the composite grant, construct new classrooms, etc. Also, the managing committee's approval is required to sanction medical leaves of teachers, give 20 years' benefit to the teachers, and in many such important matters. But, for the last 2-3 years (say from December 2018 to May 2021) there is no President as well as valid managing committees in thousands of schools in the state. Hence, all the development works of those schools have been halted.

In the present survey, a question was asked to know the attitude of the respondents. The majority of respondents (36.02%) are aware of the situation that there are no valid managing committees in many schools in the state, while about a quarter of respondents (23.65%) are unaware of it. Quite naturally a similar number of respondents 26.07 percent said "Maybe", and 14.24 percent of people kept silent in this question.

Table: 6.18 Do you know many High Schools in Bengal have not valid Managing Committee?

Opinion	Number of respondents	%

Yes	134	36.02
No	88	23.65
Maybe	97	26.07
Non respondents	53	14.24
Total	372	100

Source: Survey data

In the run-up to the Lok Sabha elections, the prime minister Narendra Modi had blamed the Mamata-led government for imposing what he called a Triple T: 'Trinamool Tolabaji Tax'. Tolabaji stands for organized extortion. He went on to claim that the Centre had approved infrastructure projects worth Rs. 90,000 crore for West Bengal, but the state government was not interested in implementing them because the 'syndicate raj' there did not get their cut. Varieties of newspapers have been vocal in 2019 after the chief minister herself announced her party comrades to return the cut money, they extracted, to the people.

Newspaper reports highlighted that, corruption has plumbed such depths that even widows or relatives of the dead were not spared. For example, the current rate card for releasing Rs. 2,000 the state government gives to the poor to cremate a relative is Rs. 200. And a widow cannot access her right to a monthly pension of Rs. 1,000 if she fails to pay a bribe of Rs. 2,000 to Rs 3,000 to the local Trinamool dada. But the tide is slowly turning with public anger forcing Trinamool panchayat members to commit in writing that they would refund the bribe money. When Modi and the Left accused the CM of institutionalizing corruption, Mamata brushed them off, hoping the charges won't stick. After ceding space to the BJP in the Lok Sabha elections, she appears to have realized the groundswell of resentment against the Trinamool's extortionists and wanted to cleanse her image, hence the call to return the cut money. By distancing herself from the wrongdoers, she was also trying to create a halo of being a saint who was untouched by the party's political filth. Whether or not people see her as St. Mamata will be known when civic body polls happen next year.[29]

The TMC government has become a synonym of corrupted government. Many of its leaders are alleged to have links with criminal and corruption activities. It often complains that a section of government officials are involved in corruption. Bribe-taking has become a normal practice in several departments in the State. When asked if people support the corrupt practices of the government officers sitting in various departments, only a small percentage of people (6.45%) supported, how did they support – it is beyond anyone's knowledge; while the majority of the respondents (72.04%) quite naturally did not support the corrupt practices of some government departments. Only 7.24 percent of respondents said "Maybe" and 14.24 percent of respondents did not respond.

Table: 6.19 Do you support the corrupt practices of some government departments?

Opinion	Number of respondents	%
Yes	24	6.45
No	268	72.04
May be	27	7.25
Non respondents	53	14.24
Total	372	100

Source: Survey data

There were whispers in the party's inner circles that Mamata had been advised by the poll strategist Prashant Kishore to publicly acknowledge the cut-money racket to portray a clean image. But after the initial steps to repay the cut money by the TMC members and office bearers, it seemed the government became silent and, in turn, inspired the party workers and leaders to be more corrupted. Mamata Banerjee has been known for her very clean image and she is also renowned for her anti-corruption image throughout the country. But being the chief minister, if she does not control the corruption of the departments, officials, and party leaders, it exposes her inability. And this, in turn, allows people to consider her weak, or supportive of the corrupt practices of her 'own people'.

Newspaper reperts[30] even in 2014 highlighted that the CBI probe into Saradha and Rose Valley scams has already embarrassed the Trinamool Congress, along with the arrest of its senior leaders. Also, the handing over of probe into the Narada sting operation scandal to the Central Bureau of Investigation was the third big blow to chief minister Mamata Banerjee within three years of her chief ministership. In Saradha blow Madam Mitra, the then Sports and transport minister and a confidante of the CM was arrested on December 12, 2014. Rajya Sabha MP Srinjoy Bose, Vice-president Rajat Majumder were also jailed. The then high-profile leader of TMC Mukul Roy was also grilled. People watched on television screens to take about Rs. 5 lakh by Trinamool leaders in Narada videos. Further, in 2016 Mamata Banerjee's government faced a major controversy when the under-construction Vivekananda Road flyover in North Kolkata was collapsed that killed 27 people.

When asked to the people "Do you believe that the present government is indifferent to controlling the corruption?" 45.96 percent of respondents responded "Yes", but 20.43 percent of respondents did not believe in that. On the other hand, 12.90 percent of respondents said "Maybe" and 20.68 percent of respondents did not reply at all. Respondents say that the highest authorities are involved in corruption. Another respondent uttered that, "I think that the government should hike the salaries of the employees with the effect of pay commission because employees are not satisfied with the present pay of the state government."

Table: 6.20 Do you believe that the present government is indifferent to controlling the corruption?

Opinion	Number of respondents	%
Yes	171	45.96
No	76	20.43
Maybe	48	12.90
Non respondents	77	20.68
Total	372	100

Source: Survey data

The chief minister became very visible and overactive, and her sudden visit to different hospitals, markets, and offices showed her intention to give transparent and corruption-free governance. But after a few months, she was not visible on roads as was seen in the initial few months of her headship. From the survey data, it was found that the majority of the respondents (53.49%) believed that the chief minister was not as much stricter as she exhibited after winning in 2011. On the other hand, only 18.27 percent of respondents felt that she was equally strict as she was before the 2011 elections. On the other hand, 16.39 percent of respondents said, "Maybe", while 11.81 percent of respondents did not make any response at all.

Table: 6.21 Do you believe that the Chief Minister is not as stricter as she shown after winning in 2011?

Opinion	Number of respondents	%
Yes	199	53.49
No	68	18.27
Maybe	61	16.39
Non respondents	44	11.81
Total	372	100

Source: Survey data

The vigorous election campaignings in West Bengal indicated a tough war between the Trinamool Congress and the Bharatiya Janat Party. The CPI (M) and Indian National Congress parties had little relevance in the State as they lost public confidence in the last seven decades. Besides, these two parties were not seen in any movements, or inaction of public assistance in different emergency works such as in natural calamities like Amphan, or COVID-19 pandemic victims. The BJP made a strategy to win the hearts of Bengal's electorates by declaring scores of expensive and lucrative development schemes from farmers to fishermen. However, people of this State were in a dilemma if the TMC will be able to continue good governance, or the BJP will be able to give better governance with transparency. From the survey data, it came to light that, majority of the respondents (50.53%) believed that the government will not be able to give good governance with transparency in its 3rd phase, if it comes back in power in 2021 elections, while 13.97 percent respondents did not believe so. On the other hand, a small percentage of respondents i.e., 16.39 percent said "Maybe", while 19.08 percent of respondents did not make any response at all.

Table: 6.22 Do you believe this government will be able to give good governance with transparency in its third phase, if it wins in 2021 elections?

Opinion	Number of respondents	%
Yes	52	13.97
No	188	50.53
Maybe	61	16.39
Non respondents	71	19.08
Total	372	100

Source: Survey data

A different view was expressed by a large number of respondents. The majority of respondents (52.95%) believed that, if the BJP comes to power in 2021 it will be able to give better governance with transparency, while 31.72 percent of respondents did not believe so. On the other hand, only 7.25 percent of respondents said "Maybe", and a mere 8.06 percent of respondents did not respond at all.

Table: 6.23 Do you believe the BJP will be able o give better governance with transparency if it wins in 2021 elections?

Opinion	Number of respondents	%
Yes	197	52.95
No	118	31.72
Maybe	27	7.25
Non respondents	30	8.06
Total	372	100

Source: Survey data

Al last the respondents were asked "Do you believe that the BJP is the best alternative in West Bengal in 2021?", the majority of respondents 51.34 percent replied in affirmative while only 12.09 percent of respondents said "No". On the other hand, 11.82 percent of respondents said it might be, and the question was completely avoided by 24.72 percent of respondents.

Table: 6.24 Do you believe that the BJP is the best alternative in West Bengal in 2021?

Opinion	Number of respondents	%
Yes	191	51.34
No	45	12.09
Maybe	44	11.82
Non respondents	92	24.72
Total	372	100

Source: Survey data

Conclusions

This chapter highlights the perception of the respondents on various issues that came up prior to the general elections of West Bengal in 2021. A few more significant issues came up later with the approach of the election dates. As the survey was conducted online between September to November 2020, many momentous issues such as an arrest of the TMC coal mafia by CID, change of party by Suvendu Adhikary, and others from TMC to BJP, fracture of the leg of the chief minister, etc. remained out of the plate of the respondents. However, the survey data show that the majority of respondents were not satisfied with the performance of the Trinamool Congress government as a whole, and particularly with a large number of its leaders, and policies that were compartmentalized with certain sections of society. The issues of cut money, tolabaji of a section of its leaders, corruption in recruitment, gender inequality, women's security, mismanagement of school administration, lack of opportunity in decent jobs for the educated youths in the State made a large number of respondents, though the sample size was very small in comparison to the population of the State, dissatisfied with the government. This trend was transparent, the public judgment was also clearly indicative in favor of a change. The pre-election hyped and colorful campaign of BJP, the rush for joining by MLAs, MPs, and Ministers of TMC and others in the BJP camp, and jump into action by the whole of BJP stalwarts in Bengal created an affirmative atmosphere in Bengal. And the BJP appeared to be the best alternative to the present government. But with the approach of election dates the rise of hope and aspirations of electors in Bengal could not be held high and honored by the BJP. Are the policies of BJP's top leadership responsible for such a debacle in Bengal? Are the electors turned aversed apathetic to the turncoat and tainted leaders of BJP? Was language a problem for the Bengal's electors? To know the reasons at length let us read the following chapter.

Chapter – VII

Arguments for BJP's Debacle in Assembly Elections

"Don't worry when you are not recognized, but strive to be worthy of recognition."

- *Abraham Lincoln*

Introduction

West Bengal, along with three other states viz. Kerala, Tamil Nadu, Assam, and one Union Territory (UT) Puducherry, concluded the elections of 294 members of Legislative Assembly on 29 April, and results of all States and UT came out on the 2nd day of May. There were a few exceptional incidents in these elections. The most significant aspect of the latest Assembly elections in Kerala was the comeback of the Left Democratic Front (LDF) led by Chief Minister Pinaryi Vijayan for the second consecutive term 'in a state that had not returned an incumbent government in four decades.'[1]Interestingly, the Bharatiya Janata Party could not open its account in the state. So, Kerala is now the only state Assembly House in India that has no representative from the BJP. On the other hand, with the entire team of BJP, it was badly defeated in Bengal. However, in the case of Kerala, experts believe that the prompt and able handling of the Covid-19 pandemic brought back Vijayan for the second term.

However, in Tamil Nadu, the DMK and its allies including the Indian National Congress won a landslide victory in the 234-seat House defeating its bitter opponent, the AIADMK which had been ruling since 2011. To form the government, a party or an alliance needed 118 seats, and the DMK alone under the strong leadership of Muthuvel Karunanidhi Stalin, in short, MK Stalin alone won 133 seats while its opponent, the ruling AIADMK, won only 66 seats. In Assam, the BJP-led NDA retained its power. In the 126-member Assembly House, the Bharatiya Janata Party had won 60 seats alone, while its allies

Asom Gana Parishad won 9 seats, and the United People's Party Liberal won 6 seats. Among the 33 seats of Puducherry's Legislative Assembly, the National Democratic Alliance comprising All India NR Congress won in 10 seats, the AIADMK and the BJP won in 6 seats. The NDA attained a clear majority in the elections.

The most interesting election results came from West Bengal. The BJP, despite putting its full focus, strength, and attention on Bengal, failed to cross three digits which proved true to the words of Prashant Kishore, the poll strategist who challenged the BJP ab initio citing if it (BJP) crosses three digits, he will leave his profession. Such was the level of self-confidence, credence, and boldness of a professional poll strategist like PK before whom the entire BJP team was flattened on the ground. At the end of the day, the scoreboard showed that Mamata Banerjee, the TMC supremo, for whom PK worked as a strategist, alone won in 213 seats, 2 seats more than that she won in 2016, and the BJP had to satisfy itself with only 77 seats. Another striking fact was that the CPI(M) made an alliance with the decaying Indian National Congress party, and insignificant Rashtriya Secular Majlis Party, while both the two former parties failed to open their account in Bengal, which is again a record in Bengal politics since independence for both the INC and the CPI(M). All the leaders of these two parties were seen to fall flat on their faces with the declaration of election results. This indicated the fall of the tyrannical and disruptive politics and bad governance in Bengal rendered by both the Left and the Right parties in two cycles from 1947 to 1977, and from 1977 to 2011; and the absolute rejection of slogans like '*Bhenge dao, guriye dao*' (break down, Smash down), '*Manchi na, Manbo na*' (Not obeying, will not obey), '*Cholche na, Cholbe na*' (is not running, will not run); and disruptive politics of '*Chakka Jam*' (shut down of wheels), bandhs, hartals and frequent strikes of the Left and the ultra-Left parties. The dismantling and destroying political agenda of the Left parties were discarded incompletely by the people in 2011 partly and absolutely in 2021.

The most eye-catching part and focus of the 2021 elections in Bengal was centered around Mamata Banerjee on the one hand, and the combination of the Prime Minister, Home Minister, party president J.P. Nadda, a bunch of BJP Chief Ministers, and Union Ministers together on the other. The frequent visit of Prime Minister, Home Minister, and

J.P. Nadda for campaigning in favor of their candidates roused a mixed reaction of astonishment and curiosity among the common electors of Bengal. Considering their regular visits in Bengal to fight against Mamata Banerjee, a substantial number of people in the state in particular and in the country as a whole including media houses gave them the epithet of 'daily passengers' and compared them with Chengis Khan, or Nadir Shah, who invaded India several times with an aim to loot its valuable treasures.

The enticement to opponent leaders and accommodating them in the party and finally giving tickets to many of them without checking their credentialties was boomeranged to the BJP because it hurt the dignity, labor, and aspiration of the BJP workers who have been working sincerely and faced all hardships in the soil of Bengal. The joining in BJP by hundreds and thousands of TMC supporters and members including sitting Ministers like Suvendu Adhikary, Rajib Banerjee, and MLAs such as Baishali Dalmia, Sonali Guha, Sital Sardar, Dipendu Biswas, Rabindranath Bhattacharya, Jatu Lahiri, and others increased the enthusiasm and aspiration of the high-ranking saffron leaders, and they started day-dreaming of winning in 'more than 200 seats' to conquer the Nabanna. The former MLA and Kolkata Mayor Sovan Chatterjee along with his girlfriend Baishakhi Banerjee, Debashree Roy, the MLA of Raidighi left the hand of Mamata Banerjee and joined the BJP in search of fortune, but their dream shattered in bites. The same was the misfortune to many turncoat MLAs. They lost everything – the love and affection of Mamata Banerjee; the faith of their supporters; and their chances of coming back in mainstream politics forever. They remained nowhere. Against the above backdrop, the elections of 2021 were fought by the Bharatiya Janata Party. Now, let us examine the reasons why the party was defeated in the elections? Let us explore the omnifarious and presumptive consideration in short.

Reasons for Deplorable Defeat of the BJP in Bengal

Despite all the apparently veritable and explicit wave of affirmation, the final verdict of the Janta Janardhan (electorate) went in disfavor of the BJP. Close scrutiny of the ground situation from the eyes of an independent researcher can be highlighted here.

1. BJP opened wide its doors for tainted persons on the eve of elections

On the eve of Legislative Assembly elections the BJP, an upstart in Bengal opened wide its doors and windows facilitating all persons including persons with "tainted image", "Turncoat image", "Corrupted image" and such from all parties to enter in its "bedroom". Though Dilip Ghosh, the president of Bengal's BJP, initially aired his perception saying "Whom we shall allow in our bedroom, and whom to keep at our drawing-room, and ultimately whom we will allow up to our kitchen, we will decide" ultimately accepted and welcomed them, maybe, by pressure from Delhi Head Quarters (I presume); he ultimately failed to stop the flow of *'Beno Jal'* in the clean watery image of Bengal BJP.

2. Fielded many corrupted leaders of its own and of TMC

Fielding many corrupted leaders, the BJP campaigned against Corruption. It was ridiculous to the voters. The poll rights group Association for Democratic Reforms (ADR) released a report analyzing all 191 candidates contested in the first phase of the election.[2] It indicated that "12 (41%) out of 29 candidates analyzed from Bharatiya Janata Party (BJP)" have declared themselves with criminal cases in their affidavits, while its most prominent rival TMC filed 10 (35%), tainted candidates, out of 29 total. Another report published in the Anandabazar Patrika[3] highlighting a joint report prepared by West Bengal Election Watch and Association for Democratic Reforms (ADR) pointed out that there was 20 percent of candidates contested in the latest elections had criminal charges. More shockingly it exposed that most of the criminal cases were pending against the BJP candidates. Out of 293 candidates of the BJP candidates, 144 candidates are having serious criminal charges; that indicated almost half of their candidates were seriously charged in various criminal cases. Out of TMC's 209 candidates, 98 candidates had serious cases pending against them. Interestingly, the CPIM is also not much behind their other above-mentioned counterparts. They fielded 58 candidates out of their total 139 who had serious criminal charges against them.

3. BJP fielded many 'outsiders and turncoats' in the elections

Fielding many 'outsiders and turncoats' by the BJP in the elections created confusion and anguish amongst the traditional hardcore BJP leaders and workers. It hurt the sentiment of the local leaders and supporters who had been working for long in the aspiration of getting tickets to contest in elections. When the BJP accepted Suvendu Adhikary, Rajib Banerjee, Baishali Dalmia, Dinesh Trivedi, Biswajit Kundu, Jitender Tiwari, and others and gave them tickets to fight the elections from different constituencies; it did not think for a moment, nor examined the pros and cons about the 'patriots', 'supporters' and 'workers' who had been fighting for making ground in Bengal inch by inch for last one decade or more. This made a lot of BJP workers and supporters either indifferent or anti-BJP in Bengal. It made a negative impact on the election results. In the aftermath of the election results, the blame game was apparent within the BJP. It came to light that, "Inside the BJP, a blame-game is on over giving nominations to those who came from other parties on a priority basis. A senior state unit leader, who spoke on the condition of anonymity, cited how workers broke out in agitations in most of these losing seats soon after the outgoing MLAs from other parties were named as the BJP candidate."[4] One week before the elections in Bengal, around 70 BJP workers from Kalna Assembly in East Burdwan joined Trinamool Congress to express their disgust with the BJP for nominating controversial Trinamool turncoat Biswajit. One Prabir Mondal of the team said, "We left six years ago for the BJp to protest Kundu's corruption. We were shocked when Kundu joined the BJP and got the ticket."[5]

4. BJP puzzled its own workers as well as supporters of turncoats

The BJP leadership was puzzled by the huge influx of TMC MLAs. Total 34 TMC legislators joined the ranks of BJP after leaving Mamata Banerjee's hand, but only 13 of them got tickets from BJP. "As the race to the West Bengal elections heats up, there has been a flurry of leaders from the ruling Trinamool Congress (TMC) joining the ranks of the Bharatiya Janata Party (BJP). The list of leaders leaving TMC for the BJP includes some prominent names like Suvendu Adhikari, Mukul Roy, and celebrity-turned-politician Mithun Chakraborty."[6] The BJP leadership was puzzled as to what to do and how to accommodate these huge numbers of turncoat MLAs. These legislators left the TMC either due to differences with the party, being denied a ticket by the TMC this time, or due to the belief that their future lies with the BJP and not the TMC. But when they did not get a ticket from BJP their future hung in gigantic uncertainty, and it caused anger and dissatisfaction among the aspirant MLAs as well as their supporters. Without getting tickets from BJP, the TMC-left out MLAs turned to merely a single elector, while the supporters of these MLAs were perplexed as to whom they would extend their support. Thus the votes of all the supporters of newly joined TMC MLAs are cast in the basket of TMC.

5. The Election Manifesto was published late

The BJP has a record of publishing its Manifesto late as was seen in the 2014 Lok Sabha elections also. The Hindustan Times[7] reported as quoted by the then Spokesperson of BJP Smt. Nirmala Sitharaman: "The party manifesto will be released on April 7 (the first day of polling in the nine-phase general elections that will end on May 12)." In the case of West Bengal, it was published on the evening of 21st March, and named "Sonar Bangla Sankalp Patra 2021," while the elections started on 27th March. Also, it was published in Hindi and English. The majority of West Bengal's general people neither can read English nor Hindi, and most of them failed to grasp the meaning of it. Besides, the publication and circulation manager, if any, of BJP failed to distribute it among the workers in every booth of all the 294 Legislative Assembly constituencies.

6. Manifesto and its contents were not properly disseminated.

It is learned that neither all the leaders and workers of every Gram Panchayat, Block, or Booth/Municipality word of 23 districts including the candidates received the Manifesto, nor did they memorize the same. If they themselves did not clearly understand the contents – the real treasures - of the manifesto, how could they disseminate the same amongst the voters? And if the electors were not savvy of the developmental schemes and benefits the BJP was going to deliver and those benefits were much higher, more attractive, and more inclusive than that of the TMC manifesto, how could the electors cast their votes in favor of BJP candidates?

7. Fear of losing family pension by government employees

The greatest bait of the 7th Pay Commission was rejected by the government employees in the state. Why? It happened because the panic of losing family pension grasped them all, while it might be the single agendum that could cast favorable votes through postal ballots in favor of BJP candidates. In the 21st century, it is folly to judge the Bengalee people as 'idiots' because they keep a close eye on every activity and action of the Union Government in other states - the latest example is Tripura, our neighboring state. Hence, the words or promises of not withdrawing family pension scheme in the Manifesto from Bengal could give better dividends to the BJP in the election results. The artifice act of the manifesto makers was caught by the intellectuals in the state. Hence, the government employees desisted from casting postal ballots to the BJP's basket.

8. The Income Tax (IT) policy of the Union government annoyed the employees

Up to Rs.2.5 lakh income, IT for an individual taxpayer is free; in the second slab from Rs.2.5 lakh to Rs.5.00 lakh IT to be paid is 5%; then comes the big jump - from 5% to 20% income tax payment for individuals earning yearly from Rs.5.01 lakh to Rs.10 lakh. And as soon as one's yearly income crosses Rs.10 lakh, he has to pay 30% of his income to the Government as IT. The highest saving option is only up to Rs.1.5 lakh, which has been prevailing for more than a decade. This system needs revision considering the benefit of the employees. If you pay greater benefit to the government employees they will, in turn, give you a greater number of votes – this is a simple equation. But the opposite action of the BJP government in Delhi annoyed the government employees in Bengal too, which was reflected in the EVM causing lower postal ballots from the government employees to the BJP's tray.

9. The wave of farmers' movement in Delhi broke on the shore of the Bay of Bengal.

The BJP through its manifesto of 2021 promised to pay financial assistance to the farmers –"We will implement PM Kisan Samman Nidhi with the increased financial assistance of Rs. 10,000 per year to each of the 75 lakh farmers in the first cabinet meeting."[8] The Home Minister, the Prime Minister, and the BJP president told in some campaigns in a few places, and in a television interview in ABP Ananda (with Sri Amit Shah) that the BJP, if comes in power, would pay Rs.6000 x 3 months = Rs.18,000 plus Rs.10,000 at a time to all the farmers. On the other hand, the TMC declared "to pay Rs. 10,000 per acre support to be provided to 68 Lakh small and marginal farmers under the Krishak Bandhu Scheme."[9] Further, the Prime Minister said at Haripal, Hooghly that, "…When Bengal's BJP chief minister, Bengal's BJP government will take the oath, I'll surely attend that ceremony: I'll come and tell the new chief minister that brother, I have to send this money from Delhi, please implement this fast in the first cabinet (meeting)… And listen, every farmer of Bengal… will be getting the total arrears of Rs. 18,000 in his bank account… I'll say that before Durga Puja the money should reach the accounts of every farmer."[10] Why did the farmers' choose TMC's offer, instead of BJP's? The reasons are 1. Maybe the farmers did not understand the promises of Hindi-speaking star campaigners – PM Modi, and HM Shah; 2. Maybe the BJP leaders failed to reach out with this message of BJP's manifesto to the farmers; 3. Maybe the Farmers' movement in Delhi created an atmosphere of disbelief on the BJP's promises.

The leaders of the farmers' movement came to West Bengal and campaigned heavily for 'No vote to BJP' in the pre-election period. Quite naturally they were happy when the election result went in favor of TMC. When the Trinamool Congress Party was getting more seats and was ahead of BJP in Bengal on 2nd May, the day of the counting of votes, the farmers from Punjab and Haryana reacted first by distributing laddoos to the neighbors as the Samyukt Kisan Morcha (SKM), an umbrella body of farmers' unions, had held 'No vote to BJP' rallies in West Bengal to protest against the three farm laws. The farmers also celebrated the defeat of the BJP at Delhi's Singh and Tikri borders. A news report, written by Kusum Arora citing comment of Jagseer Singh, a farmer associated with BKU (*Ekta Ugrahan*) from Bhatinda, was published in The Wire that suggests: "The BJP's loss in Bengal is a big boost to the farmers' protest, as SKM leaders campaigned against them. [Narendra] Modi's arrogance has taken a toll on his own party. Had the Modi government listened to farmers and repealed the three black laws, they might have won Bengal. Even now it is not too late and the Central government should scrap these laws, else they should get ready to face a complete rout in Uttar Pradesh in the 2022 assembly elections."[11]

10. Mamata's card of *Bahiragata* created a sense of nationalism among the Bengalees

A recent report of India Today reveals that the issue of 'Bahiragata' not only created a sensation among the supporters of TMC, but it ultimately played a catalytic role in giving birth to nationalism among the rank and file of Bengal's voters. Ananya Bhattacharya wrote, "Week after week, as BJP national leaders went out to talk religious identity in Hindi, Mamata addressed the masses in coarse Bangla, the Bangla they understand. Every time the average Bengali saw the respected Prime Minister take digs against their CM, Mamata consolidated her base. And then, the final nail in the coffin for Bengal BJP flew in on the sturdy arms of a virus."[12]

11. PM's gesture was unacceptable to the people

Moreover, the Hon'ble PM's gesture and throwing of the words "Didi - O - Didi" with a long pronouncement, and "Clapping with two hands" were not accepted by the gentry of Bengal irrespective of political ideology. A section of scholars, teachers, and government officers said in private, "This is unmatched with the stature of a PM of India when compared with Jawaharlal Nehru, Atal Behari Vajpayee, or Dr. Manmohan Singh, his predecessors". The Indian Express quoted Sashi Panja, a TMC state minister, who in a press conference expressed her disgust and anguish: "Today, we are all perturbed that the prime minister and home minister of the country are not respecting their positions. The prime minister is speaking in a leering, joking tone much of a hater of women he is. It is quite unfortunate that it is clear from his speeches how the prime minister is using this kind of language...... Can you speak like this about someone? Is it correct? Can a Prime

Minister speak publicly about a chief minister in this manner? Why should the prime minister stoop so low that one is compelled to call him a harasser and provoker of women?"[13] The same views were expressed by Medinipur's TMC candidate actress June Malia. She said, "This is not just an insult to Mamata Banerjee but to ll the women of Bengal this is an insult to the concept of womanhood. For 25 years, Mamata Banerjee was an MP and also a minister several times. To date, no prime minister has insulted her the way the current prime minister has. This shows the level to which the JP has sunk."

When the Prime Minister and his team were busy campaigning in Bengal, the young internet lover electors in Bengal found an uncanny picture and videos of north India wherefiom Modiji, Amit Shah and Yogi Adityanath ascended. "They saw scenes of dead bodies piling up outside crematoiics in North India. The BJP-ruled Uttar Pradesh; Delhi, where PM Modi sits (no one quite cares about Kejriwal), were overflowing with the sick and the dead."[14] When Yogi Adityanath warned the goons of TMC to face criminals in UP, the goons were united against the BJP. What actually Adityanath said? "Once the BJP forms a government in Bengal, the TMC goons will meet the same fate as the goons in UP. They will be on their knees after poll results. Goons sheltered by the TMC will be tracked and sent behind bars within a month o the formation of the new government. We will punish those who are part of the syndicate raj and demand cut money from people.[15]

Further, the Indian Expressed reported in its April 8 Kolkata issue that, Uttar Pradesh chief minister Yogi Adityanath in a public meeting in Hooghly district expressed his apprehension for women's safety in the State. So, he asserted that anti-Romeo squads will be formed in West Bengal once the BJP forms a government in West Bengal.[16] The majority of youths of this state did not accept his promise of forming 'Anti-Romeo' squads to evict loving couples from parks and other places of the State.

12. BJP's *hindutva* card turned as a boomerang

The card of Hindutva played by the Prime Minister, the Home Minister, and Yogi Adityanath in Bengal was not accepted by the people en bloc. The visit of the Prime Minister to Orankandi in Bangladesh and the tall promises to the Matua voters could not wet the minds of the so-called backward people. This too much-polarized politics and articulation of the same by the Hon'ble Prime Minister and Home Minister were not accepted by the liberal electorates in Bengal. See what happened to the Muslim voters, Matua voters, and many Hindi-speaking voters in Kolkata, and its surrounding districts such as North and South 24 Parganas. They turned their faces away from the BJP as a whole.

13. Wooing religious leaders with allurement proved fatal

A futile attempt was taken by BJP to woo the religious leaders. In response to the promise of Mamata Banerjee's government to give a monthly stipend of Rs. 1000 to 8000 poor Brahmin priests facing a financial crisis and provide houses to those who need one'17 and providing houses to those who need one and her announcement of earlier stipend (in 2012) of Rs. 2500 to the Imams of all mosques; the BJP through its manifesto declared that "We will set up a Purohit Welfare Board where all the purohits across West Bengal will be given a monthly honorarium of Rs. 3000."[18]

14. Use of CBI and ED before elections was a handiwork of BJP

The use of Central agencies prior to the assembly elections was not liked by the general voters in Bengal and other states. It was claimed by the Congress in Puducherry that the Union Government has been misusing its agencies to pull down its elected governments in the state. Puducherry Congress in-charge Dinesh Gundu Rao expressed his anxiety that, the actions of the BJP ruled central government using agencies such as CBI, I-T department, ED, who have threatened, blackmailed, and coerced their MLAs.[19]

The Enforcement Directorate has sent notices to Principal Secretary to the Chief Minister Gautam Sanyal and Additional Chief Secretary of Animal Resources Development Department BP Gopalika in connection with the probe of the Metro Dairy case when the election was knocking at the door. Earlier also notice was served to state Home Secretary H.K. Dwivedi by the ED in this connection. The investigating agency has also summoned state Security Advisor and former Director-General Surajit Kar Purkayastha and another IPS officer Rajat Majumdar in connection with the Saradha chit fund scam. The investigating agencies have summoned many more politicians, bureaucrats, and officers of West Bengal just prior to the elections which indicates the ill-intention of the central agencies.[20]

The act of mere calling the main opposition leaders (sometimes symbolically a few of its own party leaders who were corrupted and were charged so earlier), their supporters, and high-rank governmental officials without taking any final actions made it a child's play to the voters in Bengal. People started questioning as to why the CBI and ED call the tainted and corrupted leaders, politicians, bureaucrats, and others from the Opposition party before the elections only. Where do they remain throughout the year? Why only the selected opponent party leaders are house arrested or called prior to the elections? Are they acting on behalf of the Union Government led by BJP? Were they sleeping throughout the years? Thus, this over-activism of the central agencies posed a negative impact upon the general voters in Bengal, which was reflected in the vote-box.

15. BJP's failure to give dummy agents

In almost every Assembly Constituency there were one or more dummy candidates of the TMC party who contested with the different symbol(s). They were also eligible to nominate booth agents equally along with the main candidates. These dummy candidates and their election agents also nominated booth agents, and counting agents who were actually the TMC party insiders, and they often assisted the other booth agents of TMC's principal candidate within the booth; sometimes jammed the booths, or helped in identifying the blind or infirm voters; offered cold drinks and biriyani packets or fed chicken/mutton curry with rice to the polling officers; supplied tea as many times as desired by the polling teams; intimidated the Presiding Officers or other Polling Officers within the booth, and finally cast votes in the afternoon for those who were debarred (often threatened on the eve of election day for not to come to the polling booths for casting votes) to attend in the polling booth to cast their votes. Also, the agents of dummy candidates attended the counting process. These disguised agents often, being many in numbers of the same party in different names or for different candidates, take the advantageous position and try to influence the counting officers, or endeavor to manipulate the counting process. The BJP has failed to counter these efforts of the TMC party.

16. Faulty campaign strategy

BJP's focus of the campaign was faulty. All the prominent campaigners in Bengal came from a Hindi-speaking zone, and they all spoke in Hindi except for PM's *'tuti-futi'* Bengali and Smriti Irani's un-intellectual public speech in Bengali. The UP model or Bihar model or Gujarat model of campaigning was not percipient and admissible in Bengal, which the topmost BJP leaders failed to understand. This caused more damage to the public sentiment. There was a lack of ardent appeal from the Prime Minister, Home Minister, and other speakers for casting votes in favor of all the BJP candidates only. There was the absence of developmental promises and schemes from the speeches of high-ranking leaders. There was no comparative analysis of achievements of other BJP ruled states with that of Bengal's Mamata Banerjee government. India's success story in the last 6 years, its industrialization, economic development, and increase of GDP could not be highlighted in comparison with Bengal's growth story. Instead of that, almost all the top leaders focused on blaming the chief minister and her nephew – calling Pishi and Bhaipo. In addition to that, the citation of Anti Romeo squad by Yogi Adityanath was not accepted by Bengal's average youths. Besides, the words like *'ghuspetia'*, *'tustikaran'*, *'bhrastachar'*, *'chiriya'*, *'sankalpa patra'*, etc. used by Hon'ble PM, HM and J.P. Nadda and other Hindi-speaking star campaigners of BJP with different pronouncement styles were not understood by the common masses who gathered in the meetings, and rallies as well as the people who watched the rallies on the television screen. People watched colorful TV programs and the stunning spread of rose petals by the Home Minister on the roads of Bengal created a negative impact upon the minds of electors.

17. Eight-phase elections were unscientific during the COVID-19 pandemic

The declaration of elections in 8 phases by the Election Commission, and not clubbing the last 3 phases together during the super-spread of Corona Virus in Bengal, intensified the tension, anxiety, and anger of the people against the Union Government, which was made an issue by the TMC supremo. But the counter-narrative, though issued by the Election Commission, was not produced by the BJP intellectuals or its party spokespersons and leaders everywhere. It was a failure of the BJP leadership.

It was clearly informed by the Election Commission well in advance in the first week of March that massive violence was the only reason behind such month-long elections in Bengal, which the BJP leaders failed to propagate among its voters in Bengal. The Hindustan Times (March 4, 2021) reported that there have been at least 1,500 incidents of political violence between mid-2019 and the end of 2020, resulting in 118 deaths. Of the three other states and the Union territory of Puducherry that went to polls around the same time, Kerala, Tamil Nadu, and Puducherry will vote in a single-phase; Assam will vote in three. The last assembly elections in Bengal, in 2016, were held in 6 phases; and the one before that, in 2011, was held in 6 phases as well. The assessment, which was provided on January 9, 2021, captured the extent of the violence that took place during the 2018 panchayat elections, the parliamentary elections in 2019, and the run-up to the 2021 assembly polls. Overall, 693 election-related violent incidents were observed around polling dates in 2019. This resulted in the EC taking up such a decision. But were the BJP leaders successful in making the voters understood this fact fully and clearly?

18. Abnormal hike in the price of petrol and cooking gas angered electors

The abnormal hike in the price of Gas, petrol, edible oil, and some other essential commodities during the elections angered the common electors in Bengal, and it was fanned skillfully and artistically by the TMC leadership. Mamata Banerjee successfully raised the issue before her voters, but the BJP failed to counter her argument with a proper explanation. Maybe the reasons were not adequately known by the BJP leaders, or unaware of the fact behind the price hike. The price of LPG has doubled from Rs. 410.5 per 14.5-kg cylinder on March 1, 2014 to Rs. 835 on 6.5.2021; kerosene sold to the poor through the public distribution system (PDS) has risen from Rs.14.96 per liter in March 2014 to Rs.35.35 in March, 2021.[21] Similarly the price of petrol is now almost Rs. 95.00 per liter. As a result, the entire annoyance of common house-makers as well as vehicle owners went against the Union Government and particularly the Prime Minister and

Finance Minister, which was not addressed by the BJP leadership in rural as well as urban areas properly and squarely. This was also reflected in the ballot units in polling booths.

19. The BJP failed to counter TMC's propaganda

In West Bengal women voters were increased to 49.1 percent. Mamata Banerjee was a woman. After the bad performance in the 2019 Lok Sabha polls, Mamata Banerjee appointed *'Bongo Janani'*, a political front of the TMC whose main motto was to reach out to women by highlighting the developmental schemes of her government and 'rise in crimes against women in the BJP-ruled States. The BJP fielded Smriti Irani, who was politically novice to Mamata Banerjee. Besides, BJP's several announcements in its manifesto related to women's and girls' empowerment that touched 33 percent reservation for women in government jobs, increased pension to widows, free transport, and free education from KG to PG level was not circulated and popularized through any channel to the real beneficiaries. Mamata Banerjee's Kanyashree Prokolpo which has received global acclamation and benefitted lakhs of girl students were repeatedly told to the women audience in the campaign period. The BJP failed to counter it properly and efficiently with its lately received schemes published through the Sankolpo Potro 2021.

20. Bengal's Chanakya' Mukul Roy was wrongly used

By fielding 'Bengal's Chanakya' Mukul Roy to fight from Krishnanagar Assembly Constituency, Sri Amit Shahji made a great mistake. The National General Secretary of BJP and its Bengal unit in charge Kailash Vijayvargiya also openly acknowledged the fact at a public meeting at Keshiyari in Purba Medinipur. He said, "BJP vice-president Mulul (Roy) da is here with us. He is the 'Chanakya' of Bengal. Together we will certainly oust Banerjee's government this time."[22]

He (Roy), Suvendu Adhikary, Rajib Banerjee, Sonali Guha, Sovan Chatterjee are the persons who know all the strengths as well as loopholes of Mamata Banerjee. Mukul Roy is the key person and the second man of Mamata Banerjee who could give the best suggestions to the BJP if utilized properly. But, by keeping him away from engaging solely in making schemes, strategies, and plans for victory, the BJP facilitated the TMC party indirectly. Roy knows all the key persons in West Bengal; he knows all the areas, their strengths, and weaknesses; but remained isolated and hidden during the entire election period paving way for TMC's massive win.

Besides, if Mamata Banerjee is termed as the 'Tigress of Bengal,' Dilip Ghosh can be called the "Royal Bengal Tiger". He is the only person who can speak with Mamata Banerjee by keeping his eyes open and straight at her. But, by sidelining this "brave and skillful" leader from the focal point of campaigning and without projecting him as the 'Chief Minister', the top leader(s) in Delhi hurt public emotion. The BJP central leadership failed to strictly follow the simple principle of Management study – 'Right man should be placed in the right position.'

21. Weak and lowly informed campaigners crowded in BJP camp

There were mostly weak and lowly informed campaigners in the BJP camp. The champion campaigners were the Prime Minister and the Home Minister. They realized that by suppressing or by shadowing the Bengal's leaders they could win over the minds and hearts of Bengal's electors. Mere throwing of rose petals and showing Victory signs do not melt the minds of electors of Bengal; rather the hard words and challenging attitude of Dilip Ghosh, Raju Bandopadhyay, Mukul Roy, Sonali Guha, Baishali Dalmiya, Suvendu Adhikary, Rajib Bandopadhyay, Sovan Chatterjee could bring more dividend for BJP. But the central leadership failed to gauge the strengths, and measure the level of acceptance of these indigenous leaders of Bengal who fortunately or unfortunately came under the umbrella of BJP before elections with a view to getting respite from the misrule of the TMC government (or misbehavior of its supremo), and oppression of a section of TMC rowdies, miscreants and *tolabaj* leaders.

It was reported in various newspapers and discussed in many television channels and also complained by some BJP central leadership that the Trinamool Congress's 10-year rule was actually 'a a misrule'. Defence Minister Rajnath Singh while addressing an election rally in Joypur district on the last day of campaigning before the first phase of voting set to take place on 27th March, said, "When entire India is living in a new century, the 21st century, West Bengal is living in the 19th century. This is all because of decades of misrule by the Left parties and TMC."[23] Further, the Prime Minister upheld that, "Mamata Banerjee's government turned out to be a rebirth of the Left Front rule and the misrule and lawlessness under this regime was a far more fearful than that of the Left Front government....The government empowered corruptionists and *tolabaaji* (extortion) and ensured that Bengal lagged behind in progress when compared to other states in the region."[24]

The BJP leadership fell through to reap the benefit of the situation. Also, the dream of all newly joined leaders, workers, common electors, intellectuals, and others was torn by the faulty decisions and policies of the BJP leaders in Delhi. Why blame the central leaders? It is to be understood that, in a disciplined party structure, the members, and state-level leaders cannot raise their voice or say anything against the central leadership. They had to digest the trickle-down policies of the higher authorities.

22. The BJP leaders were daydreaming

The crowd in the meetings does never reflect the support and turning the support base into the ballot boxes. The best example of a 21-party led pre-election Brigade meeting called by Mamata Banerjee in 2019; this year's Brigade meeting of our honorable PM, as well as CPI(M)-Congress-ISF combined rally at Brigade Parade Ground. The BJP leaders were living in daydreams; instead of extensive campaigning and public contact, they were satisfied with the huge roadside mass gathering in their rallies where they assumed the role of a demigod with Victory signs and artificial smiles. This culture has not yet proven congenial in Bengal.

23. False empathy and show of love & respect for the downtrodden

The eating of BJP leaders in poor families was symbolic and a show-cause of love and respect for the backward and farmer families, which was also adopted by Rahul Gandhi in Uttar Pradesh. The Home Minister Amit Shah along with his entourage had lunch at the house of a farmer in West Bengal's Paschim Medinipur district as part of his exercise to strengthen relations with the agriculturists ahead of the Assembly elections in the state. Prior to that, in November 2020 he also had lunch at the residence of a tribal BJP worker in Bankura and the house of a 'matua' community member in North 24 Parganas.[25] What a funny act of a crorepati Home Minister of India! But this tactic is not laudable and appreciated in Bengal. Picking up a child while campaigning, and having lunch in a hut of the poor farmers may satisfy the feelings of the rich and powerful, but it gives birth to hatred and disgust for the VIP guests in most of the minds of the same caste people in society, which is a psychological game that was failed to realize by the BJP leaders.

24. BJP failed to prove Abhishek's involvement as coal mafia

The BJP leaders often raised the issue of the coal mafia connection of Abhishek Banerjee. Suvendu Adhikary released an audiotape of the conversation between an unidentified person and the main accused in the coal pilferage case Anup Majhi's aide Ganesh Bagaria and alleged Banerjee's involvement. But there was no concrete proof against Banerjee. Further, the BJP stalwarts tried to threaten and panic Abhishek Banerjee and alleged the involvement of TMC MP Abhishek Banerjee in a coal pilferage case. While Banerjee in turn challenged the Union Government and its leaders the BJP failed to prove his involvement. This proved the BJP's dirty game of maligning an Opposition party MP and leader, who happens to be the nephew of the chief minister. Banerjee upheld, "All coal assets fall directly under Centre and are guarded by the Central agencies. If BJP thinks TMC leaders got money from those illegally operating the coal assets, then what's stopping Centre from investigating all culprits who failed to manage these national assets?"[26] A very pertinent question the BJP failed to respond to properly and boldly. This became a boomerang for the BJP.

25. The BJP candidates of Bengal were dolls in the hands of (in)visible men

The BJP candidates of Bengal were not given free hand. They were encircled by some 'outside observers' or what may be called them I do not know. This mistrust of the candidates or projecting silent watchmen worked negatively upon the minds and actions of the candidates themselves. One candidate expressed that there were eight *'pheus'* behind him in a major constituency in mainland Kolkata. Also, it was observed by this author in some other constituencies of Kolkata. Why were those 'non-Bengalee' observers attached in every constituency? What function did they do? What result did they give? Could they produce any positive impact upon the candidates or electorates in the state? Were there no assistants or politically, socially, culturally, and educationally sound scholars/researchers/teachers/workers/supporters within the BJP from Bengal itself that you had to hire them from outside of this state? This was an insult and ignoring of the indigenous scholars on the one side, and wastage of money of the party, and labor of those people arrived from outside, on the other. The Party leadership in Bengal and central leaders neither take any initiative to find out the best brains from society or from academia, authors of development studies in universities, or private researchers, teachers from schools, colleges and universities, technocrats, and other eminent persons who were eager to extend their all-out assistance to the party without any money or any expectation. Some lowly qualified, lowly knowledgeable, and lowly familiar faces but sycophants came to limelight, who took the party to the door of the Hell, instead of the electorate.

Though it was an appreciable act that the BJP appointed observers, co-observers, and conveners in the districts prior to the Assembly elections, they were not properly utilized, and given free hand to make a proper plans, and act according to their plan. But the more distressing phenomenon was that it appointed five central observers to look after the party's organization. The party's General Secretary (organization) BL Santhosh, BJP decided the state would be divided into five organizational zones, and each zone will be under the control of a central leader. It was reported that "Sunil Deodhar would look after the Medinipur zone while Vinod Sonkar would be in charge of the Rarh Bongo zone. BJP national general secretary Harish Dwivedi will be in charge of the North Bengal zone, while the Kolkata Zone will be under national general secretary Dushyant Kumar Gautam. Vinod Taorey will be in charge of the Nabadwip zone."[27] Nitin Gadkari, Shivraj Singh Chowhan, and Rajnath Singh are to be added in the Great War against a woman. When the BJP fielded the entire team in Bengal, only Mamata Banerjee was alone with her Bhaipo standing beside her. This arrangement was also not accepted by the intellectuals, civil society, and citizens in general, which caused their defeat.

26. Worthless, inept, and ignorant *pundits* worked as guides in BJP

All 'outside pundits' of BJP were worthless and ignorant of Bengal's culture, heartbeat, and feeling. They all were male; they all were like migrant birds. See the list first. Sunil Deodhar, National Secretary was basically from Maharashtra; Vinod Tawde, another national secretary was from Maharashtra, Vinod Sonkar, a National Secretary and MP from Kausambhi, UP was from Allahabad. His election affidavit says that he has four cases pending against him, where he has been charged with promoting enmity between different groups on grounds of religion, race, place of birth, residence, and language, and bribery and illegal payments during elections. Harish Dwivedi, National secretary, and MP from Basti, UP was born in Basti district. There were five cases against him, where he has been accused of rioting, wrongful restraint, and confinement, intentional assault to provide a breach of peach, obstruction of public way, and assault on a public servant. He became in charge of the north Bengal zone. Dushyant Gautam, another National general secretary, and Rajya Sabha member who was hailed from Delhi played the role of in-charge of the Calcutta zone. All these above 'five Pandavas came prior to the first phase of elections in Bengal and after touring in their respective zones returned to Delhi to report JP Nadda and Amit Shah.

That was not all. Another 13 numbers of 'outsiders' with zero knowledge of Bengal came to examine the status of Bengal. (i). Sunil Bansal, a General Secretary (organization), UP, from Rajasthan, came to Bengal to coordinate and oversee the Bengal BJP's Calcutta zone. (ii) Ravindra Raju, General Secretary (organization), Haryana played the role of looking after the Burdwan zone. (iii) Bhikhubhai Dalsaniya, General secretary (organization), Gujarat was the in-charge of the Nabadwip zone. (iv) Ratnakar, Joint general secretary (organization) Bihar originally from Deoria in UP, played the role of a Head of the north Bengal zone. (v) Pavan Rana, General Secretary (organization), Himachal Pradesh, an RS pracharak, handled the BJP's Howrah-Hooghly-Midnapore zone. (vi) Sanjeev Balyan, an MP from Muzaffarnagar, UP, Union minister of state for animal husbandry, dairying, and fisheries. (vii) Gajendra Singh Shekhawat, an MP from

Jodhpur, Rajasthan, Union minister for water resources, river development, and Ganga rejuvenation, was originally from Sikar district of Rajasthan. (viii) Nityanand Rai, an MP from Ujjarpur, Bihar, Union minister of state for home, (ix) Arjun Munda, MP from Khunti, Jharkhand, and Union minister for tribal affairs, (x) Dr. Narottam Mishra, Cabinet minister for home, law and legislative affairs, prisons and parliamentary affairs in Madhya Pradesh, (xi) Kesav Prasad Maurya, a Deputy chief minister of Uttar Pradesh, was originally from Sirathu in Uttar Pradesh, (xii) Prahlad Singh Patel, an MP from Damoh, Madhya Pradesh, Union minister of state (independent charge) for tourism and culture, and (xii) Mansukh L. Mandaviya, a Rajya Sabha member from Gujarat and Union minister of state (independent charge) for port, shipping and waterways, chemicals and fertilizers.[28]

27. BJP played trick with Bengal's electorate by not declaring a strong chief ministerial candidate

There was not a strong chief ministerial face before the electors in Bengal. It was also reported in some newspapers as "The biggest problem of the BJP in West Bengal is the same as in Delhi. The party lacks a credible face in the state when pitted against the image of firebrand street-fighter and able administrator Mamata Banerjee."[29] The election in West Bengal was fought between incumbent chief minister Mamata Banerjee vs. a 'Bhumiputra'. What a foolish act it was! The election was fought between a very strong and well-known face vs an unknown and unnamed faceless candidate. Still, people cast their votes on the party and their candidates. Is it not surprising? It is considered that the greatest asininity of top leaders in Delhi was keeping secret the name of would-be Chief Minister in Bengal. The party failed to project a consensus Chief Ministerial face in Bengal before elections. It was like a beautiful woman going to marry a faceless man by the words of her parents. This may happen in some other states, but not in Bengal.

The Bengalee people always wanted to know who would be their chief minister; what are his or her education level, family background, social identity, cultural bent, and such other things. Dr. Swapan Dasgupta could be an accepted face in Bengal. Dilip Ghosh could be a more familiar and well-accepted face in Bengal, because, it is he (Ghosh), and not Kailash Vijayvargiya who had brought the party to the present height within such a short period of time. Dr. Dasgupata could also be projected beforehand, and he might be fielded from Kolkata, instead of the Tarakeshwar constituency.

28. Unwise selection of candidates

The selection of candidates was also full of flaws. The BJP's decision to field four sitting MPs, including junior minister Babul Supriyo, Locket Chatterjee and Nishith Pramanik and Rajya Sabha MP Swapan Dasgupta in the upcoming assembly elections in West Bengal has surprised many political pundits of India.[30] Surprisingly all the three MPs, except Nishith Pramanik, were defeated in the elections. Fielding of sitting MPs in Assembly elections was not a wise decision. The MPs might be in the second line of campaigners, who could help in supporting the candidates in all the constituencies; while the third-line speakers ought to be the central leaders. The PM or the HM might be campaigned in VVIP seats only such as Dum Dum constituency, Siliguri constituency, and others, and definitely not come and go regularly and get the epitaph of "daily passengers'. They thus lowered their dignity and belittled their position before the general people of Bengal, nay in India as a whole. I remember, the then PM Dr. Manmohan Singh campaigned for Bratya Basu in Dum Dum Constituency in 2011.

29. Internal strife and ego-problem among the intellectuals

The internal strife and ego-problem amongst Bengal-BJP's intellectuals caused great damage to the party. Not only within the intellectuals, but there were also clashes and violence within two groups – old and new members – in Bardhaman and Asansol even in front of the senior leadership.31 Further, it was revealed in a newspaper report that, there had been murmurs of internal rumblings within the BJP but all that boiled over on 23rd October when state president Dilip Ghosh unilaterally dissolved all district committees of the party's Yuva Morcha formed just a day earlier by Lok Sabha MP, Saumitra Khan, a turncoat from TMC.[32] The two men were at the loggerheads for a while before the 2021 assembly elections in Bengal. In addition to the above, "The inner fight within the BJP's local leadership is not unknown to the citizens. Bengal BJP chief Dilip Ghosh has continuously been at loggerheads with the state General Secretary Mukul Roy."[33] The selection of close but unworthy or lowly qualified people in different posts hurt the sentiment of others. This election was not fought together by all. There were leg-pulling and backbiting against each other in personal or small group talks, which was not an indication of a good sign.

30. Paralyzed many general members of the party

The people who became members of BJP in the last 2-3 years in Bengal after having been attracted by the charismatic qualities of the Prime Minister and his enigmatic feats were never activated either virtually or personally. One person who took online membership of BJP in 2018 frustratingly told that only before the elections (2021) one Hindi-speaking tele-caller asked for his name, age, date of birth, name of constituency, name of a word, and other information, which merely created confusion to the Member because, in the time of online frauds, scores of people did not want to share their details with those tele-callers. Moreover, the online callers, mostly Hindi-speaking persons, failed to understand Bengali, and in turn, many of them could not make the members understood their intentions of inquiry. Thus, the system turned into a mess. Besides, the basic meaning of participatory democracy was meaningless to thousands of BJP members in the state, who were averse to cast their votes in favor of BJP candidates.

31. BJP failed to accommodate workers and agents in every booth

The party was successful in making many (temporary) leaders; but it failed to increase the numbers of supporters, workers, and agents in every booth of Gram Panchayat; every word of Municipalities, and borough of Corporations, who could fight for the leaders and act as spokesperson of the party in local areas. They could disseminate the information of developmental schemes mentioned in the Manifesto to the general voters in their respective areas. Besides, they could respond to the violence and threatening of the 'TMC goons' and leaders who debarred thousands of BJP supporters and voters on the Election Day, or P -1 day from casting votes.

32. Failure to combat the false propaganda of the TMC

The BJP leaders in Bengal could not combat the false propaganda of the TMC party regarding the cleverly renaming of central-government-sponsored schemes that have ubiquitous effects on rural livelihood. The renaming of some schemes such as from the *Pradhan Mantri Gram Sadak Yojana* (PMGSY) to *'Banglar Gramin Sadak Yojana'*, by the TMC government facilitated the village transportation, made ease of doing business, helped even rickshaw pullers to smoothly pull the rickshaws, and the maintenance cost of personal cars, motorcycles, bicycles, rickshaw-van, trolly, Toto, etc. of rural people was reduced to a lot. This ease of life and livelihood helped Mamata Banerjee to reap the benefit through ballot boxes. Similarly, the *Pradhan Mantri Awas Yojana-Grameen* was transformed by Mamata Banerjee as *'Banglar Griha Prakalpa'* in Bengal; Prime Minister Narendra Modi's pet project of *Swaohh Bharat Mission* (Gramin) is known in Bengal as *'Mission Nirmal Bangla'*. *Ajeevika* (National Rural Livelihood Mission) has been renamed as *'Ananda Dhara* (The State Rural Livelihood Mission) by the State Government.

It proves that State BJP has a little number of intellectuals and scholar advisors or *'Diknirdeshaks'* who could extend necessary policy recommendations or put forward concrete suggestions for countering the false propaganda of the TMC-led Government. In a letter dated 12.04.2017 Saurav Kumar Das, the then Additional Chief Secretary to the Government of West Bengal gave a circular to all the District Magistrates of the state highlighting that "(A) Use only these state government assigned names in all correspondences – both with the state and stakeholders at the district and sub-district level. (B) Popularize these names in course of all interactions with the local stakeholders – at worksites, in the institutions, and in course of community mobilization. (C) Develop posters, banners, hoardings, leaflets, and IEC materials to propagate the schemes and associated benefits. (D) Promote awareness among the people on the eligibility for getting assistance from the schemes, procedures for the selection of recipients, support provided to the individuals/households/groups and the community under the scheme, etc. (E) West Bengal's performance as a state and your district's performance in implementation of the scheme may also be suitably highlighted in course of any promotional campaign."[34] The TMC's argument in favor of its renaming is that, as the state government is now paying 40 percent of its share, 'the schemes cannot have only the stamp of the Central government.' Though the Opposition parties criticized the act of the State government and called the trend "Unethical", but the BJP leaders in Bengal failed to prevent the maneuver of the TMC Government.

33. Lastly, it must be pointed out that the rift between *'adi* BJP' (old BJP) and *'nabya* BJP' (new BJP) put the last nail to the coffin of BJP's hope of winning the elections.

Conclusions

Though several reasons for the defeat of BJP in Bengal have been delineated above, which are no doubt negative in nature, and those might add salt to the injury of BJP leadership in both Bengal and Delhi, but a closer investigation into the above-mentioned shortcomings with inquisitiveness might open up doors of Nabanna for the BJP leaders. History always teaches us lessons to so that we may make the right decision at the right time, and it is the failure from which the BJP might learn some good lessons. Bengal is unlike many other states of India. One should not mix up Bengal with states of North or West. The history of the freedom movement and the contribution of Bengal might be kept in mind by the BJP leadership. Bengal's fight against the anti-partition movement in 1905; Netaji's resolute attitude for attaining complete freedom; the methodological rift between Gandhi and Bose – one from Gujarat and the other from Bengal – reminds us of the repetition of History. The lack of in-depth homework; insufficiency of wit and knowledge of history, culture, and self-esteem of Bengalees; and above all 'language disorder' by most of the star campaigners flown off from Delhi, Mumbai, UP, and other 'planets' brought catastrophic result for the much ambitious team of BJP. It is hoped that the BJP leaders – central and state level - will sit together, and examine the deficiencies, pointed out above, to find the solutions and formulate more scientific strategies with the help of sincere researchers, developmental thinkers, authors, Political Scientists, Economists, and other academicians of the State, to win over the hearts of average Bengalee voters in the days to come. The more sincere they are in seeking the help of just mentioned 'academicians and other exclusive people' of society the more mellifluous of their chances to come in power in Bengal, and prior to that, of course, in 2024 in India.

Only one simple prescription for the topmost BJP leaders is: concentrate in strengthening at least 20 unflinching and clean-imaged Pracharaks, and 2 strong agents in every booth of the State i.e. 1,01,790 (booths) X 20 (pracharaks) = 20,35,800 Pracharaks and 1,01,790 (booths) X 2 (agents) = 20,35,80 (as per 2021 election data). However, the following chapter deals with the perception of the people regarding various deficits of the Left Front Government.

Chapter – VIII

Understanding the Rise and Fall of CPI(M) and

Congress in Bengal

"No folly is more costly than the folly of intolerant idealism."

- *Winston Churchill*

Introduction

This chapter deals with the significant rise of the Indian National Congress and the CPI(M)-led Left Front (LF) and the miserable downfall of both. In 2010, I conducted a research study in four districts of West Bengal. The survey was conducted in different politically headed Zilla Parishads. North 24 Parganas and Paschim Medinipur Zilla Parishads were headed by Women Sabhadhipatis while Bankura and Nadia were headed by male Sabhadhipatis. One thing common in all the districts was that they were bordering districts. The influx of people from other states and countries was a common phenomenon. It sometimes created problems and even brought about disturbances and even instability in some pockets of West Bengal. The climate, land, and means of livelihood, nature of occupation, caste-base, and originality of the people hold a decisive role in shaping the character of a state. The demand and supply level determines the political stability of a state as well as a country. If there is a crisis in supplying the bare necessities to the majority of people, it is sure to spring a crisis that even can upside down an existing government. Besides, when there is massive oppression of one class by another in a given society, revolution is sure to come. Also, if a particular political party remains in power for more than two consecutive terms, one kind of 'don't care attitude', 'haughtiness', 'rudeness', 'corruption', 'inertia' are some common ailments that are sure to come. The CPI(M)-led Left Front ruled the state for 34 years at a stretch.

However, with a view to examine the people's attitude and perception regarding the performance of the Left Front (LF) government, and particularly its ministers, leaders, and other party members, supporters, and opponents, some questions were framed in a structured questionnaire, and the language of the questionnaire was Bengali so that the respondents feel free to respond it without any hiccup. The researcher personally met all the respondents and sought answers from them so that they could speak openly and without hesitation about the problems they were facing which needed immediate attention by the Government. Most of the persons initially hesitated to answer the political questions, but when they were assured that it would be used only exclusively for the research purpose, they became relieved and spoke even more than what was asked through the questionnaire. Thus, it is necessary to present the additional comments, wherever available, of the respondents separately at the end of each analysis of each table. But the tables are not given here with a view to shed off the length of the chapter and, to avoid boring repetition of the same which were published in my previous book *West Bengal Government: The Issues and Constraints of Development* in 2010.

Now let us examine the perception of both male and female respondents about the Left Front (LF) government. At first, the respondents were asked about the nature and ways of functioning of the government in the last 2-3 years i.e. prior to the elections in 2011. When asked whether they are satisfied with the style of functioning of the government or not, most of the respondents (Males - 67.85% and Females – 45.58%) answered that they are not satisfied with the method of functioning of the then LF government, while less than quarter respondents consisting of 19.28 percent males and 31.66 percent females believed that the LF government was working satisfactorily. On the other hand, 12.85 percent of males and 22.5 percent of females did not respond. Maybe they did not think it wise to disclose their opinion regarding the matter. Some were in fear, while others hesitated to speak openly about their perception regarding the performance of the government.

As it was one of the purposes of the study to examine the then perception of the people towards the nature and functioning of political leaders of the Left Front in particular and the Government as a whole, the questionnaire was framed in accordance with the objective of the study. How people were viewing the steps the government was taking and decisions being made to resolve various crises were endeavored to ascertain. It was the people who always decide the fate of the government. Hence, what people felt and what they thought about the government's actions needed to be discussed.

Interestingly, when it was asked whether the LF government had been working properly for the last 2-3 years as it had been working since 1977, a mixed reaction was received from different people in this regard. Trinamool Congress supporters and Socialist Unity Centre of India (SUCI) along with other leaders and supporters felt that the Left Front Government never did well for the poor and landless people of this state. One Trinamool Congress supporter Naresh Biswas[1] of 1 No., Natun Fulia, Nadia felt that "They never did any good to the people". The opposite view was expressed by a School Mistress.[2] She believed that *"Uchu matha kaj kore, kintu chyalara kaj kore na"* (The higher-level leaders work, but the lower-level workers are not working). This view was corroborated by another teacher.[3] He felt that *"Ekebare kaj kore ni ta noi"* (It was not that government did not perform at all).

On the other hand, more interestingly it was observed that some Congress supporters even felt that the Left government had done well for the common people in the last 33 years, but recently it was not working well. Similarly, government officials and especially the senior officers considered that the government had done well. One bank employee felt that the recent problem had started from the last five years while one physician[4] expressed that, "Dhara paribartan haoa darkar" (It was necessary to bring about a change). However, it was observed that a substantial number of young college students were dissatisfied with the performance of the LF government. One such college student5 cited that, *'Kintu ami mane kori gata tin bachere bamfront sarkar garib manuser chahida mato kaj korche na"* (The Left Government had not been working for the poor people for the last 2-3 years).

In regard to the question of whether the government had been successful in providing security of life and property to the people, most of the respondents (Males – 72.85% and Females – 63.33%) felt that it failed to give adequate security to the life and property of all the people in the state. This was a serious allegation against the government. Most of the respondents felt that the government failed to provide security to the property, and protect land, and life to the people of the state. When continuous murders, chaos, turmoil, and agitations went on in some parts of the state, the heat was definitely felt by others. However, a few percentages of respondents i.e. 20.71 percent males and 26.66 percent females felt that the government was providing necessary security and safety to the people. On the other hand, 6.42 percent of males and 10.00 percent of females did not respond at all.

Madan Das[6] the then president of Daspur Mandal Committee of BJP felt that "*Ain shrinkhla bhenge poreche. Narider kono nirapatta nei*" (Law and order has been broken down, women have no security in our state). He also added that "*Manush beporoa hoea geche*" (People have become unrestrained or indisciplined, while the head clerk[7] of a municipality does not hold the same view. He considered that "*Sarkar bhaloi dicche*" (the government was providing good administration and safeguarding the life and property of the people). Almost all the aged people above 70 years old have been told that the then LF government was failing to provide security to the people and they were dissatisfied with the activities and decisions of the then LF government. They visualized the black days of the seventies when this type of anarchy prevailed in the state administration.

It was asked to the respondents whether the government was providing good governance. Again a mixed opinion of the people was reflected. It was evident from available data, that most of the respondents (Males – 65.00% and Females 63.33%) felt that the government had not been providing good governance to the people especially for the last 2-3 years (2007 -2010) while 15.71 percent males and 15.83 percent females believed that the government was providing good governance. But, 19.28 percent of males and 20.83 percent of females did not think it right to comment in this regard.

One farmer[8] believed that "*Ei sarkar pratham panchis bachar bhalo kaj korechilo. Ekhan era bhalo prasashan o janaganer jiban o sampattir nirapatta dite parche na*" (The government gave good governance up to the first twenty-five years of its rule. And presently it was failing to give good governance and providing security of property and life of the people). He also considered that the political leaders of the ruling party members started the works as brokers where there was a setting up of industries.

If the government was failing to provide proper security and guarantee the protection of life and property to the people; if the type of governance was not satisfactory, then what will be done by the government sitting at the Writers' Buildings? Naturally, the next question came about the chances of the government to come back in power in the next Assembly elections went to the polls in 2011. If people did not feel safe, and if people could not enjoy their basic Right to Freedom mentioned in the Constitution due to movements, agitations, and disruption of law and order, it needed a government that could ensure all the basic amenities to the people, and maintain the safety of people, and stability in the state. Survey data showed that only 22.85 percent of males and 15.0 percent of females believed that the government will come back in power in the assembly elections (2011). But most of the respondents i.e. 68.57 percent male and 65.83 percent female respondents considered that there was no chance of the LF government to come back in power, and form government after the end of that tenure, because they believed that, people's Constitutional rights like the Right to Freedom of Speech and Expression, Right to Life, and Right to Education of Children between the age of 6-14 years old and several others were being violated. In a word, the law and order situation had been broken down, though in certain parts of the State only. Common people did not like these troubles; they needed peace, and they wished to live happily. However, it came to light from the data that 8.57 percent of males and 19.16 percent of females did not put their comments on the issue. Those respondents, however, were puzzled about the chances of the existing government come into power. Many among those non-respondents were former supporters or sympathizers of the LF government. However, the extra opinions of the respondents – both for and against the government – are given below.

A Government Librarian[9] told that "*Khanikta asambhab bole mone hochhe gati-pakriti dekhe*" (It seemed from the course of happenings that there was little chance of the government to come back in power in the next assembly elections). Mr. Bhabadeb

Biswas[10] a senior bureaucrat, also expressed that *"Seta nao aste pare"* (It may not come back in power). Most of the college teachers felt that it was being impossible for the Government to come back to power in the next Assembly elections. Again a few cautious teachers[11] expressed that, "Still there is enough chance and something miracle can happen." The same view was expressed by Prof. Dipti Sarkar.12 However, another retired college teacher13 felt differently. He told that *"Ek kathai uttar deoa jai na, prai du bachare je damage hoeche seta recover kara jabe kina seta nischit noi"* (It was not certain whether the damage caused during the previous two years could be recovered or not). One housewife[14] Mina Kar, wife of a Head Master viewed that, *"Duschinta ache"* (There was confusion regarding come back in the power of the government). On the other hand, Dr. Ashok Chakraborty[15] expressed that, *"Sarkarer ferar asa niye ami ashabadi"* (I'm optimistic of the Government's coming back). He loved the party blindly.

On the other hand, some sympathizers, who also sympathized with the party but, in view of the then developments, expressed their anxiety regarding the future of the LF government. *"kichui bojha jai na"* (Nothing was understood) – another housewife16 asserted. While another woman respondent[17] felt that, "The present government will not come back within next ten years." Another house wife and network business agent18 felt, *"Mane hoi ar asbe na"* (It seemed that it would not come back to power in the next elections). A van rickshaw puller[19] felt, *"Jadi churi kare tabe asbe kshamatai"* (If the government manipulates in the elections, then only it would come back in power). Tapan Samanta, a farmer[20] told that *"Amra paribartan chai"* (We need change). Similarly, another farmer[21] expressed that, *"Ora lokke mithya pratisruti dei, saijanyei ei sarkarer patan ghatbe"* (They gave false assurance to the people and that's why the Government will fall down).

One Insurance Executive[22] of Maxwell Newyork Life Insurance of Belighata, Daspur (in Paschim Medinipur) asserted a few reasons for not coming to power of the LF government in the next assembly elections. Reasons he mentioned were: "1. *Nicher sanghataner netader sikshagata jyogyata kam, tara kshamatar apabyabahar korche o nirapekshata bajay rakhte parche na* (Though the LF government had satisfied a lot of demands of the people, it failed to keep direct contact with its lower-level leaders.

Besides, their (lower-level leaders) educational qualifications were low. As a result, they had misused power and failed to keep up impartiality). 2. *Manusher mane ekta bhul dharan gethe deoa hoeche* (A misconception regarding the government had been fixed up in the minds of people). 3. *Bamfront sarkar siddhanta nite durbalata dekheieche o deri koreche* (LF government showed weaknesses, and delayed in taking decisions). 4. *Siksha byabasthake sathik karar kshetre durbalata dekhicehe* (it showed a lack of intention to improve the education system). However, he in the same breath asserted that *Amader paribartan sunischit, kintu paribartan kamya noi* (Though the change was inevitable, it was not desired). Because he has raised some valid and important questions: 1. *Paribartaner par ki, je dal kshamatai asbe tader chintadharar madhya kono paribartan lakshya kara jachhe*? (was there any change in the attitude and activities of the existing opposition party, who are going to be the next ruling party?) 2. *Tara ki kono daityasil sarkar gathan korte parbe*? (Will they be able to form a responsible government?) 3. *Tara kshamatai ele ki khunoknuni bandha hobe*? (Will there be an end of murders if they come in power?) 4. *Tara kshamatai ele ki garib manuser swartha surakshita hobe*? (Will the interests of the poor people be safeguarded?) 5. *Tara ki kono sunirdista sanghatan korte parbe*? (Will they be successful in forming the right organization?) 6. *Tara ki silper unnati korte parbe*? (Will they be successful in bringing about industrialization?) The person had very rightly raised some important questions. Those are the demands of the people which are reflected in his words. Whosoever may govern the state, general people expect all these facilities from the people in power.

Gram Sabhas and *Gram Sansads* were formed in every Gram Panchayat of West Bengal. The meetings of Gram Sansads were supposed to take place twice a year where all the voters of a booth would sit together and take decisions for the development of their respective villages. Similarly, every December the meeting of Gram Sabha was scheduled to take place where all the voters of the Gram Panchayat were the members. Likewise, in every Urban Local Body (ULB), there was Ward Committee; they were also supposed to sit regularly for taking decisions regarding the development of their locality/ward. But often complaints rose that the meetings were not happening regularly. Even if the meetings were called, only a few selected partymen were invited to take decisions regarding the whole of the locality. Thus, people's participation in the local decision-making bodies was not actualized. In the survey also most of the respondents (Males – 90.62 and Females – 86.07%) considered that people's participation in grassroots organizations was not taking place in reality. But contrary to that view, 6.24 percent males and 7.58 percent females did not believe in that, and 3.12 percent males and 6.32 percent females, with or without knowing about the happenings, did not talk about it.

From the interactions with the respondents, it came to light that, the meetings of ward committees were not taking place regularly. In Ghatal Municipality areas, the ward meetings were not taking place regularly till 2010. One Head Master observed that "In last five years, in 15-number ward of Ghatal Municipality only two meetings with members i.e. the common ward members had taken place."[23] The opinion of the Head Master was substantiated by one Councilor. He stated that "The meetings of Ward Committees were not held regularly. The meetings of Ward Committees were held after two-three months."[24] It was then a mandatory rule in rural local governance to abide by the decisions of the Gram Sansads and Gram Sabhas. Prabhat Datta[25] in a book wrote that *"Gram Sansad ebong Gram Sabhar siddhanta Gram Panchayat mene nite badhya"* (Gram Panchayat is compelled to act according to the decisions of the Gram Sansad and Gram Sabha). The local government was also not much vital in the United States of America. Some seek to strengthen local government power. Gerald E. Frug considers that "A strong local government is vital to "public freedom."[26]

The fast growth of India's economy in recent years has increased stress on physical infrastructure such as rural electricity, roads, irrigation, health, rural water supply, etc. "Infrastructure could serve as a true Engine of Growth and can provide the much-needed impetus to the economy in this time of crisis."[27] Regarding the condition of village roads 85.41 percent males and 79.74 percent females stated that the village roads were not so good and in many villages, there were not morrum, or good conditioned metalled roads. Many rural roads, during rainy seasons, became muddy and un-walkable and unplayable. But 10.40 percent of males and 11.39 percent of females did not support the statement. They felt that the conditions of roads were better than before. Where there were no roads at all earlier, there were new roads, and many newly constructed rural roads have been connected with the main roads through the Rajiv Gandhi Gram Sadak Yojana (RGGSY). Interestingly, a few respondents (Males – 4.16% and Females – 6.32%) did not open their mouths in this regard. However, one senior government bureaucrat[28] told that "Ager theke anek unnata." (It was much better than before). Still, India has many nonconnected habitations. To upgrade rural infrastructure, the government of India has planned to construct 1,46,185 km of road under Bharat Nirman Prakalpa.[29] But it should be remembered that "The road network in India remains poorly funded for meeting the maintenance requirement for current roads."[30]

Rural drinking water is one of the six components of Bharat Nirman. The data on the problems of potable water in some villages tend to demonstrate that there was still the problem of potable water in some villages of this state. In the survey area 89.58 per cent males and 89.87 per cent females believed that the problems of potable water still existed in some villages. On the other hand, 9.36 percent of males and 6.32 percent of women considered that there was no such problem in their villages, and 1.04 percent of males and 7.79 percent of females did not respond. The problems of potable water were not the problems of West Bengal alone; it is the problem of the country as a whole.

The government might provide funds to mitigate the water crisis. But there was corruption during the LF government in the water scheme too. In this regard, a student uttered that, *"Amader grame anek paniya jaler samasya ache. Nalkup ache, kintu tate jal ase na. Amader gramer CPI(M) partir Pradhaner Swajal Dhara Prakalpe jaler byabastha karar katha chilo, kinto sai taka se atmasat koreche"*[31] (In our village there was a scarcity of drinking water. We have a tube well, but there was no water in it. The Panchayat Pradhan of our village had taken money for Swajal Dhara Prakalpa, but he has misappropriated that fund). On the other hand, another respondent, who was a Physician by profession, expressed that, "In our place, the distribution and availability of water is o.k."[32]

But in general, there was a problem with potable water in the villages. It became clear from the words of an Assistant Teacher. He held that "About 150-200 people depend on one tube well in their village (Bural, under Sabang Panchayat Samity, Paschim

Medinipur). When it gets defective and does not work, people have to use pond water for drinking, cooking, cleaning of utensils and for other purposes."[33]

The spiraling rise of essential commodities was a massive problem for the poor and middle-class people in the state. And this problem is, it seems, never-ending. The price of vegetables, petrol, medicines, and edible oil has caused the lives of millions of general people miserable. This has touched almost every section of society, and the happenings indicated that "Neither the Centre nor the State had shown seriousness in controlling the price of essential commodities" – expressed an existing councilor.[34] One ex-serviceman of Navy[35] felt that "In all the cold storages the potatoes were kept or hoarded by the Party Cadres and leaders. As a result, the Government failed to control the prices of potatoes."

The quality of education has deteriorated during the Left Front government. Almost every government and its education minister experimented with the future of our students. In terms of lower quality of education, one Left-minded Assistant Teacher of a Higher Secondary School[36] expressed that, "*Sarkar chesta koreche, kintu jara sarkarer pratinidhi tara bastabayita hote dei nai*" (Though the government has been trying, its representatives did not allow it to materialize). The view was corroborated by another retired college teacher. He was also known as a sympathizer of the Communist Party of India (Marxist). He believed that, "Government has taken measures, but those were not implemented properly."[37] On the other hand, one councillor38 felt that "*Kichu koreche matra*" (The existing government has done a little bit only). However, one ex-Army[39] concluded by saying that, "*Sab to sambhab noi, kichu hoeche*" (All were not possible, but something had really been actualized)."

It was not only necessary to increase the rate of literacy in the state; rather increasing the quality of education was more important. If there is a mere increase in numbers of students, and the State fails to keep up the quality of education; do not uphold the morality and self-esteem of students; and shows dilly-dally attitude to inculcate among the students the lessons on discipline, punctuality, honesty, respect for others, tolerance, patriotism, etc. the ill-effect is sure to run into every section in society including family and even every government department – from Finance to Urban Local Bodies. Both quantitative and qualitative education together is important for the development of a nation as well as a State. A recent study by the Pratichi Trust regarding the condition of primary education in the state also highlighted the same problems of poor quality of primary education in the state. A Class VI pass student of a high school could not write his name and address in English, the examinees of Head Mastership were getting poor marks in English in written examinations, while a lot of administrative officers failed to understand the meaning of circulars and letters written in English in the state, and in this way taking much time to finish their daily works. For all these reasons, 89.58 percent of males and 92.40 percent of females believed that the quality of education in the state had deteriorated. But 8.32 percent of males and 2.52 percent of females did not believe so and 3.12 percent of males and 4.16 percent of females did not make even a comment in this regard.

Public opinion on the issue was captured in the study. It was expressed through the comments they made while taking the interview. A student[40] told that, "*Adhikangsha professorera passer classer prati abahela dekhai. Seta to thik noi. Jehetu se sikshak sehetu tar sakalkai siksha deoa uchit. Karan sikshaker kaj holo tar gyan bhandar theke gyan niye siksharthir janya bhandar purna kara*" (Most of the college teachers were not giving importance to the classes of Pass subjects. As a teacher, it became one's responsibility to take care of all classes in both Pass subjects as well as Honors subjects. Because the job of a teacher is to fill up the store of students from his own). But an opposite view was uttered by a college teacher.[41] He questioned why a large number of the students were not attending the classes regularly need to be identified and provided solutions. Besides, there should be arrangements for vocational training in general college also. So the students could avail of jobs after completion of their education.

Moon Moon Bera,[42] a college student asserted that "The present government has brought down the quality of education to such an extent where a well, sensitive person will be ill at once. Today a lot of class eight-pass students cannot write their own names and addresses in English. But they were getting promotions from one class to another without learning up to his or her standard of class. The government was only interested to see the maximum number of students getting promoted just to show off others about the higher percentage of literacy rate in the State. But, have they ever thought that how much loss they have done to the ignorant and poor students? What profit have we made, and for whom? We feel shame to tell the students of other states that we have passed 10th even when reading in college. It is completely my personal experience. So it seems to me that instead of increasing merely the rate of literacy; if the government would have taken much care to increase the quality of education; to me, it would have been better. The condition of the education system would not have been so miserable. Now in this education system, those who have money could continue only education and get prosperity in life because of their pursuit of education in English medium reputed schools. On the other hand, we, the common, poor, and middle-class students go the substandard government schools, colleges and come back home in the evening after gossiping the whole day. In the name of studying, we are doing a hoax."

In relation to the worsening education scenario, a High School teacher[43] expressed that, "The system of conducting unit tests in high schools was defective. Besides, within the existing system and infrastructure, four to five students were sitting on one bench. Naturally, the scope for copying from each other's answer script was high and most of the students were asking and copying and getting high marks. We found it difficult to distinguish between a good and a poor student. The girl who did not prepare her daily lessons was scoring good marks in unit tests. The system might be good for low merit students, but not for meritorious and serious students. Secondly, as there was examination now in almost every month, we could not explain the lessons properly because we were in a hurry to finish the syllabus."

A college teacher asserted that "The internal assessment in the Under Graduate (For both Pass and Honours) and Post Graduate level was not desired by them."[44] Reason behind was that when in Pass Course there was a shortage of teachers it became very difficult to assess the answer scripts. For example, in Ghatal R.S. College there were only two part-time teachers in Education Department whereas the numbers of students were approximately 1200. How much time does it take to examine the answer scripts carefully and properly for all those students? It became very difficult for them to examine the answer scripts accurately and timely too.

One primary school teacher[45] pointed out that, "There was lack of teachers in primary schools. There was a total of 140 students and the number of teachers was only 4. Though there was Mother-Teacher Association in schools, the mothers did not like to come spontaneously. We had to call them from home. Besides, the grants for 85 percent of students were coming only, whereas in some schools the attendance of students was about 100 percent. Moreover, the primary teachers were doing a variety of works other than teaching. It included census duty, and preparing, and correcting electoral rolls, etc. Sometimes village survey works were also getting done by us."

In addition to the above matters, a few deficiencies of the Left Front government can be highlighted hereunder, which all played catalytic roles in driving out the Communist rulers from the Writers' Buildings. The party by virtue of staying in power uninterruptedly for more than three decades turned to "People's Boss" in place of "Public Servant'. The middle of top-level leaders even did not hesitate to abuse or even slap publicly the dignified doctors, teachers, and others who dared to express opponent views in front of them. Sushanta Ghosh in Garbeta, Manirul Islam in Birbhum, Laksman Seth in Medinipur, Tarit Baran Topdar in Barrackpore, Anil Basu in Arambagh, and scores of such leaders created a reign of terror. There were very few brave people to file nomination papers for contesting in the Panchayat elections in rural Bengal. The threatening of one ex-MLA and Minister of CPI(M) went to such an extent to the women in rural Medinipur that he openly declared, 'if you cast vote to any opposition party candidate, you will have to wear white saree' (while saree symbolizes the widowhood in West Bengal).

The college and university students' unions were mostly dominated by the Students' Federation of India (SFI). The Chatra Parishad students had to fight a lot and suffer from bloodshed before filing nomination forms to contest in elections of college unions. Corruption was there in almost every Gram Panchayat and Municipality office. Besides, without bribes, no file would move from one table to another in many departments of government. People were disgusted and suffered in the hands of ruling party leaders, office bearers, and other ultra-supporters of the party. People's anger fell in the ballot boxes in the 2011 assembly elections. The honorarium of office bearers during the

CPI(M) rule was very low. The educational qualification of many MLAs and Local Body representatives were very poor causing delays in their delivery of services. Violent bandhs, and frequent strikes, and *'chakka jam'* policies of the Communist parties created abhorrence and disgust for the LF candidates and MLAs. People started to look for an alternative prior to the elections. Primary Teachers' Training Institutions (PTTI) were running in the state without adequate affiliation from the National quality control agency. This hampered the life and career of a substantial number of students who were undergoing training for Bachelor of Education (B. Ed.) Degree. Frequent load-shedding created a great problem in West Bengal during the LF government. It impeded the study of students, the operation of patients in hospitals, and production in factories. The quality of roads was so bad that during the rainy season many of them either turned to small ponds, and the potholes caused frequent road accidents and deaths of human beings.

Health infrastructure was hellish. Government hospitals were dirty, and lack of doctors and nurses. The industry was almost doomed during the disruptive political atmosphere in Bengal under Communist rule. The anti-industry image of the Communist workers, and leaders, and their pro-labor policy reduced West Bengal to a mere agrarian State and its erstwhile big industrialists either closed their plants or shifted to other States. The Central government-sponsored schemes were not properly implemented. The Central funds were not utilized timely and appropriately by the State government. And finally, the ideological difference and often dispute with the Union government drag the State behind many of its counterparts during the 34-year long rule of the Communist Party-led Left Front government.

The Buddhadeb Bhattacharjee government became weak and indecisive. West Bengal witnessed tremendous political chaos and instability and lack of peace in Jangal Mahal. The rise of Maoism and the failure of the then government was a major cause of the fall of the Buddhadeb Bhattacharjee government in 2011. Deprivation and non-development were primarily responsible for Maoism's uprising. In this regard, Abhijit Guha wrote, "Just four years before the Maoism armed struggle began in the area Mr. Chandan Sinha, the then-District Magistrate submitted a Report to the Government of West Bengal which revealed that a large number of a small village inhabited by the scheduled tribes had neither drinking water sources nor irrigation facility…. No development work took place at the grass root and the Maoists extorted money and food grains from the poor villagers and also forced people to join their meetings."[46]

Reasons for Withering Away of the Left Front and the Congress from West Bengal Legislative Assembly in 2021

The 2021 assembly elections in West Bengal created a war-like political ambiance, where the principal contestants were the ruling All India Trinamool Congress Party and the Bharatiya Janata Party. The Left Front including the Communist Party of India (Marxist), Communist Party of India, All India Forward Bloc, Revolutionary Socialist Party, and Marxist Forward Bloc made an alliance with the Indian Secular Front of Abbas Siddiqui. Again these two fronts allied with the Indian National Congress Party with a view to deterring 'fascist TMC' and 'communal BJP'. What a despicable and wicked alliance it was! Why it was vile and gruesome? It was because the Congress and the communists are born-enemies in India since the pre-independence period, though Nehru had a Soviet tilting. In 2021 also the two major opponents in Kerala were the INC-led UDF and the CPI(M)-led LDF. Have people forgotten that the UPA-II government was at stake in 2019 only due to the pulling out of LF's support from the Union government? Abbas Siddique is completely a religious leader and is notorious for his instigating and unconstitutional speeches. This was one of the most unholy alliances ever made in political history in Bengal, and probably in India. Now let us go back to history and have a peep into the political scenario in Bengal.

Rise and fall of Congress and CPIM: a historical perspective

In the first Government of 1937 in the pre-independence period, the Indian National Congress party secured only 22 percent of total seats and acted as the main Opposition Party in the Assembly. But since Independence, the Indian National Congress Party in Bengal was strong with pan India, and it ruled the State so far as it had a strong and wise party leadership in Bengal. But with the demise of chief minister Dr. Bidhan Chandra Roy in 1962, a vacuum was created in the political leadership of the Congress party. Besides, the Congress in West Bengal was always faction-ridden and was not the dominant political outfit during colonial rule too, and only after partition, it emerged as an unchallenging and dominant party. But, Dr. Bidhan Chandra Roy was a great politician and a renowned physician with his simplistic and humane character. He was also a deft administrator who handled the problems of refugees, who came from East Pakistan after the partition (from 1947-55). Also, he efficiently tackled the food crisis. But after his death (1st July 1962), the inept handling of the crisis by his successor Prafulla Chandra Sen (1962-1967) marked the beginning of the decay of Congress strength in Bengal. In this regard, Prof. Shibaji Pratim Basu wrote in one of his articles that, "The price of rice reached Rs.5/ per kg that year. Kerosene, the main domestic fuel for the village people and the city-poor became more and more scarce. To cap it all, Prafulla Sen, the new C.M. after the demise of B.C. Roy made a unique suggestion in a speech. In view of the growing scarcity of rice, he advised the people of the state to change their food habits. He suggested that people should shift in their choice: from rice to wheat/flour. He also argued that they could also live on "green-bananas" because they had more nutrition value than potatoes."[47] But his advice was not well accepted by the Bengalees in the State. We, the Bengalees, are famous for eating 'rice and fish'. So, to suggest the opposite was only to bring its debacle.

Thus we find that after the death of Bidhan Chandra Roy his immediate successor failed to fulfill the expectations of the Bengalee electors through his works and words. The food crisis could not be handled properly by the chief minister Prafulla Chandra Sen, and subsequently, the Congress party lost power in 1967. The next decade (1967-77) was infested with several severe social, political, and economic crises. This is considered the black decade in the political history of Bengal. After defeating the Indian National Congress in 1967 assembly elections for the first time in Bengal the United Front government was formed on 25 February 1967. The United Front government was formed with the leadership of the Bangla Congress' chief Ajoy Mukherjee, who became the chief minister, and the United Left Front led Jyoti Basu, who became the deputy chief minister. This upstart United Front government could not survive for more than two years. The first UF government ruled for only 265 days (from 1st March 1967 to 21st November 1967).

West Bengal politics was never tranquil. Due to political upheaval, atrocities, and disruption of normal life and government property the State came under President's Rule several times. The following part seeks to focus on the reasons. In the sixties, West Bengal witnessed an uprising of Naxalite movements in the northern part of the State with the leadership of Charu Majumder and Kanu Sanyal. Many young and bright students of colleges and Universities were engaged in the Naxalite movement with a view to 'Change the society and political system'. But they adopted violent methods in their political actions. The top Naxal leaders were almost similar to 'terror' in Bengal at that time. They built up a power base inside the party ranks and acquired firearms to initiate larger struggles to occupy excess lands in Naxalbari. The United Front government's Left partners started the politics of 'gherao' that caused anger and dissatisfaction among the industrialists. The numbers of gheraos in May 1967 were 151 in West Bengal, while these numbers were 32 in March. However, it went up to 194 in September, the same year. How horrible was the *gherao* politics of the Left Front! They are notorious for their disruptive politics throughout the world. The internal disturbances and atrocities in politics reached such an extent that, chief minister Prafulla Chandra Ghosh had to resign from his ministerial post. He broke up relations with the United Front and formed a new party, the Progressive Democratic Front along with 16 other members of the Legislative Assembly. Ghosh's intention to form the government was supported by Congress. The Governor ordered chief minister Ajoy Mukherjee to prove his majority in the legislative assembly, but he failed to do so. On 16 November Dharma Vira, the then Governor of West Bengal dismissed the United Front cabinet and let Prafulla Ghosh form a new cabinet.48 The UF government was not satisfied with the action of the Governor and called for civil disobedience across the state, where 3500 persons were arrested during the campaign including 14 assembly members. The violent incidents continued. Hence, in February 1968 President's Rule was declared in West Bengal that continued till 25 February 1969. After 1 year and 5 days of Presiden's Rule, a mid-term election was held in 1969, and the second Ajoy Mukherjee Ministry (consisting of a 12-party coalition government) was formed in Bengal that lasted only for 13 months from 25 February 1969 to 16 March 1970. Again Jyoti Basu became the deputy chief minister from the Left Front.

The fifth assembly with the chief ministership of Ajoy Mukherjee's Bangla Congress was dominated by Left Front. As per the pre-election understanding, instead of Jyoti Basu Ajoy Mukherjj became the chief minister. However, after coming to power the CPI(M) initiated a land reform movement, that widened the widespread confrontation across the State. Through popular mobilization, 300,000 acres of land were redistributed, and clashes occurred among different political parties in the state. Wealthy landlords, in resistance against the United Front parties and the Naxalites, set up their own private paramilitaries.[49] Also, there was infighting between the CPI(M) and CPI, who charged against the former saying they adopted a 'domineering and dictatorial attitude' towards its coalition partners and CPI in particular. In September 1969 the CPI West Bengal State Council issued a resolution that accused CPI(M) of following a 'bankrupt opportunistic line' and claimed CPI(M) had created a 'reign of terror' in the Baranagar against CPI activists.[50] This rift among the different front partners created a chaotic atmosphere in Bengal. Later on 19 February 1970, three ministers belonging to the Bangla Congress (Sushil Kumar Dhara, Charu Mihir Sarkar, and Bhabatosh Soren) submitted their resignations to their party. Ajoy Mukherjee presented had no other option than to tender his resignation on 16 March 1970. Thereafter, the government was dismissed on 19 March, 1970.[51]

President's Rule was imposed again in West Bengal from 29 June 1971 to 20 March 1972. At the end of the President's Rule, a general election was held in the West Bengal legislative assembly and the Congress party came back in power for the last time in 1972. Siddhartha Shankar Ray, a barrister, and political stalwart became the 7th chief minister in the State (from 20 March 1972 to 30 April 1977). He took office at such a time when the Bangladesh Liberation War was just finished. Millions of Bengalees migrated from Bangladesh to India and particularly in West Bengal. Therefore, his administration was faced with the massive problem of resetting over a million refugees in various parts of the State. The crackdown on Naxalites also took place during this period.[52]

At the capacity of a renowned Barrister, he advised Prime Minister Indira Gandhi to impose an 'Internal emergency' under Article 352, and also drafted a letter for the President to issue the proclamation and showed her how democratic freedom could be suspended while remaining within the ambit of the Constitution.[53]   In post-independence Bengal, the period 1967 to 1972 was the most turbulent one. World Bank President Robert McNamara's plane was not allowed to land at Kolkata's Dum Dum airport. The frequent resort to gherao led to a flight of capital from Bengal.[54] The Hindu reported that "Mr. Ray was West Bengal's Chief Minister between 1972 and 1977 during the Naxal movement. He is credited with having quelled the movement, which, having started as a peasant uprising took the route of annihilation, causing a rift within his party's ranks and leadership.[55] It was Siddhartha Shankar Ray, who gave respite from violence to the people in Bengal by starting his policy of "fake encounters" in 1972 to eliminate the Naxalites.[56]

The order of emergency bestowed upon the Prime Minister the authority to rule by decree, allowing elections to be canceled and civil liberties were suspended. Most of Indira Gandhi's opponents were either imprisoned or they themselves went underground. There were massive violations of human rights. Prime Minister's younger son Sanjay Gandhi campaigned for massive forced sterilization. Under the national emergency between 1975-77, the Congress despite having continued to exert power and succeeding to quell the Naxalite agitation and movements in Bengal and cowing down other communists, the "tanashahi" (dictatorship) of Indira Gandhi enabled the Communists to return to power in 1977 and hold on till 2011.[57] Siddhartha Shankar Ray stayed in office for complete 5 years and 41 days. The assembly was dissolved on the 30th of April, 1977, and the vacant office was brought under President's Rule for the fifth time, though for an expanse of only 51 days. On June 21, 1977, the newly elected chief minister, Jyoti Basu assumed the office that marked the beginning of the three-decade-long communist rule in Bengal.[58]

Why did the CPI(M) Vanish in the 2021 Assembly Elections?

If we look back we will find that out of 250 seats the united Communist Party sec three seats in the 1946 elections of the Bengal Legislative Assembly and it was British-trained jurist, Jyoti Basu. We have discussed how the Left Front had fur as part of the United Front government since 1967. During the seventies under th Front government, the State witnessed anarchic Naxalite movements led

Majumber and Kanu Sanyal. The vice-chancellor of Jadavpur University, Gopal Sen, was murdered along with some other innocent people. Jawhar Sircar expressed in an article titled 'In a Calcutta Gripped With Naxal Violence and Police Brutality, People Lost Sons, Brothers and Friends' that, "….all of a sudden, in May that year, armed tribals rose in revolt and killed landlords and policemen in broad daylight somewhere near Siliguri. It took a while to understand that this was an act of an extreme left group of communists, and not by the left government itself — which was actually embarrassed by it. But soon, these villages where the peasants' movement had erupted, Naxalbari, Kharibari, and Phansidewa, became widely known, as did the leaders of the insurrection, Charu Mazumdar, Kanu Sanyal, and Jangal Santhal."[59] This total chaos and anarchy helped bring Congress back in power in 1972. But the elections were rigged, Jyoti Basu was defeated and a large number of communist leaders had to leave West Bengal and many others were forced to go underground.[60]

Sarkar further wrote that, in April 1969 the second UF government after coming to power released top Naxalite leaders from jail, as a gesture of goodwill. This backfired, and the entire disparate extreme left groups soon grouped together to form a new party, the Communist Party of India (Marxist Leninist). This CPI(ML) became the sworn enemy of its own earlier parent party, the CPI(M). Kolkata started witnessing regular bloody street battles between the ruling Marxists and their breakaway extremists, the Naxalites. No one was ever sure where bombs would be thrown next and who would die or be injured as 'collateral damage'. During classes, we would often hear deafening slogans just outside, *'Amaar Naam Tomaar Naam: Vietnam, Vietnam'*, rising in a crescendo. Teachers would often have to wait, some quite impatiently, as the sloganeers usually took their own time and would occasionally start giving speeches.[61]

The Communists were opposed to the introduction of computers in LIC. They had anti-machine sentiment. They were totally against industrialization. Only a change of their industrialization policy was found in the last term of the Buddhadeb Bhattacherjee government from 2006 to 2011. Moreover, after Jyoti Basu, there was not a single chief minister who could exert such command over the electors of Bengal. A close look at Jyoti's career shows that he had good schooling at St. Xavier, and college at Presidency,

Calcutta. He studied B.A. Honors in English there, and Bar at Law from Middle Temple, London. In London, he came in close association with Harry Pollitt, Rajani Palme Dutt, Ben Bradley, and other leaders of the Communist Party of Great Britain. He was the secretary of the West Bengal Provincial Committee of the Communist Party of India and was elected to the Bengal Legislative Assembly in 1946. After Independence, he was elected to the West Bengal Legislative Assembly 11 times in 1952, 1957, 1962, 1967, 1969, 1971, 1977, 1982, 1987, 1991, and 1996. He served as the Opposition Leader in the West Bengal Legislative Assembly from 1957 to 1967. He was deputy chief minister of the two United Front governments in West Bengal in 1967 and 1969.[62] Was there such a leader in West Bengal to match him to date? This is a major reason for CPIM's smaller number of seats to Nil seats in the Assembly Elections in 2021.

Himadri Ghosh wrote a beautiful article in The Wire that reads as: "the Communist Party of India (Marxist)-led Left Front failed to win even a single seat in the West Bengal assembly election. In a first since independence, there won't be a Left representative in the Bengal state assembly. The Left Front lost a deposit in 158 of 177 seats it contested. It didn't end here, in only four seats, CPI(M) secured a second position, the worst was 7th in the Darjeeling seat. A party, which uninterruptedly ruled Bengal for 34 years from 1977 to 2011, was reduced to zero in merely ten years."[63] A very pertinent question comes into the minds of millions of its previous and present workers, supporters, and members including party leaders and MLAs. Let us investigate the matter.

Was ISF a deciding factor for CPI(M)-Congress failure?

The most striking electoral gimmick of 2021 was CPI(M)'s an alliance with the newly formed Indian Secular Front of Abbas Siddiqui, an influential cleric of Hooghly's Furfura Sharif, who launched his new party just three months ahead of elections. The Left Front, Indian National Congress, and Indian Secular Front jointly held a rally in Kolkata's Brigade Parade ground, which was considered as the state's largest political gatherings over decades, which made the alliance leaders enthusiastic and workers rejuvenated. But the election result showed that their presence in the rally did not reflect into ballot boxes. Why? Because the banner they put read: Amrai Bikalpa, Amara Dharmanirapeksha. Amari Bhobishyat." It meant, "We are the alternative. We are secular. And we are the future." Though the name of Siddiqui's party is Indian Secular Front, it has earned the reputation of being a fundamentalist group, largely due to comments he made during the myriad religious speeches. By making an alliance with the ISF the Left did a mistake as it is complained by a section of its supporters and workers that, "The Left has damaged its secular credential."[64]

Further Himadri Ghosh wrote, "Several Bengal Left leaders who contested elections recently have already shown their discontentment against the alliance after the electoral debacle. Party veteran and state committee member Kanti Ganguly in an interview to a regional news channel said, "Alliance with ISF was never discussed in the state committee. At least, I was not part of any such discussion." It came to light after the election result was out that the party candidates were also not satisfied with the alliance of the Congress party. It was reported in The Wire that, "Not all Left Front partners were enthused by the alliance with the Congress and the ISF, but it was the CPI(M) leadership which pushed it. It was an opportunistic alliance, which neither had any progressive program nor had a smooth seat-sharing deal. It was largely perceived by the people as a spoiler.[65]

Too much contemplation and little action by the CPI(M) leadership

Many leaders of the Left parties and political commentators publicly opined that the biggest issue with the CPI(M) leadership was that they continued to introspect but didn't do much-needed course correction. Even after their consistent electoral failures, not a single party leader took responsibility for it. The Left Front takes too much time to discuss and take action.

Escapist theory of 'joint responsibility' of the CPI(M)

The CPI(M) talks about the 'joint responsibility.' The leaders are very clever. When they started defeating in election after election, they said it was no one's fault; rather it was the fault of everybody. Nobody within the CPI(M) has ever been held accountable for their consecutive electoral setbacks. There was never any real introspection on why they lost power in West Bengal in 2011. I doubt there is any smart and very highly educated political scientist in the party who has detail knowledge other than Marxism and Leninism or Maoism.

The top leaders are too old to revive the partymen

The top leaders of the CPI(M) never quit from their posts – thus they rarely allow other new blood to come into their bodies. Party's top leaders such as CPI(M) state secretary Surya Kanta Mishra, Left Front chairman Biman Bose, and other politburo members from Bengal like Md. Salim, Hannan Mollah, and Nilotpal Basu, observers say, made no efforts to revive the party and strengthen the organization in Bengal.

Widening gap between the grassroots workers and top leaders

While toured in different districts of the state during the research on gender empowerment and political participation of women, it was found by this researcher that there is little interaction and contact between the district or state leadership and local committee members. A few zonal committee members and secretaries often tried to contact in their personal choice, but there were many who did not like that. Many of them turned from proletariat to bourgeoise. The largest communist party in the country, however, has not made any effort to bridge the gap of leadership and its cadres on the ground.

Deviation from the ideology

The Left leaders in West Bengal kept on harping that theirs is an ideology-based party and their stance on policies or any socio-economic issues was driven by ideology. The same party forged an alliance with their arch-rival Congress in 2016 with a singular aim to defeat Mamata Banerjee's Trinamool Congress. The alliance didn't work. CPI(M)'s vote share reduced from 30% in 2011 to 19.7% in 2016. They only won 26 seats, a fall of 14 from 2011.

Culture of protest

Abhijit Guha in the book wrote that "Another important characteristic feature of communist ideology is revealed through its culture of protest. The communists give primacy to protest and rebellion before taking up or giving any thought to planning their future development agenda. Take, for example, the demand for giving land to the poor through land reforms in West Bengal. When the communists were not in power they undertook forcible capture of land from the big landlords to distribute the same to the landless and after coming to power they used the state machinery to expedite the process without giving an iota of importance towards the formation of farmer's cooperatives, and ecologically sustainable mode of agriculture growth, which if previously planned would have been more congruent with their socialistic ideal."[66]

Final verdict of the people in the elections

All the factors mentioned above played a catalytic role in bringing down the CPI(M) to zero. On the basis of all the reasons, the Left-Congress could not win in a single seat from anywhere out of 294 seats in the West Bengal Legislative Assembly. While their ally Indian Secular Front won only one seat in the elections. This was a stark decline from the 2016 general assembly election, where the alliance won 74 seats. In the 2019 Lok Sabha polls, the TMC won 42 seats, The INC got 2 seats and the BJP succeeded in 18 seats. The noteworthy point was the TMC's share of the vote went up by 3 percent, from 40 to 43 percent in the 2019 Lok Sabha elections. But the latest election result shows that the BJP has made inroads in the legislative assembly with 77 seats (later 2 MLAs resigned and returned to Lok Sabha), while the TMC's vote share in 2021 has gone up to 48.3 percent having secured a 9 percent lead over the BJP. Both the Congress and the CPM have become irrelevant with their combined vote share coming down to less than 10 percent.

Conclusions

From the above discussion, it can be concluded that the background was ready in 2010 for the defeat of the Communist Party of India (Marxist)-led Left Front government. The political, social, economic, and bureaucratic tussle between the Union and State government ultimately diminished the performance of the State government, lowered the living standard of the general public, and spoiled political culture in the State. Moreover, their destructive political agenda; borrowed and outdated ideology; and anti-industry policy relegated Bengal to the subordinate position in terms of industry, trade, and economic growth. The prolonged enjoyment of absolute power by the Left Front MLAs, Ministers, and party leaders automatically transformed them from "Public Servant to Political Boss." The evil effect of this fake self-assessment of the CPI(M) leaders brought about their ultimate debacle in the elections of 2011. The said election ensured the downfall of the 'red citadel' in Bengal and the rise of TMC as a phoenix. The Communist Party of India got only 40 seats in 2011, while the Trinamool Congress Party won 184 seats alone out of 294. Further, within a decade, the people of India witnessed another unbelievable result in the assembly elections of 2021, when the once-most-powerful party in Bengal lost all the seats and was reduced to merely a Party in the name.

Chapter – IX

Conclusion and Way Out

"Let noble thoughts come to us from all sides."

- *Rig Veda*

Introduction

From the foregoing discussions, it can be concluded that West Bengal is a state with high cultural, economic, political, and natural resources. The State is unique for various reasons. Being the capital of the then British Empire till 1911, Bengal and its capital Kolkata boasts of its Monument, Race Course, Victoria Memorial, National Library, Museum, and many others. West Bengal's rich heritage, culture, architecture, sculpture, and natural beauty have bestowed it an unparalleled position in the world. Its mineral resources, forests, sea beach, and hill stations attract foreign tourists as well as Indians from across the country. Despite all these bragging things, Bengal is notorious, nay famous for its revolutionary activities and contribution to the national freedom movement. Protesting vehemently against the tyrannical British rulers; non-cooperation with the foreign tradesmen; playing a major role in the national movement, and finally, the translucent rift between Subhas Chandra Bose and Mahatma Gandhi are well-known facts to any student of History. It seems that opposing the 'outsiders' is a perpetual desire and unabated tendency of the Bengalees. Despite all these facts, West Bengal and its people are unmatched in literature, economics, poetry, music, art, film, theatre, and above all in noble thoughts.

With all the beauty and rich culture of this State, politics in Bengal was never so smooth and idealistic except for a few years after Independence. West Bengal witnessed umpteen intra-party and inter-party ups and downs of the Indian National Congress and the Communist Party of India. The unseparated rule of the Indian National Congress from 1947 to 1967 is considered as the only perihelion period of the party. Further, after a brief rule (for only 90 days) of the Progressive Democratic Front led by Prafulla Chandra Ghosh, West Bengal witnessed political turmoil with two times of Presidential Rule from 1968 to 1971. Again Bengal underwent political anarchy. The reign of terror and political chaos started under the (mis)rule of the Indian National Congress led by Barrister Siddhartha Shankar Ray from 1972 to 1977. The heyday of the Communist Party of India (Marxist) started with Jyoti Basu, who ruled Bengal with a clear majority for 23 years from 1977 – 2000, and his successor Buddhadeb Bhattacharjee reigned for 11 more years from 2000 to 2011. The Trinamool Congress party led by its supremo Mamata Banerjee came to the Writers' Buildings in 2011 after defeating the once very powerful Communist Rulers in Bengal, and she has been enjoying power since then with the astounding majority. She retained her control over Bengal in the 2021 assembly elections also, after winning a thumping majority of 213 seats.

After conducting an empirical research on the performance of the State government a decade ago, the researcher conducted another study in 2020. The principal aim of the study was to examine how far the people of the state are satisfied with the performance of the present government. What are the problems being faced by the people, and, what are their suggestions for 'the people in power?' After exploring the perception of the people regarding various issues on good governance, politics, economy, society, health, education, etc., it was intended by the author to know the suggestions of the respondents for overall improvement and development of the State. Only highlighting the problems does not give any benefit to the people; rather tracing out the problems and extending concrete solutions is the best component of research. It is because only then the State would be able to change its policies for better governance and provide corruption-free services to the general public of the State. Now, let us examine the recommendations extended by the respondents to the *'People in Power'*. After discussing the general recommendations, we will enumerate the specific prescriptions of the respondents at the end.

General recommendations

The people were asked to express their opinions regarding some issues that touched upon their lives and livelihood. Hence, the majority of the respondents extended some recommendations to the State government for establishing good governance, ensuring transparency, and providing decent job opportunities for the youths of the state. The following table (Table 9.1) shows that majority of the respondents are against the distribution of free ration to all the people of this state. The teachers, the bureaucrats, the businessmen, the traders, the film actors, the judges, the lawyers, the defense personnel, the retired government employees, the professors – all were included in the scheme. Do they need at all the free ration items such as rice, coarse flour, etc? It is considered an insult to the people of middle, upper-middle, and high-income groups in the state. When a Professor of Calcutta University travels abroad by airplane abroad if his co-passenger asks him, "Do you receive free rice and coarse flour from the state government?" How would he feel? It lowered the dignity of a certain category of people in this state. The majority of respondents (68.81%) in the survey report also did not approve the free rationing system for all people in the State. On the other hand, a mere 15.59 percent of people considered the action of the government as appropriate. But a small percentage of respondents (7.52%) told that they were not sure about it, while 8.06 percent of respondents abstained from responding to the question.

Table: 9.1 Free ration is to be distributed only to the needy families

Opinion	Number of respondents	%
Yes	256	68.81
No	58	15.59
Maybe	28	7.52
Non respondents	30	8.06
Total	372	100

Source: Survey data

The Government of India has recently given the emphasis on skill development, the Make in India program, Aatmanirbhar Bharat (Self-reliant India), and the promotion of Micro Small Medium Enterprises. Hence, it is necessary to emphasize skill development training i.e. vocational courses from school life. Skilled students mean skilled India. Therefore, a great number of respondents (68.81%) enthusiastically told that they wish the present government should make all efforts to implement vocational courses i.e. skill development training on dozens of subjects from Class VI to University level. The Education Policy 2020 has also mentioned the introduction of vocational skill development from the School to the University level. Though the majority of the respondents agreed to implement the skill development training, small numbers of people (4.30%) were not supportive of the policy. But, 9.94 percent of respondents said it might be, and another 16.93 percent of people did not respond at all. One unanimous respondent pointed out that, "For this purpose, the government needs to build sufficient infrastructure and recruit efficient teachers first." Another respondent suggested that "Our youths should enhance their skills first."

Table: 9.2 All efforts should be made to implement vocational training on dozens of subjects from Class VI to University with proper subject teachers

Opinion	Number of respondents	%
Yes	256	68.81
No	16	4.30
Maybe	37	9.94
Non respondents	63	16.93
Total	372	100

Source: Survey data

Under the "House for All" and "Pradhan Mantri Gramin Awas Yojana" schemes there are provisions for constructing houses with toilet facilities in rural and urban areas by the local governments. Instead of paying direct cash through local governments to the beneficiaries, the government should construct single, double, or three-storied buildings for the local poor. It is suggested by people that, the poor may be given monetary support initially, but when the financial status of the people will be stable or better, the money spent for building the house should be repaid to the government by the poor-of-yesterday beneficiaries. However, the majority of respondents (52.95%) consider it necessary for building houses for the poor and homeless people in both rural and urban areas, but a small number of people (14.24%) did not approve the recommendation. Interestingly, 84 respondents (22.58%) neither confirmed nor denied the suggestion, while 10.21 percent of respondents avoided the question completely by not replying to it.

Table: 9.3 There should be 'House for All'

Opinion	No. of respondents	%
Yes	197	52.95
No	53	14.24
Maybe	84	22.58
Non respondents	38	10.21
Total	372	100

Source: Survey data

India is the land of young people. But, millions of educated youths are workless now. "Micro, Small, and Medium Enterprises (MSMEs) are regarded as the growth accelerators of the Indian economy, and more so for the rural economy as more than half of the MSMEs operate in rural India. MSMEs contribute about 30 percent in the national GDP, contribute about 40 percent to the overall exports and employ nearly 110 million people across the country."[1] As it is not possible to provide government jobs to the huge pool of unemployed youths, the government must encourage MSMEs to make our youths economically self-reliant. Hence, a question was asked to know from the people how these youths could be economically independent. The majority of the respondents - a total of 245 in number with 65.86% - consider that the challenge of unemployment can be met up with the setting up of Micro, Small, and Medium Scale Industries in the State. But some 33 people consisting of 8.87 percent did not support entrepreneurship for Indian unemployed youths; rather they were in favor of government decent jobs. However, 25 people (6.72%) could not decide about the issue, while 69 respondents (18.54%) remained completely silent in the question.

Table: 9.4 The Setting up of Micro, Small and Medium Scale industries is to be encouraged in true sense

Opinion	Number of respondents	%
Yes	245	65.86
No	33	8.87
Maybe	25	6.72
Non respondents	69	18.54
Total	372	100

Source: Survey data

Often complaints are received from the rural entrepreneurs that the nationalized banks harass them and other poor people in giving loans for setting up small businesses. Hence, it is necessary to make such a policy that the banks give loans to the persons for setting up small and medium scale industries and businesses. It is evident from the following table (Table 9.5) that a total of 236 respondents (63.44%) recommend concrete government policy and instruction for the nationalized banks for releasing loans without hassle to set up Micro Small Medium Enterprises, but this view was not supported by 7.52 percent respondents, and substantial number (66) of respondents comprising 17.74 percent were not sure if the government should formulate a policy for assisting entrepreneurs to set up MSMEs. On the other hand, 11.82 percent of respondents did not respond to the question.

Table: 9.5 The Government must make policy and instruct the nationalized banks to release loans without hassles to set up MSMEs

Opinion	Number of respondents	%
Yes	236	63.44

No	28	7.52
Maybe	66	17.74
Non respondents	44	11.82
Total	372	100

Source: Survey data

The number of quality researches in universities is negligible, and the position of colleges is very frustrating in West Bengal. The study highlights that majority of respondents 248 in number comprising 66.66 percent believe that all Universities and Colleges in the state should give more emphasis on research and innovation, but this view was not supported by 8.60 percent of respondents, while 11.02 percent respondents said "Maybe". A small percentage (13.70%) of respondents did not put their comments on the following question. One respondent urged, "And there must be an arrangement for campus interview."

Table: 9.6 All Universities and Colleges should give more emphasis on research and innovation

Opinion	Number of respondents	%
Yes	248	66.66
No	32	8.60
Maybe	41	11.02
Non respondents	51	13.70
Total	372	100

Source: Survey data

An interesting fact revealed by the study was that, a large number of respondents i.e. the 50.00 percent in all recommended for the research opportunities to be extended to school levels too. There are thousands are scholarly teachers in Schools, who can do better research works if opportunities and funds are provided to them from both Centre and State governments. But this view was not supported by 16.66 percent of respondents. One respondent, however, pointed out that, "Schools should be left for basic education." In this regard, only 5.10 percent of respondents were hesitant to decide, while a large number of respondents (28.22%) remained silent in regard to the extension of research facilities in schools.

Table: 9.7 The research opportunities should be extended to School levels too

Opinion	Number of respondents	%
Yes	186	50.00
No	62	16.66
Maybe	19	5.10
Non respondents	105	28.22
Total	372	100

Source: Survey data

During the reign of the Trinamool Congress party, the School Management Committees are dominated by local MLAs and councilors in Municipalities and Panchayat Members in rural areas. There is little freedom of work for the Head of the Institutions. As a result, a pertinent suggestion was sought from the respondents – The School administration should be completely free from political interference. In this sphere, the majority of the respondents (70.43%) replied in affirmative, but 7.79 percent of respondents still believed that in the schools, political interventions should have existed for the better governance of schools. A small number of respondents (7.52%) were indecisive, and a little more than one-tenth of respondents (14.24%) considered it better to remain silent. One respondent, however, pragmatically said that, "In West Bengal, it is not possible," while another unanimous respondent uttered that, "Not only school but also all college administration should be freed from political interference."

Table: 9.8 The School administrations should be completely free from political interference

Opinion	Number of respondents	%
Yes	262	70.43
No	29	7.79
Maybe	28	7.52

| Non respondents | 53 | 14.24 |
| Total | 372 | 100 |

Source: Survey data

In many High/Higher Secondary schools of West Bengal, the Managing Committee was set up only once i.e. in 2015/2016. And, since then no new President was appointed by the government. After the expiration of their term after three years from inception many tendered their resignation, and the School Managing Committees became dysfunctional. The term of the existing committees was extended by government notification after notification. In many schools, there are only administrators or DDOs. Hence, the majority of respondents (58.60%) recommended that there should be the President of every Managing Committee in Schools for smooth functioning of the administrative as well as financial activities, but it was not supported by 5.37 percent respondents, while 16.93 percent respondents said it might be set up. On the other hand, 19.08 percent of respondents did not think it proper to comment on this issue. One person recommended that "School is only for school teachers and students. Hence, there should not be any Managing Committee." The Head of the Institution with the help of some knowledgeable and energetic teachers should look after the administration and finance of the school.

Table: 9.9 All Schools should be provided with Managing Committee presidents and other government nominees immediately

Opinion	Number of respondents	%
Yes	218	58.60
No	20	5.37
Maybe	63	16.93
Non respondents	71	19.08
Total	372	100

Source: Survey data

Discrimination is going on in relation to giving 2 additional increments to the school teachers having Ph. D. Degrees. After 2005, the facility of giving 2 additional increments was withdrawn by government law. But still, a lot of teachers, who have attained a Ph. D. Degree before 2005, are getting the financial benefit of 2 additional increments. Hence, a large number of respondents (38.44%) feel it is necessary to give 2 additional increments to all the teachers having Ph. D. Degrees; but this view was no supported by 14.24 percent of respondents. However, 25.80 percent of respondents consider it "Maybe", and another 21.50 percent of respondents remained unanswered.

Table: 9.10 All the teachers with Ph. D. Degrees in Schools should be given two additional increments

Opinion	Number of respondents	%
Yes	143	38.44
No	53	14.24
Maybe	96	25.80
Non respondents	80	21.50
Total	372	100

Source: Survey data

If India wants to be an Aatmanirbhar Bharat there should be a rejuvenation of the rural economy. Unless the rural economy is not getting strong, India's dream of a $5 trillion economies will remain a distant dream. Therefore, it is necessary to set up industries in every village in India. The majority of respondents (72.04%) in the study extended support for setting up at least some small-scale industries to meet the local needs, but this view was not supported by 4.83 percent respondents, and 12.09 percent respondents remained indecisive. And unfortunately, 11.02 percent of respondents did not say anything in this matter.

Table: 9.11 All villages should have at least some small industries to meet the local needs

Opinion	Number of respondents	%
Yes	268	72.04
No	18	4.83
Maybe	45	12.09
Non respondents	41	11.02
Total	372	100

Source: Survey data

Not only the Micro Small and Medium Enterprises (MSMEs), it is necessary to set up big labor-intensive industries in every block and Subdivision of this State. Without industrialization, there will not be opened wide the employment opportunities for our youths; and without decent job opportunities and social security facilities, they will feel a kind of deprivation, which might turn fatal for the future growth of our State and the country as a whole. Therefore, the majority of the respondents (56.18%) in the study suggest that big labor-intensive industries should be set up in Bengal to meet the demands of huge unemployed youths of the state, unfortunately, a small number of respondents (7.52%) did not support the proposal, and 20.43 percent respondents did neither fully confirm nor reject the importance of the big labor-intensive industries. However, 15.86 percent of respondents did not answer at all.

Table: 9.12 Big labor intensive industries are to be set up

Opinion	Number of respondents	%
Yes	209	56.18
No	28	7.52
May be	76	20.43
Non respondents	59	15.86
Total	372	100

Source: Survey data

A large number of our students at present are not aware of our Constitution, its ideals, our freedoms and limitations, and the ideals of our freedom fighters. Besides, the sense of discipline, punctuality, self-respect, fellow-feeling, tolerance, respect for others, and above all patriotism is almost missing from the syllabus of Indian schools and our State is not an exception. Due to lack of this basic knowledge and education, our students and large numbers of (future) our citizens are engaged in disruptive and anti-national activities. These qualities are considered soft skills. And with these skills, every student of today will be a good and responsible citizen of tomorrow. They all will be our assets, instead of liabilities and burdens of society. It is learned from the following table (Table 9.13) that, 66.66 percent of respondents want to see the development of skills or capacities of the Indian youths through the early implementation of the National Education Policy-2020, but this view was no corroborated by 8.60 percent of respondents. On the other hand, 10.21 percent of respondents said it might be, and 14.51 percent of them did not say anything in this regard.

Table: 9.13 Skills or capacities of Indian youths should be enhanced through the implementation of National Education Policy-2020

Opinion	Number of respondents	%
Yes	248	66.66
No	32	8.60
Maybe	38	10.21
Non respondents	54	14.51
Total	372	100

Source: Survey data

Always there is a debate with the concept of population. One group of scholars considers it is wealth to the nation, while the other group thinks that the population must be controlled. However, it comes to light from this study that, 67.74 percent of respondents recommend stringent measures to control the population growth of the state. On the other hand, 9.67 percent of people do not think so. Interestingly 14.24 percent of respondents are not sure if the population should be controlled at all, while a small number of people did not respond to the question

(8.33%). One unanimous respondent proposed that "Two-child norm should be strictly implemented in the State in government jobs and getting elected as members of local bodies and Legislative Assembly."

Table: 9.14 Stringent measures must be taken to control population of this state

Opinion	Number of respondents	%
Yes	252	67.74
No	36	9.67
May be	53	14.24
Non respondents	31	8.33
Total	372	100

Source: Survey data

West Bengal being a bordering state foreign infiltration has become a regular phenomenon. This has been running since the bifurcation of the two independent nations – Pakistan and India in 1947. Assam, West Bengal, and some other states witness infiltration of Bangladeshi people from across the border. In West Bengal infiltration is a major problem since the time of Independence. The infiltrators, after coming to India and this bordering state of West Bengal, often seek to destabilize peace and normalcy in the State. Moreover, they share a substantial chunk of the developmental pie of the State government. It is found that the majority of the respondents 58.04 percent people did not support illegal infiltration. Hence, a large number of respondents (216 respondents) opined that no illegal infiltration should be allowed in the State. Only a small number of respondents (15 persons) supported illegal infiltration while 68 people (18.27%) were undecided and 16.93 percent of respondents did not reply to the question. One respondent wonders "Whether it is at all possible by either the Centre or the state government to stop illegal infiltration."

Table: 9.15 No illegal infiltrations should be allowed in the State

Opinion	Number of respondents	%
Yes	216	58.04

No	15	4.03
May be	68	18.27
Non respondents	63	16.93
Total	372	100

Source: Survey data

A new trend in West Bengal arose during the last 10 years rule of Mamata Banerjee i.e. to distribute money to the clubs. People's money is being distributed from the government exchequer to the clubs. What fun the rulers are making with public money! Hence, quite naturally this action of the government was not supported by 70.16 percent of respondents, while only 8.60 percent of respondents supported the government's policy of giving away public money to the clubs, who often did not utilize the same inappropriate manner and purpose. However, 12.36 percent of respondents were undecided about the state government's action, and a negligible percentage of respondents (1.34%) kept themselves away from responding to the question.

Table: 9.16 Clubs must not be given any government money

Opinion	Number of respondents	%
Yes	261	70.16
No	32	8.60
Maybe	46	12.36
Non respondents	33	8.87
Total	372	100

Source: Survey data

The TMC government initiated distributing doles to different sections of people on different pretexts. As if its own hard-earned money is being distributed at the sweet will of the government. The suggestions as revealed through the survey highlight that, majority of people (48.92%) do not like government doles. A lot of respondents feel that government must stop giving away doles. It makes people mentally paralyzed, and dependent on the government's charity. But 9.94 percent of respondents do not think it is right to stopping government doles to the people. On the other hand, 20.16 percent of respondents were confused to give a proper reply in either affirmative or negative, and another 20.96 percent of respondents remained non-respondents. However, "Doles can be given only to the old, helpless and disabled persons", one respondent suggested.

Table: 9.17 The government doles must be stopped

Opinion	Number of respondents	%
Yes	182	48.92
No	37	9.94
May be	75	20.16
Non respondents	19 78	20.96
Total	372	100

Source: Survey data

The aim of learning is earning. If there are not decent job opportunities after attaining educational the highest University qualifications, then what is the meaning of studying hard in colleges and universities? Why do parents spend money on children's education? Has the government ever thought over it seriously? Hence, the majority of the respondents (68.81%) proposed more decent jobs for the educated youths of Bengal, while 6.45 percent respondents were happy with the temporary or contractual nature of jobs being provided by the state government in civic police, education department, fire service, and other departments. However, 11.55 percent of respondents could not decide what is right and what is not, while 13.17 percent of respondents were nonrespondents in this regard.

Table: 9.18 More decent jobs should be provided to the educated youths

Opinion	Number of respondents	%
Yes	256	68.81
No	24	6.45
Maybe	43	11.55
Non respondents	49	13.17

| Total | 372 | 100 |

Source: Survey data

The West Bengal government has recruited a lot of civic volunteers in the State. The chief minister increased the salary of Civic volunteers from Rs. 8000.00 per month to Rs. 9,000.00 from September, 2020.[2] On the other hand, the salary of a West Bengal Constable (male) is on the pay scale of Rs. 5,400-25,200. They are entitled to receive a salary in the Pay Band 2 with a Grade Pay of Rs. 2,600.00. Hence, the civic volunteers need to be given permanent status and their salary should be equal to a constable in the State. The survey result shows that the majority of respondents were in favor of the interest of the civic volunteers. A large section of respondents (41.12%) suggest that the temporary civic volunteers should be made permanent, and on the other hand, more than a quarter of respondents (28.96%) do not support the proposition. 16.39 percent of respondents were undecided in the matter, but 21.50 percent of respondents remained non-respondents. One respondent said, "Civic volunteers should be made permanent after proper training," while another respondent pointed out that, "All due examinations must be conducted in all recruitments." Another person said, "They must undergo proper training."

Table: 9.19 The temporary civic volunteers should be made permanent

Opinion	Number of respondents	%
Yes	153	41.12
No	78	28.96
Maybe	61	16.39
Non respondents	80	21.50
Total	372	100

Source: Survey data

Health is wealth. In West Bengal, it is often complained by people that emergency hospital services are provided through some intermediaries. In many cases, those who have no connection with political leaders cannot avail of the services properly. Hence, people demanded that hospitals should be freed from political dadas (elder brothers). More than one-third of respondents (73.11%) suggested in the survey that, hospitals should be freed from political intervention, while 8.33 percent of respondents disagreed with them, and 6.18 percent considered it might be necessary, while 12.36 percent people remained Non-respondents.

Table: 9.20 Hospitals should be freed from political intervention

Opinion	Number of respondents	%
Yes	272	73.11
No	31	8.33
May be	23	6.18
Non respondents	18 46	12.36
Total	372	100

Source: Survey data

Since 2013 West Bengal has been attracting national public attention for corruption. The most interesting fact is that the chief minister in almost all the big cases came forward to rescue the corrupt officers and leaders. An IAS officer Godala Kiran Kumar, while working as the CEO of the Siliguri Jalpaiguri Development Authority (SJDA) from 2011-2013, it was alleged that he siphoned off Rs.80 crore in a scam involving Rs.200 crore.[3] After his arrest and compulsory waiting, the chief minister reinstated him as the Joint Secretary of the Statistics department in 2016. Later he was suspended and sentenced to jail.

Further, the TMC leaders, MPs, MLAs have been seen on the television screens take bribes in 2016. This became a great issue before the assembly elections of 2021. BJP Rajya Sabha MP Swapan Dasgupta, who was a probable chief ministerial face in Bengal, claimed that corruption in West Bengal has reached sky-high.[4] On the other hand, Suman Nath wrote in an article in the Economic and Political Weekly[5] that, "Trinamool Congress's decisive second term in West Bengal in 2016, even after serious corruption charges were levied on the party, makes it clear that corruption is not important as was thought by the opposition." Again, he wrote that "A fortnight before the 2016 assembly elections in West Bengal, Narada News brought forth video clippings of 12 key Trinamool Congress (TMC) leaders, purportedly accepting bribes from an unidentified person. The impact of this sting operation made the TMC supremo Mamata Banerjee acknowledged making a mistake in selecting candidates for the election (Hindustan Times 2016)." However, the issue of 'corruption became a very serious weapon of the BJP before the 2021 state legislative assembly elections. Therefore, 76.34 percent of respondents suggested that corruption must be traced and rooted out from government offices. But 4.30 percent of respondents did not approve the proposition, and only 2.15 percent of respondents were hesitant to prescribe it, and 17.20 percent of respondents remained silent.

Table: 9.21 Corruption to be traced and rooted out from government offices

Opinion	Number of respondents	%
Yes	284	76.34
No	16	4.30
May be	8	2.15
Non respondents	64	17.20
Total	372	100

Source: Survey data

Corruption has eaten up Bengal's recruitment process – as is complained by a majority of respondents. It is reported in various electronic and print media that some middlemen or political leaders are taking bribes of Rs. 20-25 lakhs for giving the job of a High School Teacher and this rate is a little less in case of Primary School Teachers. This study also reveals the reflection of the same opinion of the people. Majority of the respondents recommended fair and free recruitments in all government departments. More than one-third of respondents (75.53%) extended their view that all recruitments in Bengal should be free and fair, while 6.45 percent of people did not recommend that, and 4.83 percent were hesitant, and 13.17 percent respondents remained silent. In personal interaction, most of the respondents expressed in favor of the motion. One respondent, in reply to the proposition, said that "Definitely, but it will never have happened."

Table: 9.22 All recruitments should be free and fair

Opinion	Number of respondents	%
Yes	281	75.53
No	24	6.45
May be	18	4.83
Non respondents	49	13.17
Total	372	100

Source: Survey data

Specific recommendations

At the end of the questionnaire, numerous respondents have mentioned a lot of suggestions. These were done with the hope of improving the existing socio-economic and political situation; controlling the level and extent of corruption, and ensuring good governance in the State. But there were asymmetry and incoherence in their prescriptions. Moreover, a lot of suggestions were analogous to others. Therefore, after filtering the manifold suggestions a few specific recommendations, which were not included in the questionnaire, have been enumerated hereunder. Health and education are the two most significant pillars of development that should be strengthened with more budgetary allocation. It is a fact that health is wealthier than wealth, and education is the backbone of a society. Hence, the State government must allocate more funds in these two sectors for the holistic development of the human capital of the State. The school buildings, which are dilapidated, should be repaired regularly; teachers should be recruited as per requirement through free and fair examinations of the School Service Commission (SSC), and orientation programs of teachers should be implemented for their professional upgradation. All schools must be provided with a valid Managing Committee, and the Presidents and other members must be highly qualified (in place of existing graduates, they should be at least Master Degree holders) and with the significant academic and social contribution to society. The Teachers with Ph. D. Degrees should be given two additional increments. There should be a reservation of seats for existing school teachers in College and University teaching posts. Age bar for recruitment of School Teachers should be withdrawn in time of recruitment in Higher Education Department. The age of retirement of teachers should be extended from the present 60 to 65. The National Education Policy 2020 should be implemented at the earliest so that students can avail themselves of the scope to learn Constitutional duties, Fundamental Rights, and reasonable restrictions on the Rights and Freedoms. Besides, morality, discipline, lessons on patriotism, and many such ideals could be inculcated among the young minds of our students through the implementation of the said Policy. This will bring about an affirmative change in the society, family, and the State as a whole within a few decades.

The shortage of doctors and nurses must be immediately filled up with setting up more medical colleges at least one in every district. More pathological laboratories with trained technicians should be opened. There should be uniformity in the fees of each type of testing. Medicine manufacturing companies must be invited to West Bengal. The manufacturing of costly and life-saving medicines, vaccines, medical equipment such as PPE, oxygen, oxymeters, gloves, masks, etc. should be encouraged. Research and innovation in the medical sector are highly required at this hour of a pandemic. All the blocks in West Bengal should have a medium-sized hospital with all facilities, and rural hospitals should be equipped with the necessary infrastructure, doctors, nurses, and pathological facilities.

Providing decent jobs can only be possible through setting up more small, medium, and large-scale industries. More electronic and software, as well as hardware manufacturing companies, should be set up. The agro-based industries can be scattered in every district. The rural produce is to be upgraded through continuous training and interaction with the farmers and producers. Local demand has to be created through local governments for locally made goods. Let the youths of villages be skilled in hundreds of soft and hard trades. The use of technology in agriculture can be both profitable and lucrative to the educated youths. If agriculture is our base, the industry is our future. Hence, both agriculture and industry should be developed equivocally. All the old and left out industries in the State should be rejuvenated. Foreign Direct Investment must be invited and taking cut money from the industrialists should be stopped at any cost. Trace out the Bengalee industrialists from across the world, and request them to set up industries in the State for the holistic development of our youths.

The government and particularly the chief minister must not stand by the corrupt leaders. There are two different narratives in this regard. To stand by the bribe-takers, and dishonest leaders and officers reflect the chief minister's personal empathy and love and affection for them. The other narrative is that it indicates her direct support for corruption and corrupted leaders. This has a larger negative impact upon the minds of general people in India and particularly among the educated and cultural citizens of this State. The open support for (allegedly) corrupted and arrested leaders and officers since 2013 by the de facto Head of the State does not indicate the good health of state administration. Moreover, defending the corrupt (or allegedly corrupted) ministers, leaders, and officers with government money, and using Constitutional capacity is unjustified, unfair, and unconstitutional too.

Not punishing the lawbreakers indicates weak and impotent administration. Punishing a selective few for violating the same law is also termed as partial administration, which is equal to the violation of Constitutional duties. The King should be impartial. Moreover, remaining silent when a section of agitated mob burnt railway stations, train compartments, public vehicles including an ambulance the government remained silent in 2019. Was the act matched with the personality and chair of a chief minister and particularly of Mamata Banerjee? As a result, the image of the State government was tarnished before the country. The government should think about it and act accordingly so that nothing serious law and order problem takes place in the future.

In West Bengal, a very clownish act is found that, if a member or an office-bearer of the ruling party breaks a law, commits a crime, or uses words that are prohibited in the Constitution as 'Reasonable Restrictions,' he is protected by the ruling party, and exempted from getting punishment by police and law of the land. Instead, it was seen that, at best, he was verbally or by mere 'showcase letter' punished by the Party only for violating the law of land. It is very odd and abominable. This was observed during the Left Front regime too. The police have, to a great extent, lost their image because people have witnessed them on some occasions to remain silent spectators in front of law-breakers. They too may be imparted regular training and brought under orientation program. And the law should be equally applied to every citizen - from ruling party workers, members, and leaders to opposition party leaders, members, and supporters, and VIPs or common citizens. Police must act instantly and strongly while there will be any law and order problem. They should be given free hand to perform their duties.

The pre-poll and post-poll violence must be stopped at any cost. The participation of subaltern people in the political process is good and desirable too, but their over-engagement in political agitations and movements is dangerous for democracy. They are mostly ignorant people; they should be handled properly and carefully. The political leaders must not do this mistake that "these men and women are ours, and they will continue to dance as per our direction forever". If they think so they are merely living in 'the paradise of fools.' Today one particular section of people in a locality may swim into action at the indication of your eyes, or instigation of yours, but nobody can guarantee that the same 'men and women of yours' will not turn their face and camp once you are no more in power and position. The attack on political leaders including Central ministers, MPs, MLAs, and even common citizens (often on opposition party leaders and members), damaging their cars with stones and lathis; torturing the opponents, oppressing them, abusing them, insulting them openly, and even deporting from their homes for merely 'not seeing eye to eye with you, or not behaving as directed by you' should be stopped immediately by the government for the larger interest of the general people in the State. Peace, harmony, and co-existence of people must be established with an iron hand.

The domination of some lumpens in the TMC party should be controlled before it crosses its all limits. Except a few amongst these faces such as Jogen Chowdhury, Subhaprasanna, Mahasweta Devi, Aparna Sen, Dipak Ghosh, Prof. Sugata Bose, mentor group members of Presidency University, Dr. Amit Mitra, Prof. Sunanda Sanyal, and the like are almost missing from the list of TMC party. A party depending mostly on the lower strata of society cannot run for long period; there should be a representation of all sections of society. Though it gives political empowerment to the marginal sections of society, it dampens the spirit of a lettered and enlightened section of society. The chief minister too is becoming parochial in her outlook. Therefore, it is high time that the government and chief minister should prevent the dampening spirit of the middle and upper strata of the society and brings down the gap between gentry and rustic citizens equally in the political process. It must be remembered that, "The right man should be placed in the right position".

The acts of tolabaji and taking cut money should be stopped. A section of dishonest government employees is taking bribes regularly from their customers and general people who come to their office for any specific work. Many of the local TMC leaders also ask for cut money from newcomers, businessmen, rent-seekers, shop-keepers, and many such people. The payment of cut money for availing of government beneficiary schemes is sure to make damage to the party in the days to come. It must be traced and rooted out from society in no time.

The people who are running the show of state administration in the three-tier system of governance -state, district, and local level – should be honest, sincere, and wise, educated, and people-friendly. The Councillors, Panchayat members, MLAs – all have to work for the interest of the people only and not for their own. Many of the Chairpersons of Municipalities, heads of the three-tier *Panchayati Raj* System are not aware of the laws and rules of Municipal affairs as well as rules of Gram Panchayats. Some of them are very parochial and do give any importance to the schools and others working under their jurisdiction. This situation should be improved in the State. Giving a particular section of society too much relaxation and imposing restrictions on others is unfair. The government and TMC leaders must treat all people and institutions of society equally. Besides, nepotism should be stopped everywhere.

In a television discussion at Swabhumi, Salt Lake organized by ABP Ananda prior to the 2021 elections (dt.8.01.2021, time 8.00 p.m - 9.15 p.m) where Sukhendu Sarkar of Trinamool Congress, Adhir Ranjan Chowdhury of National Congress party, Sujan Chakraborty of CPI(M), and Dilip Ghosh of Bharatiya Janata Party were sitting in one row and the opposite row was occupied by Rudranil Ghosh, actor; Tilottama Majumder, writer; Anindya Chatterjee, singer, etc. while in the audience there were some eminent (non) political persons of Bengal. The "common citizens" of Kolkata asked some basic questions to the political leaders, if any of them come (will surely come) to power, and urged them to fulfill or address the minimum requirements of "common people". The proposals and views of all the persons sitting in the "common citizens' row" can be summed up as hereunder.

1.   The political leaders, being members of the larger society, should be available not only before the elections, rather throughout the year as and when asked to at least hear the words of common people.

2.   When Deshbandhu Chittaranjan Das was the Mayor of Calcutta Municipal Corporation, in 1923 a young councilor was elected and offered Rs. 3000.00 as monthly salary. The young councilor humbly returned the offer and urged the Mayor to make half of his monthly salary to Rs.1500.00. This kind of honesty and selfless service was sought from the present political leaders of Bengal.

3.   Let all political leaders stop blaming and throwing mud at each other before elections. The use of language should be made judiciously and wisely by the leaders of all political parties.

4.   The culture of considering themselves (the political leaders) as 'persons of the special category' should be replaced with the 'persons of the general category' and the sole intention should be public service.

5.   The roads should be garbage-free, poverty should be reduced and people's skills and capabilities should be increased.

6.   One singer (Anindya Chatterjee) told with folded hands to stop quoting Rabindranath Tagore's poems wrongly. Also, the use of words by many political leaders of contesting parties should be polite and intellectual; rather than foul and abusive.

7.   Any person in West Bengal should have a choice of his own in regard to eat food, wear a dress, make love, and enjoy life in his own way. This should be respected by anybody who may come to power.

8.   Instead of visiting with some goons before the elections, they should be visited the places with professors, academicians, artists, and respected persons of society.

9.   The police should be used only for maintaining the law and order of the land, and they should not be used for personal purposes. The morale of the police should be brought back in the state.

10.   By giving people dole, the government is making them paralyzed; instead people should be made economically independent so that they can afford their own needs with their hard-earned money.

11.   Giving all people free health facility and rice @Rs.2 only reflect the poverty of planning of the government. All people do not require the facility, but this facility is making Bengal's people insulted and belittled them before the world.

12.   The BJP is taking all TMC leaders including some tainted and corrupted leaders. If they give tickets to all of them, then the TMC leaders in the guise of BJP will rule in the same pattern and style in the state government. How will the BJP check this trend? Will the old BJP not be deprived and frustrated?

13.   Why so many poor laborers are leaving Bengal? If there were earning opportunities in the State, would they leave Bengal? This reflects Bengal's poor employment facility and infrastructure.

14.   If Bengal is better in medical services, as is claimed by the ruling TMC Party, why do the people from Bengal go to Chennai, Vellore, Madras for medical treatment?

15.   If Bengal's education system is better, why students are not coping with other students in all Indian competitive examinations such as UPSC Civil Service?

16.   Why Bengal's students are going out of this state for higher studies and for seeking employment in other states if there were enough opportunities for decent jobs here?

17.   Both the ruling and opposition parties should work together, after the election is over, for the holistic development of the state.

Conclusions

From the above discussion, it comes to light that a lot of recommendations have been put forward by the general respondents through the survey data, which were discussed thoroughly in the first part of this chapter, while the second part highlighted some specific recommendations of the respondents and some 'common citizens' of this State. These prescriptions and opinions extended by the general electors on the eve of the assembly elections regarding the poor state of affairs, the weird behavioral pattern of political leaders, misquote of Tagore and others, negligible job opportunities, unfortunate health services, infertile education management, pitiful condition of migrant laborers, cleanliness of Kolkata and cities, the exodus of Bengal's youths to other states in search of job and employment, the unproductive impact of dole politics on society and human life, etc. threw a bunch of new challenges to the existing and future rulers of this State. The recommendations and views though expressed by a small group of people from different walks of life actually reflected the inherent aspirations and demands of the common citizenry to the forthcoming rulers. One may find a touch of indignation in the free opinions of the 'common electors of this state.' to the political leaders of the major contesting parties, but actually, those were the aspirations and demands of the common people to the 'people in power.' General people want very little from the leaders of the State. They want to see the State as developed, progressive, and corruption-free. The main concern of the majority of people is skill development of our youths, their decent job opportunities through the proper and fair examination process. The major emphasis was given to the improvement of the health and education sectors. Unfortunately, none of the prominent political leaders of Bengal was so people-friendly, or service-prone. The political leaders, irrespective of any party, talk big but deliver little. Initially (after coming to power) they merely show off their respect for public sentiment and delivering good governance with transparency; but in no time most of them turn to haughty, out of touch with common people, and corrupted. Soon, they take a U-turn from 'public servant' to 'public master'.

However, it is hoped that after the elections both the ruling and opposition party leaders should work shoulder to shoulder to provide service to the general people in the state.

There should not be any kind of violence between groups, castes, and communities. The leaders of either party must desist from encouraging their supporters, and workers to take retaliation. All the political parties must respect the participation and liking of every voter in society. Anyone can vote for any party, any person can shout slogans for any candidate, and any elector can campaign for any candidate or party. It is his or her fundamental right. But, if the winner beats and burns the losers after the elections, it only increases the hate and cruelty in society. Today's losers will be tomorrow's winners and vice versa. If they also take the same course of action what would happen, then? So, please remember that we all are brothers and sisters. Hence, there should be no violence, no oppression by one another, no beating to anyone, or no burning of any house, or no torturing on any of our neighbors. Let us hope that, there will be a marriage between the State and the Union government, and the State government should work hand in hand with the Central government for attaining the Sustainable Development Goals to be attained by 2030. It is cooperation and not confrontation that can bring about lasting peace and prosperity in the State. Let us stay together, help each other and make our loving State the best one in the world.

References:

<u>**Chapter - I**</u>

1. Bryan S. Turner, Max Weber: From History to Modernity, Routledge, New York, p. Preface viii.

2. Robert A. Dahl, 2001, On Democracy, East-West Press, New Delhi, p.60.

3. Robert A. Dahl, 2001, On Democracy, East-West Press, New Delhi, p.61.

4. "Left-Congress ally with ISF's Abbas Siddiqui: Who is the Muslim cleric and what impact will he have on polls?" Times Now digital, March 1, 2021.

5. 'PM Modi, Shah focus on Bengal's glorious past on election eve', The Hindustan Times, Kolkata, February 19, 2021.

6. "Bengal's decadal population growth dips to 14%", BusinessLine, April 6, 2011.

7. Census of India, 2011.

8. Census of India, 2011.

9. "Kolkata records year's highest temperature at 39.6 deg C", Business Standard, Kolkata, June 14, 2019.

10. Geology and Mineral Resources of the States of India: Part I - West Bengal, 1999,

   the Director-General, Geological Survey of India, Calcutta, p. 20.

Chapter -2

1. Keshab Chandra Mandal, 2021, National Education Policy 2020, The Key to Development in India, Notion Press, p. 1.

2. Keshab Chandra Mandal, 2014, The Thoughts of an Unknown Indian, Scholars' Press, Germany, p. 132.

3. Anil Kumar Biswas, Universalization of Education, Kurukshetra, May 2011.

4. B. K. Pramakin and Madan Mohan Singh, Sarva Shikhya Abhiyan and Inclusion Education, Kurukshetra, May 2011, p. 16.

5. Maulana Abul Kalam Azad was quoted by B.K. Pramanik and Madan Mohan Singh, Sarva Shikhya Abhiyan and Inclusion Education, Kurukshetra, May 2011, p. 17.

6. D.D. Headey and A. Hodge, 2009, was quoted by E. Wesley, F. Peterson, in their article 'The Role of Population in Economic Growth,' Vol. 7, Issue 4, October 11, 2017', https://us.sagepub.com/en-us/nam/open-access-at-sage.

7. Baker, D., Delong, J. B., Krugman, P. R. (2005). Asset returns and economic growth. Brookings Papers on Economic Activity, 1, pp. 289-330.

8. Linden, E. (2017, June). Remember the population bomb? It's still ticking. New York Times: Sunday Review, 4.

9. Atul Thakur, 'How and why West Bengal fell behind India,' The Times of India, April 6, 2021.

10. India Brand Equity Foundation, 'West Bengal State Presentation and Economy Growth Report', May 17, 2021.

11. Biswamoy Mukherjee, 'Bengal government introduces a number of industry-friendly policies in 2019', United News of India, Kolkata, December 25, 2019.

12. India Brand Equity Foundation, 'West Bengal State Presentation and Economy Growth Report', May 17, 2021, Retrieved from https://www.ibef.org/states/west-bengal-presentation on 19.06.2021.

13. Economic Survey 2020-21, Vol. 1, Government of India, Ministry of Finance Department of Economic Affairs, New Delhi, p. 121.

14. Economic Survey 2020-21, Vol. 1, Government of India, Ministry of Finance Department of Economic Affairs, New Delhi, p. 121.

15. Maitreesh Ghatak, 'The Story of Bengal's Economy', The Hindustan Times, April 15, 2021.

16. SDGs India Index, 'List of Indian states and union territories by poverty rate', December 31, 2019.

17. 'Indian States by GDP', 1st March 2021, Ministry of Statistics and Programme, Government of India.

18.   Keshab Chandra Mandal, 2010, Empowerment of Women and Panchayat Raj: Experiences from West Bengal, Sarat Book Distributors, Kolkata, p. 38.

19. Rehana Jhapvala, 'Empowerment and the Indian Working Woman', 2001, in Promilla Kapur (ed.), Empowering the Indian Women,   The Director, Publications Division, Ministry of Information and Broadcasting, Government of India, New Delhi, p.56.

20. Valsamma Anthony, "Education and Employment: The Key to Women Empowerment", Kurukshetra, February 2006, Vol. 54, No. 4. P. 27.

21. Archana Singh, "Micro Finance For Women's Empowerment", Kurukshetra, April 2004, p. 34.

22. Keshab Chandra Mandal, 2019, Gender Empowerment in Local Governments: Prospects and Debates of Sustainable Development in India, Levant Books, Kolkata, p. 155.

23. Miller was quoted by Niroj Sinha (ed.), 2000, Women in Indian Politics, New Delhi, Gyan Publishing House, p. 15.

24. Lasswell was quoted by Niroj Sinha (ed.), 2000, Women in Indian Politics, New Delhi, Gyan Publishing House, p. 15.

25.   Ministry   of   Panchayati   Raj,   Government   of   India, https://pib.gov.in/PressReleaseIframePage.aspx?PRID=1658145 retrieved on 10.5.2021.

Chapter – III

1.   Dipankar Sinha, 2013, 'Same Side Goal' Politics: West Bengal's New Brand Image?'Economic and Political Weekly, Vol. 48, No. 30, July 27, p. 19.

2.   Keshab Chandra Mandal, 2010, West Bengal Government: The Issues and Constraints of Development, Levant Books, Kolkata, p. 2.

3.   Samit Kar, 'Agricultural Marketing – The Emerging Practice of Agri-Business,' Kurukshetra, August 2009, p. 36.

4.   Keshab Chandra Mandal, 2010, West Bengal Government: The Issues and Constraints of Development, Levant Books, Kolkata, p. 2.

5.   Zia Haq, 'How Bengal economy has fared over the last decade', The Hindustan Times, New Delhi, March 21, 2021.

6.   Zia Haq, 'How Bengal economy has fared over the last decade', The Hindustan Times, New Delhi, March 21, 2021.

7.   'The GST collection in West Bengal improving with growing economic activities: Official', The Economic Times, Kolkata, August 7, 2020.

8.   Economic Survey 2020-21 Vol. II, Government of India Ministry of Finance, New Delhi, p. 316.

9.   West Bengal State Portal, Government of West Bengal, https://www.wb.gov.in/about-west-bengal-at-a-glance.aspx retrieved on 12.05.2021.

10.   India Tourism Statistics, 2019, Ministry of Tourism, Government of India, p.103.

11.   ibid., pp. 104-105.

12.   India Tourism Statistics, 2019, Ministry of Tourism, Government of India, p.116.

13.   'Bengal Global Business Summit helped in improving state economy: Amit Mitra hits out at Dhankhar', The Indian Express, September 20, 2020.

14.   All India Trinamool Congress Manifesto 2021, p. 28.

15.   Namrata Acharya, 'West Bengal saw 97% decline in industries since 2010', Business Standard, Kolkata, December 28, 2013.

16.   'Bengal bags Rs. 7 kcr biz proposals in pandemic yr,' The Times of India, Kolkata, December 26, 2020.

17.   All India Trinamool Congress Manifesto 2021, p. 28.

18.   All India Trinamool Congress Manifesto 2021, pp. 22-23.

19.   All India Trinamool Congress Manifesto 2021, p. 32.

20.   Paschim Banga, Year 50, Vol. 1-3, May-July, 2017, p. IV.

21.   Department of Health and Family Welfare, Government, https://swasthyasathi.gov.in/ retrieved 13.05.2021.

22.   All India Trinamool Congress Manifesto 2021, p. 32.

23.   Sweety Kumari, 'How West Bengal Govt curbed food prices while providing better returns to farmers', The Indian Express, June 24, 2020.

24.   https://wb.gov.in/government-schemes-details-shilpasathi.aspx   retrieved 13.05.2021.

25.   Biswamoy Mukherjee, 'Bengal government introduces a number of industry-friendly policies in 2019', United News of India, Kolkata, December 25, 2019.

26.   'Bengal clears Sech Banchu Prakalpa to boost irrigation', Business Standard, 13 September 2014.

27.   https://wb.gov.in/government-schemes-details-samajikmukti.aspx   retrieved 13.05.2021.

28.   Housing   Dept.,   Govt.   of   West Bengal,https://www.wbhousing.gov.in/pages/display/77-functions retrieved 13.05.2021.

29.   https://wb.gov.in/government-schemes-details-joldharo.aspx   retrieved 13.05.2021.

30.   https://wb.gov.in/government-schemes-details-madhursneha.aspx   retrieved 13.05.2021.

31.   https://www.policeresults.com/karma-sathi-prakalpa-scheme/   retrieved 13.05.2021.

32.   https://wb.gov.in/government-schemes-details-karmatirtha.aspx   retrieved 13.02.2021

33.   West Bengal State portal, https://wb.gov.in/government-schemes-details-amarfasal.aspx retrieved 13.05.2021.

34.   Government of West Bengal, Finance Department, Budget Branch, 29 August 2014.

35.   Indrajit Kundu, India Today, August 20, 2016, Kolkata.

36.   https://www.wbmdfc.org/Home/about retrieved 25.06.2021.

37.   Health and Family Welfare Department, Govt. of India, https://swasthyasathi.gov.in/ retrieved 13.05.2021.

38.   20 Schemes that Transformed Bengal in the last 7 years, May 20, 2018, http://aitcofficial.org/aitc/20-schemes-that-transformed-bengal-in-the-last-seven-years/ retrieved on 1.11.2018.

39.   How 'Didi Ke Bolo' paved the way for 14 key Bengal programs', The Times of India, January 31, 2021.

40.   Shiv Sahay Singh, 'Visitors to West Bengal Government's outreach scheme cross 2 crores: CM', The Hindu, Kolkata January 9, 2021.

41.   Nilavro Ghosh, 'Mamata announces new neighborhood grievance redressal program', The Hindustan Times, Bolpur, December 28, 2020.

42.   Debashis Konar, 'West Bengal Plans to offer instant solutions to local problems, The Times of India, December 29, 2020.

43.   West Bengal Budget Documents 2020-21 (Annual Financial Statement, MTFP Statement); PRS.

44.   West Bengal Budget Documents 2020-21 (Annual Financial Statement, MTFP Statement); PRS.

<u>Chapter – IV</u>

1.   Robert A. Dahl, 2001, On Democracy, East-West Press, New Delhi, p. 85.

2.   Times of India, 'Highest pre-poll deployment of central forces in West Bengal', Kolkata, TNN / Updated: Mar 3, 2021, 11:13 IST.

3.   The Election Commission of India, Press Note No. ECI/PN/21/2021 dt. 3rd March 2021.

4.   The Election Commission of India, Press Note No. ECI/PN/31/2021 dt. 17th March 2021.

5.   The Election Commission of India, Press Note No. ECI/PN/45/2021 dt. 6th April 2021.

6.   The Election Commission of India, Press Note No. ECI/PN/52/2021 dt. 16th April 2021.

7.   The Election Commission of India, Press Note No. ECI/PN/52/2021 dt. 16th April 2021.

8.   The Election Commission of India, Press Note No. ECI/PN/56/2021 dt. 26th April 2021.

9.   The Election Commission of India, Press Note No. ECI/PN/53/2021 dt. 17th April 2021.

10.   The Election Commission of India, Press Note No. ECI/PN/54/2021 dt. 22nd April 2021.

11.   No. ECI/PN/56/2021 dt. 26th April 2021.

12.   The Election Commission of India, Press Note No. ECI/PN/56/2021 dt. 26th April 2021.

13.   'West Bengal Election 2021: Voting dates, election results, full poll schedule, timings, all FAQs, Business Today, April 20, 2021.

14.   The Election Commission of India, Press Note No. ECI/PN/58/2021 dt. 29th April 2021.

15.   The Election Commission of India, Press Note No. ECI/PN/30/2021 dt. 17th March 2021.

16.   The Election Commission of India, Press Note No. ECI/PN/58/2021 dt. 29th April 2021.

17.   https://eci.gov.in/mcc/ retrieved on 14.3.2021.

Chapter – V

1.   Ash Amin, 2019. Violence and Democracy, The British Academy, London, p. 6.

2.   Sohini Guha, 2019. 'Violence, Lower-caste politics and India's post-colonial democracy', in Violence and Democracy, The British Academy, London, p. 19.

3.   Sohini Guha, 2019. 'Violence, Lower-caste politics and India's post-colonial democracy', in Violence and Democracy, The British Academy, London, p. 18.

4.   Dominic Davies, 2019. 'Feelings in common: democracy as maintenance and repair', in Violence and Democracy, The British Academy, London, p. 24.

5.   Amalya Ganguli, 'The Roots of violence in Bengal', Business Standard, May 18, 2019.

6.   Sitanshu Das (1970).The Future of Indian Democracy, Fabian Society. p. 30.

7.   Aziz Ahmad and Karigoudar Ishwaran, (1 December 1973), Contributions to Asian Studies, Brill Archive. pp. 49–50, 56.

8.   Aziz Ahmad and Karigoudar Ishwaran, (1 December 1973), Contributions to Asian Studies, Brill Archive. pp. 49–50, 56.

9.   Aziz Ahmad and Karigoudar Ishwaran, (1 December 1973), Contributions to Asian Studies, Brill Archive. pp. 49–50, 56.

10.   Caesar Mandal, 'The Martial drill for Gurung's army', The Times of India, February 12, 2009.

11.   'Mamata starts 'Banga Janani Bahini' and 'Jai Hind Bahini' to counter RSS in Bengal', DNA, June 1, 2019.

12.   Sanjay Ruparelia (2015). Divided We Govern: Coalition Politics in Modern. Oxford University Press. pp. 59–60.

13.   Sanjay Ruparelia (2015). Divided We Govern: Coalition Politics in Modern. Oxford University Press. pp. 59–60.

14.   M. V. S. Koteswara Rao. Communist Parties and United Front: Experience in Kerala and West Bengal. Prajasakti Book House, Hyderabad. 2003, pp. 238-39.

15.   Aziz Ahmad and Karigoudar Ishwaran, (1 December 1973), Contributions to Asian Studies, Brill Archive. pp. 49–50, 56.

16.   M. V. S. Koteswara Rao. Communist Parties and United Front: Experience in Kerala and West Bengal. Prajasakti Book House, Hyderabad. 2003, pp.- 239-240.

17.   Subodh Verma, 'West Bengal elections: How TMC Violence against Left Opened Doors for the BJP', News Click, March 21, 2021.

18.   Subodh Verma, 'West Bengal elections: How TMC Violence against Left Opened Doors for the BJP', News Click, March 21, 2021.

19.   Apurba Vishwanath, 'Destruction of public property: What the law says, what SC directed', The Indian Express, December 18, 2019.

20.   'West Bengal Assembly passes Bill to stop vandalizing property', Business Standard, Kolkata, February 8, 2017.

21.   'Property Act amendment may include jail term', The Asian Age, Kolkata, January 31, 2017.

22.   'Railway station set on fire in West Bengal's Murshidabad by Anti-Citizenship Act protesters', The Free Press Journal, December 14, 2019.

23.   Shubhadeep Choudhury, 'List of slain BJP workers gets bigger and bigger in Bengal', Tribune, Kolkata, October 30, 2020.

24.   'More than 300 BJP workers killed in Bengal': Amit Shah', The Hindustan Times, Kolkata, December 20, 2020.

25.   'More than 300 BJP workers killed in Bengal': Amit Shah', The Hindustan Times, Kolkata, December 20, 2021.

26.   Dibyendu Mondal, 'One political party worker is killed every two days in Bengal' The Sunday Guardian, New Delhi, April 3, 2021.

27.   Meghdeep Bhattacharyya and Pranesh Sarkar, 'BJP lauds EC; TMC complains', The Telegraph, Calcutta, March 28, 2021.

28.   : Snehamoy Chakraborty and Angshuman Phadikar, 'Sporadic violence on Day One of elections', The Telegraph, Calcutta, March 28, 2021.

29. Devadeep Purohit and Anshuman Phadikar, 'Boy's tears bring firebrand back', The Telegraph, Nandigram, March 31, 2021.

30. 'Ear slashed in BJP-TMC clash in Jalpaiguri', The Telegraph, Calcutta, March 31, 2021.

31. Anshuman Phadilkar, 'BJP & CPM accuse TMC of attacks', The Telegraph, Calcutta, March 31, 2021.

32. 'BJP Prarthir upore hamla', The Anandabazar Patrika, Kolkata, April 5, 2021.

33. Sweety Kumari, 'EC receives 1605 complaints; 28 people arrested, several detained: Purba Medinipur records highest turnout at 81.23%', The Indian Express, Calcutta, April 2, 2021.

34. 'BJP's Diamond Harbour candidate, supporters attacked', The Indian Express, Calcutta, April 3, 2021.

35. 'Abhishek dares Centre to start investigation against all culprits', Indian Express, Kolkata, April 5, 2021.

36. Snehamoy Chakraborty and Subasish Chaudhuri, 'Candidates bear the brunt in new trend,' Calcutta, April 7, 2021.

37. Snehamoy Chakraborty, 'Woman dies after assault', The Telegraph, Calcutta, April 7, 2021.

38. 'Mathabhanga pick of TMC suffers injury after assault', The Indian Express, Calcutta, April 9, 2021.

39. 'BJP and TMC workers clash in Kolkata,' The Indian Express, Calcutta, April 10, 2021.

40. 'CPM urges poll panel to curb violence', The Indian Express, Calcutta, April 10, 2021.

41. Pranesh Sarkar, 'Low voter turnout, glare on violence', The Telegraph, Calcutta, April 11, 2021.

42. 'Mamata calls poll deaths 'genocide', Shah says she instigated attack', The Indian Express, Kolkata, April 1, 2021.

43. Pranesh Sarkar, 'Low voter turnout, glare on violence', The Telegraph, Calcutta, April 11, 2021.

44. 'Tension in Coch Behar after bombs recovered: reports of attacks pour in', The Indian Express, April 12, 2021.

45. The Hindu, 'West Bengal Elections: 1071 companies of Central forces deployed', Kolkata, 16 April 2021.

46.   Main Uddin Chisti, 'Central forces fun down four: Bloodstains polling in Cooch Behar', The Telegraph, Calcutta, April 11, 2021.

47.   'BJP Malda candidate shot at after meet; party worker found dead in Nadia village', The Indian Express, Calcutta, April 19, 2021.

48.   G-24 Ghanta television news, time 10.10 A.M. Date 22.04.2021.

49.   G-24 Ghanta television news, time 10.33 A.M. Date 22.04.2021.

50.   Dipak Debnath, 'Three injured in bomb attack at 15 places in Bengal's Jagatdal, BJP slams police', India Today, Kolkata, April 18, 2021.

51.   'BJP Trinamool Sangharshe ahata 6 (Six persons were injured in TMC and BJP), Anandabazar Patrika, Kolkata, April 25, 2021.

52.   'Mardhor', Trinamool neta dhrita (Beating, a TMC leader was arrested), Anandabazar Patrika, Kolkata, April 25, 2021.

53.   'BJP Malda candidate shot at after meet; party worker found dead in Nadia village', The Indian Express, Calcutta, April 19, 2021.

54.   'Jai Shri Ram' chant by official', The Indian Express, Calcutta, April 19, 2021.

55.   '1 dies in bomb explosion on eve of polling', The Indian Express, Calcutta, April 22, 2021.

56.   Snehamoy Chakraborty, 'TMC threat to chop hands: CPM plaint', The Telegraph, Calcutta, April 16, 2021.

57.   Abhro Banerjee, "Six-party workers killed, houses, shops vandalized by TMC, alleges Bengal BJP. MHA seeks report', India Today, New Delhi, May 3, 2021.

58.   Dr. Rakesh Sinha, 'What post-poll violence tells us about politics in Bengal', The Indian Express, May 13, 2021.

<u>Chapter - VI</u>

1.   Namrata Acharya, "West Bengal's debt burden rises", Business Standard, Kolkata, December 26, 2018.

2.   "Benefit poser on the Bengal club dole", The Telegraph, Kolkata, 25.01.2018.

3.   Shiv Sahay Singh, "Mamata Banerjee doubles dole to the Durga puja committees", Kolkata, September 24, 2020.

4.   Samir K. Purkayastha, "Non-Brahmin names figure in Bengal's priest dole", Kolkata, October 15, 2020.

5. Suhrid Sankar Chattopadhyay, 'West Bengal CM Mamata Banerjee announces allowance for Hindu priests' Frontline, September 14, 2020.

6. Bishwanath Ghosh, 'West Bengal fixes salaries for poorly paid guest lecturers', The Hindu, Kolkata, 25 June 2020.

7. 'West Bengal didn't handle migrants issue properly: Bombay HC', Mumbai, July 14, 2020.

8. Shiv Sahay Singh, 'Back home, migrant workers write to Mamata Banerjee seeking new job', The Hindu, Kolkata, 6 August 2020.

9. Amit Kumar Chaudhury, 'India Today investigation exposes syndicate raj in Mamata Banerjee's Bengal,' India Today, Kolkata, 28 August 2018.

10. 'Mamata running syndicate raj in Bengal, throttling democracy, says PM Modi,' Business Standard, Midnapore, 17 July 2018.

11. Ajoy Ashirwad Mahaprashasta, 'West Bengal's Syndicate Raj – a bane or boon for political parties', The Wire, 30 April 2016.

12. 'TMC govt. has imposed 'TTT' – Trinamool Tolabaji Tax in West Bengal: PM', Business Standard, 2 February 2019.

13. Madhuparna Das, '10 protests a day and counting – Mamata's cut-money 'clean-up' is scorching TMC,' The Print, Kolkata, 17 July 2019.

14. Madhuparna Das, '10 protests a day and counting – Mamata's cut-money 'clean-up' is scorching TMC,' The Print, Kolkata, 17 July 2019.

15. Mampi Bose, 'Bengal's Healthcare Has Become Dysfunctional. Here's How We Can Fix It,' The Wire, 27 June 2019.

16. Mampi Bose, 'Bengal's Healthcare Has Become Dysfunctional. Here's How We Can Fix It,' The Wire, 27 June 2019.

17. Health and Family Welfare Department, Government of West Bengal, Swasthya Bhavan, Bidhan Nagar Kolkata – 91, Government Notification No. H/F/SPSRS/20/2020 File No. HFW-14099/3/2020-SPSRC-Dept. of H &FW dated 22.04.2020.

18. The Millennium Post, Kolkata, 31 August 2020.

19. The Millennium Post, Kolkata, 31 August 2020.

20. Sudarshana Chakrabarty, 'Swastha Sathi will now include Bengal's entire population: Mamata', Down to Earth, 30 November 2020.

21. Sumati Yengkhom, 'Swastha Sathi meet: Private hospitals raise rate concerns in West Bengal,' The Times of India, Kolkata, 29 December 2020.

22.   Prithvijit Mitra, 'West Bengal govt cracks Swasthya Sathi whip on private hospitals, The Times of India, Kolkata, 10 January 2021.

23.   Indranil Banerjee, 'West Bengal CM Jyoti Basu attacks Rajib Gandhi's failure to resolve national problems', India Today, 31 March 1987.

24.   Ruhi Tewari and Krishnamurthy Ramasubbu, 'Left withdraws support, but govt sanguine', Mint, July 08,, 2008.

25.   'Protests over irregularities in recruitment of teachers', The Hindu, Kolkata, 21 February 2017.

26.   Purnima Sah, 'Women safety: a dysfunctional toll-free women helpline in West Bengal; Assam helpline lacks sufficient funds', 29 October 2020.

27.   Gopali Bandopadhyay, The Statesman, Kolkata, 16 December 2018.

28.   Snigdhendu Bhattacharya, 'Kolkata among safest cities for women but Bengal tops country in domestic violence,' The Hindustan Times, Kolkata, 1 December 2017.

29.   'Can Mamata distance herself from Trinamool's corruption racket?' The Indian Express, 25 June 2019.

30.   'Mamata Banerjee's 6-year rule riddled with Saradha, Narada, Rose Valley scams,' The Hindustan Times, March 18, 2017.

<u>Chapter – VII</u>

1.   Business Standard, 'Kerala election results 2021: LDF wins 97 seats, UDF 41; BJP draws a blank, New Delhi, May 3.

2.   Anupam Mishra, '25% of Bengal Phase 1 candidates have criminal records, Left leads with 50%, finds ADR', India Today, New Delhi, March 21, 2021.

3.   'BJP r ardhek prarthi e abhijukta (about half of the BJP's candidates are criminal) The Anandabazar Patrika, 25 April 2021.

4.   Snigdhendu Bhattacharya, 'West Bengal: Of 19 Turncoat MLAs Contesting From BJP, 13 Lost', The Wire, May 5, 2021.

5.   Snehamoy Chakraborty, 'Switch from BJP to TMC', The Telegraph, March 21, 2021.

6.   '34 West Bengal legislators went from TMC to BJP- only 13 of them got tickets to contest the election for the saffron party', Business Insider, March 25, 2021.

7.   'BJP manifesto on April 7, Congress mocks delay', The Hindustan Times, April 3, 2014.

8.   Sonar Bangla Sankalop Patra 2021, p. 11.

9.   All India Tranamool Congress Manifesto 2021, p. 21.

10.   Arkamoy Datta Majumder, 'Pre-Puja cash for farmers: PM', The Telegraph, Calcutta, Sunday, April 4, 2021.

11.   Kusum Arora, 'Thank You Bengal': Protesting Farmers Elated Over 'BJP's Defeat, Not TMC's Victory', The Wire, Jalandhar, 3 May 2021.

12.   Ananya Bhattacharya, 'Why did the BJP lose Bengal 2021?', India Today, Cooch Behar, May 3, 2021.

13.   'PM insulting women with Didi O didi digs at Mamata, says TMC', The Indian Express, Kolkata, April 5, 2021.

14.   Ananya Bhattacharya, 'Why did the BJP lose Bengal 2021?' India Today, Cooch Behar, May 3, 2021.

15.   'TMC goons will meet fate of criminals in UP: Adiyanath', The Indian Express, Kolkata, April 5, 2021.

16.   'If voted to power, BJP will form anti-Romeo squad on UP's line: Yogi', The Indian Express, Calcutta, April 9, 2021.

17.   Tanmay Chatterjee, 'Mamata Banerjee's stipend for Hindu priests a move to woo voters, says Opposition', The Hindustan Times, September 15, 2020.

18.   Sonar Bangla Sankalpo Patra, p.38.

19.   'Centre using ED, CBI, I-T department to pull down our govts: Congress', Business Standard, February 23, 2021.

20.   'BJP using ED, CPI, I-T dept to pressurize state admin: TMC', Millenniumpost, 21st March 2021.

21.   'LPG price double in 7 yrs; tax collection on petrol diesel jumps 459%, says oil minister Pradhan', The Hindustan Times, March 08, 2021.

22.   'Mukul Roy Bengal's Chanakya, Together Will Oust Mamata, Says Vijayvargiya, Asks BJP Workers to Enlist 'TMC Goons,' News 18, Kolkata, October 14, 2020.

23.   WB still living in 19th century under 'decades of misrule' by TMC: Rajnath', Business Standard, March 26, 2021.

24.   'TMC's misrule 'more fearful' than Left government, Bengal will show them 'Ram card': PM Modi', Scroll.in, February 7, 2021.

25.   'Amit Shah Eats Lunch at Farmer's House in Bengal', NDTV, December 20, 2020.

26.   'Abhishek dares Centre to start investigation against all culprits', Indian Express, Kolkata, April 5, 2021.

27.   '2021 Assembly Polls: BJP high command appoints 5 central observers in Bengal,' The Indian Express, November 18, 2020.

28.   Arkamoy Datta Majumdar, 'Outsider, That's Me', The Telegraph, Calcutta, March 31, 2021.

29.   Sayantan Ghosh, 'Why BJP is BJP's biggest enemy in Bengal,' Dailyo.in, 02.9.2020.

30.   'Why BJP decided to field sitting MPs for assembly elections in Bengal', India Today, March 15, 2021.

31.   'Internal conflict rocks Bengal BJP as groups clash with each other in Bardhaman, Asansol', The Statesman, Kolkata, January 22, 2021.

32.   Madhuparna Das, 'Ghosh vs Khan in Bengal BJP is a fight for control between old guard & Trinamool defectors', The Print, October 28, 2020.

33.   Sayantan Ghosh, 'Why BJP is BJP's biggest enemy in Bengal,' Dailyo.in, 02.9.2020.

34.   Monogya Lolwal, 'Didi vs Modi: Mamata Banerjee renames Central government schemes, BJP leader calls her Babur', India Today, Kolkata, April 24, 2017.

<u>Chapter - VIII</u>

1. Personal interview with Naresh Biswas – ex-serviceman of Navy, age 71 years, on 28.9.2009, Fulia, Nadia.

2. Personal interview with Susmita Biswas, a High School Teacher, 1 No. Natun Fulia, on 28.9.2009.

3. Personal interview with Dr. Ashok Chakraborty, an Assistant Teacher of Mathematics, on 21.9.2009.

4. Personal interview with Dr. A.K. Laha, a Homeopath Medicine Practioner, Ghatal, on 22.9.2009.

5. Personal observation of Amit Kumar Samanta, a college student from Gadighata, Daspur, while taking an interview on 2.8.2009.

6. Personal interview with Madan Das, President of Daspur Mandal Committee of BJP, on 26.8.2009.

7. Personal interview with Mr. Sisir Pore, Head Clerk, Ghatal Municipality, on 8.9.2009.

8. Personal interview with Satrughna Jana, State Council Member of Bharatiya Janata Party, Harisinghpur, Ghatal, on 26.8.2009.

9. Personal interview with Mr. Debdas Bhattacharjee, Librarian, Ghatal Town Library on 4.8.2009.

10. Personal interview with Mr. Bhabadeb Biswas, WBCS-Exe, Taherpur, Kabita Kuthir, on 26.9.2009.

11. Personal interview with Prof. Amitava Sarkar, Retired Professor of Panskura Banamali College, on 15.9.2009.

12. Personal interview with Prof. Dipti Sarkar, Retired Professor of Ghatal R.S. College, on 15.9.2009.

13. Personal interview with Prof. Pranesh Banerjee, Retired Teacher of Ghatal R.S. College, on 8.9.2009.

14. Personal interview with Mrs. Mina Kar, Ghatal, Paschim Medinipur, on 1.9.2009.

15. Personal interview with Dr. Ashok Chakraborty, an Assistant Teacher, Ghatal, on 21.9.2009.

16. Personal interview with Smt. Bela Gatait, a SHG member, Ghatal, Paschim Medinipur, on 21.8.2009.

17. Personal interview with Kakali Roy, Housewife, Dum Dum Cantonment, on 29.9.2009.

18. Personal interview with Jhuma Sarkar, 1 NO. Natun Fulia, on 29.9.2009.

19. Personal interview with Sanjit Nath, Jetia, North 24 Parganas, on 30.9.2009.

20. Personal interview with Tapan Samanta, a farmer, Harishpur, Manoharpur –I, Ghatal, on 26.8.2009

21. personal interview with Madan Das, a farmer, Dubarajpur, Daspur –I, Paschim Medinipur, on 26.8.2009.

22. Personal interview with Rajshekhar Panda, Insurance Executive of Maxwell Newyork Life Insurance, Belighata, Daspur, on 1.8.2009.

23. Personal interview with Mr. Gouri Shankar Bag, Head Master, Ghatal Y.S.S. Vidyapith (H.S.), Ghatal, Paschim Medinipur, W.B., on 11.8.2009.

24. Personal interview with Digbindu Dogra, a Councillor, Ghatal Municipality, Paschim Medinipur, on 08.09.2009.

25. Prabhat Datta, 2002, Sthaniya Sayattwasashan O Unnayan, Dasgupta and Company Pvt. Limited, Kolkata, p.41.

26. David R. Berman, 2003, Local Government and the States – Autonomy, Politics, and Policy, M.E. Sharpe, Armonk New York, London England, p. 3.

27. Dr. K. Srinivasa Rao, 'Rural Infrastructure: An Impetus to Economic Growth,' Kurukshetra, October 2009, p. 3.

28. Personal interview with Bhabadeb Biswas, W.B.C.S (Exe.), Taherpur, Nadia, on 26.09.2009.

29. Dr. K. Srinivasa Rao, 'Rural Infrastructure - An Impetus to Economic Growth', Kurukshetra, October 2009, p. 6.

30. Samir Kar, 'Managing Rural Development: Rural Roads As a Catalyst of Development,' Kurukshetra, October 2009, p. 50.

31. Personal interview with Sk. Shahalam Badsha, a 3rd-year student of Ghatal College, on 4.8.2009.

32. Personal interview with Dr. Rabindra Nath Manna, Physician, Birnagar, Nadia, on 26.09.2009.

33. Personal interview with Bankim Jana, An Assistant Teacher, Ghatal Y.S.S. Vidyapith (H.S), Ghatal, Paschim Medinipur, on 25.8.2009.

34. Personal interview with Digbindu Dogra, a Councillor, Ghatal Municipality, Paschim Medinipur, on 08.09.2009.

35. Personal interview with Naresh Biswas, 1 No. Natun Fulia, Nadia, on 28.09.2009.

36. Personal interview with Abu Jafar, Assistant Teacher, Ghatal Y.S.S. Vidyapith (H.S.), Ghatal, Paschim Medinipur, on 17.08.2009.

37. Personal interview with Prof. Pranesh Banerjee, a retired College Teacher, Ghatal, on 08.09.2009.

38. Personal interview with Digbindu Dogra, Councillor, Ghatal Municipality, Paschim Medinipur, on 8.9.2009.

39. Personal interview with Samir Ghosh, an Ex-Army, Birnagar, Nadia, on 27.09.2009

40. Personal interview with Pampa Das, a student of B.A. Third Year, Ghatal R.S. College, on 4.8.2009.

41. Personal interview with Kapotakshi Sur, an Assistant Professor of Ghatal R.S. College, Bengali Department, Ghatal, Paschim Medinipur, on 7.9.2009

42. Personal interview with Moon Moon Bera, a student of Ghatal R.S. College, Daspur, Paschim Medinipur, on 1.8.2009.

43. Personal interview with Smritikana Halder, an Assistant Teacher, Ghatal Basanta Kumari Girls' High School (H.S.), on 16.09.2009.

44. Personal interview with Murari Mohan Bera, a teacher of Ghatal R.S. College, on 07.09.2009.

45. Personal interview with Manoj Kumar Bhuniya, a teacher of Nischindipur Primary School, Ghatal, on 22.08.2009.

46. Abhijit Guha (ed), 2012, 'The Bankruptcy in the ideology and violence', in Maoism in India: Ideology and Ground Reality, Indian National Conference and Academy of Anthropologists, Jhargram, p. 90.

47. Shibaji Pratim Basu, 'West Bengal: The Food Movements of 1959 & 1966'. http://www.mcrg.ac.in/rls_pml/RLS_PM/RLS_PM_Abstracts/Sibaji.pdf   retrieved 24.05.2021.

48. M.V.S. Koresware Rao, 2003, Communist Parties and United Front: Experience in Kerala and West Bengal, prajasakti Book House, Hyderabad, pp. 240-41.

49. Aziz Ahmad; Karigoudar Ishwaran (1 December 1973). Contributions to Asian Studies. Brill Archive. pp. 49–50, 56. GGKEY:BEAUDTYBNJT.

50. Sankar Ghose (1 January 1978) Changing India, Allied Publishers, p. 136.

51. Amrita Basu (1 October 1994). Two Faces of Protest: Contrasting Modes of Women's Activism in India. University of California Press. pp. 31–32.

52. Austin, Granville (1999). Working a Democratic Constitution - A History of the Indian Experience. New Delhi: Oxford University Press.

53. Lt. Gen J.F.R. Jacob (2012). An Odyssey in War and Peace. 262: Roli Books Private Limited. p. 189.

54. Subrata Mukherjee, 'Why the BJP lost Bengal', The Indian Express, New Delhi, May 17, 2021.

55. 'Siddhartha Shankar Ray passes away', The Hindu, Kolkata, November 7, 2010.

56. Amalya Ganguli, 'The Roots of violence in Bengal', Business Standard, May 18, 2019.

57. Amalya Ganguli, 'The Roots of violence in Bengal', Business Standard, May 18, 2019.

58. Avantika, 'Revisiting the forgotten history of repeated President's Rule in West Bengal,' Yahoo.news, February 5, 2019.

59. Jawhar Sircar, 'In a Calcutta Gripped With Naxal Violence and Police Brutality, People Lost Sons, Brothers and Friends,' The Wire, March 11, 2021.

60. Subrata Mukherjee, 'Why the BJP lost Bengal', The Indian Express, New Delhi, May 17, 2021.

61. Jawhar Sircar, 'In a Calcutta Gripped With Naxal Violence and Police Brutality, People Lost Sons, Brothers and Friends,' The Wire, March 11, 2021.

62. https://www.cpim.org/content/jyoti-basu retrieved 24.05.2021.

63. Himadri Ghosh, 'Is This the End of the Road for the CPI(M) in Bengal?' The Wire, Kolkata, May 14, 2021.

64. Snigdhendu Bhattacharjee, 'Bengal: As Left and Congress Ally With Muslim Cleric's Party, Will BJP Be the Winner?' The Wire, Kolkata, February 28, 2021.

65. Himadri Ghosh, 'Is This the End of the Road for the CPI(M) in Bengal?' The Wire, Kolkata, May 14, 2021.

66. Abhijit Guha (ed), 2012, 'The Bankruptcy in the ideology and violence', in Maoism in India: Ideology and Ground Reality, Indian National Conference and Academy of Anthropologists, Jhargram, p. 92.

<u>Chapter – IX</u>

1. Dr. Jagdeep Saxena, 'Drivers of Inclusive Rural Growth', Kurukshetra, Vol. 69, No. 8, June 2021, p.8.

2. Rahul Chakraborty, Ei Somoy, September 25, 2020.

3. 'IAS officer arrested for siphoning off Rs. 80 crores in West Bengal, India Today, December 1, 2013.

4. 'Corruption sky-high in West Bengal, change in governance necessary: BJP MP Swapan Dasgupta', Financial Express, August 18, 2020.

5. Suman Nath, 'Everyday Politics, and Corruption in West Bengal', Economic & Political Weekly, vol. 52, issue 21, 27 May 2017.

Glossary

Amake dhamkaben na chamkaben na - don't threaten me, don't startle me

Amrai Bhobishyat – we are future

Amrai Bikalpa – we are the alternative

Amara Dharmanirapeksha – we are secular

Badla Noi, Badal Chai – not revenge, need change

Bahiragata - outsider

Bandhs – closures

Bargadars - sharecroppers

Beno Jal - dirty flood water

Bhadraloks – gentlemen

Bhaipo - nephew

Bhenge dao gunriye dao – break and demolish

Bhrastachar – corruption

Bhumiputra – son of soil

Biriyani – delicious food

Chakka Jam - shut down of wheels

Chatni – sauce

Chiriya – (seasonal) bird

Cholche na, cholbe na – is not going on, will not go on

Dadas - elder brothers (bosses or goons)

Dadagiri – bossism

Danga land – plain land

Duare Sarkar – government at the doorstep

Gheraos – encirclement or prevent someone to move out

Ghuspetia - infiltrator

Gram panchayats – the third tier of rural local government

Hartals – closure of shops and offices

Jala land – marshy land

Khela Hobe – there will be a game

Laddos – one kind of north Indian sweet

Lathi - stick

Manchi na, manbo na – not obeying, will not obey

Panchayat – local government

Papad – a thin Indian wafer

Paray paray samadhan – solution at locality

Pheus - secret agents

Pishi - aunt

Rasogolla - one kind of sweet

Sabhadhipatis – heads of Zilla Parishad

Sandesh – one kind of tasty sweetmeat

Syndicate Raj – an organized form of running corrupt extortion rackets

Tolabaj - extortionist

Tustikaran – sycophancy

Zilla Parishad – highest tiers of the rural local government

Tables

GSDP - Gross State Domestic Product

IAS – Indian Administrative Service

IBEF - India Brand Equity Foundation

IFCs - Industry Facilitation Centers

INC – Indian National Congress

IPC – Indian Penal Code

ISF – Indian Secular Front

IT - Information Technology

ITBP - Indo-Tibetan Border Police

LA – Legislative Assembly

LDF - Left Democratic Front

LMT – Lakh Metric Ton

LF – Left Front

LGBs - Local Government Bodies

MC – Managing Committee

MCC – Model Code of Conduct

MGNREGA – Mahatma Gandhi National Rural Employment Guarantee Scheme

MLAs – Members of Legislative Assembly

MPs – Members of Parliament

M. Phil – Master of Philosophy

MSME - Micro, Small and Medium Enterprises

NE – North East

NET - National Eligibility Test

NIEPA - National Institute of Educational Planning and Administration

NRC – National Register of Citizens

NW – North West

Ph. D. – Doctor of Philosophy

PHED - Public Health Engineering Department

R.P. (Act) – Representation of People

PTTI - Primary Teachers' Training Institutions

RSS – Rashtriya Swayamsevak Sangha

SACT - State Aided College Teachers

SAARC - South Asian Association for Regional Co-operation

SBG- State Business Summits

SC – Scheduled Caste

SET - State Eligibility Test

SI - School Inspector

SKM - Samyukt Kisan Morcha

SMCs - School Managing Committees

SNSU - Sick Newborn Stabilization Units

SOP - Standard operating procedure

SP – Superintendent of Police

SSB - Service Selection Board

SSC – School Service Commission

SUCI – Socialist Unity Centre of India

TMC – Trinamool Congress

UDF – United Democratic Front

UNESCO – United Nations Educational Scientific and Cultural Organization

UPA – United Progressive Alliance

VVIP – Very Very Important Person

VVPAT – Voter Verified Paper Audit Trail

WBIDC - West Bengal Industrial Development Corporation